GIFTS
you can make yourself

★

SECOND SERIES

GIFTS FOR ALL. *Here are only a few of the delightful gifts to be found in the pages that follow. Your leisure hours will be well spent, and enjoyed, in making something that will give lasting pleasure to your friends. There is a wide choice of subject and the crafts are varied, as can be seen by the small selection shown above.*

GIFTS
you can make yourself

SECOND SERIES

★

A SELECTION OF CHARMING GIFTS
EASY TO MAKE AT HOME

ODHAMS PRESS LTD · LONG ACRE · LONDON

Contents

GIFTS FOR CHILDREN

GIFTS FOR THE HOME

VELVET MUFF

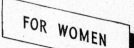

and Scarf, Trimmed with Silk Fringe

MATERIALS

2 sheets of wadding, each 45 ins. by 10 ins. approximately.

1 strip of black velvet, 27 ins. long by 14 ins. wide.

1 strip of lining silk, 16 ins. long by 11 ins. wide.

1 yd. black silk fringe.

THE MUFF

Method.—To make the foundation for the muff, take one of the strips of wadding and fold its cut ends over to meet in the centre. Fold in half again so that there are four thicknesses of wadding roughly square in shape, with two folded edges at the top. Whip these two folded edges together firmly, then make up the second sheet of wadding in the same way. Stitch the two squares together with whipping stitches at top and bottom edges then separate them at the sides to make a tube shape. Round the open ends of this tube, whip together the four thicknesses of wadding, pulling the stitches tightly to shape foundation as in Diagram 1.

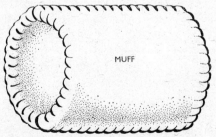

DIAGRAM 1. WADDING FOUNDATION FOR MUFF

Now take the strip of velvet and cut one end to a point about 5 ins. deep. Stitch the straight end to the top of the wadding foundation, then wrap the velvet round the foundation until the point overlaps this straight edge, en-velope-fashion. Turn in the edges of the point and stitch to the velvet beneath. Run a gathering thread along each of the side edges of the velvet, about 1 in. beyond the wadding ; draw up to fit the inside of the foundation, and tack the raw edges down.

Now stitch the fringe along the edge of the overlapping point, taking it inside the muff to the edge of the velvet on each side. Sew a second line of fringe in a V-shape about $3\frac{1}{2}$ ins. below the first.

To line the muff, stitch the two short sides of the lining oblong together to make a tube. Slip this inside the foundation ; turn in the edges at the open ends and slip-stitch them over the velvet.

THE VELVET SCARF

MATERIALS

1 square of velvet, 30 ins. to 36 ins. each way. 2 yds. of fringe.

Method.—The material must be an exact square. Fold it in half diagonally, right side outside, then turn the raw edges in towards one another and tack them together along the two straight sides. Whip over these tacked edges and remove the tacking threads, then finish the scarf with fringe stitched along the two short straight edges only.

FOR THE SMART GIRL. *This attractive velvet muff and its matching scarf will make a charming and unusual gift. The scarf is a triangular one and is trimmed with fringe along two straight edges only ; it can be worn at the neck or as a head scarf.*

THREE BLOUSE FRONTS

In Organdie and Lace

THE ORGANDIE FRONT

MATERIALS

12 ins. of 36-in. wide organdie.
1½ yds. of narrow lace or net edging.

Method.—Cut a strip of organdie 12 ins. wide and 22 ins. long and make a crease right across it, 6 ins. from the top edge. Now follow Diagram 1 to cut the neck opening. Mark the centre of the crease and round this point cut a semi-circle 2½ ins. in radius, marked B, C and D, as in the diagram. Cut through the material from C to the top edge E for the opening at the back of the neck and make a cut 4 ins. long from centre to F. The two triangles B, centre, F, and D, centre, F, will fold back to form revers.

Cut a second strip of organdie 5½ ins. wide and 14 ins. long. Leave 4½ ins. at the top of this strip plain, and pin-tuck the remainder horizontally, then cut the plain section down through the centre for 4 ins. Place this smaller strip on top of the larger one, wrong side uppermost and with the plain part to the neck edge. Stitch the two layers of organdie together along the raw edges, F to centre to D, and similarly F to centre to B on the opposite side. Snip into the corners at B, D and F, then turn inside out and press along the stitched edges. Turn in the remaining three sides of the pin-tucked strip and tack on to the organdie beneath. Hem the edges down and press the two corners of the strip down at the neck edge, to form revers, as shown in Diagram 2.

Make a narrow turning on both edges of the opening at the back of the neck, then stitch narrow lace round the curved raw edge, easing it on a little, and continue along the three sides of the pin-tucked panel and round the opposite curved neck edge. Trim the edges of the turned-back revers in the same way, then neaten the curved neck edges with

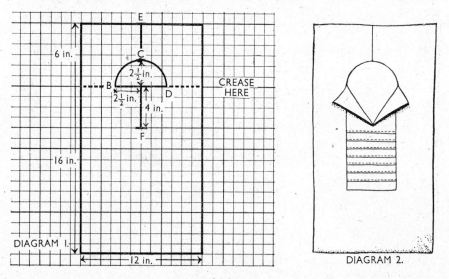

DIAGRAM I.

E

6 in.

C

2½ in.

B

2½ in.   D

4 in.

F

16 in.

CREASE HERE

12 in.

DIAGRAM 2.

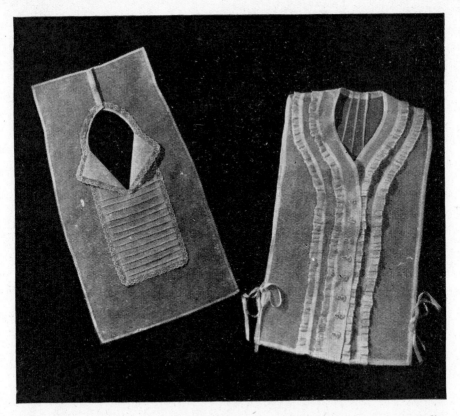

FOR THE GIRL WHO WEARS A SUIT. *Two dainty blouse fronts in organdie.*
Horizontal pin-tucks and narrow lace edging decorate the pastel shaded front on the
left, and narrow box-pleats add an attractive finishing touch to the front on the right.

narrow bias binding cut from the remaining organdie.

Finish the outer edges of the front with a narrow hem and press well, then sew press fasteners on the back opening.

THE FRILLED BLOUSE FRONT
MATERIALS

1 yd. organdie, muslin, and so on.
8 buttons. Tape.

MEASUREMENTS

Length, 22 ins.
Width, 13 ins. approximately.

To cut.—Cut two fronts as shown on the diagram, and the two facings (A—B).
Cut rectangle for back, 22½ by 14 ins.
Cut strips for frilling 1¼ ins. wide.

To make frilling.—Join strips to make 4 lengths of about 2 yds.

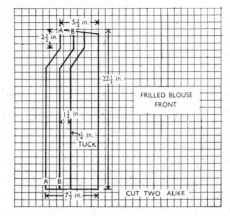

5½ in.
A—B
2¼ in.
22½ in.
FRILLED BLOUSE FRONT
1½ in.
¼ in.
TUCK
A B
7½ in.
CUT TWO ALIKE

Make a narrow hem along one edge.

Box pleat and stitch along raw edge, then machine two rows of stitching along to hold pleats in place.

To make front.—Stitch facing to wrong side of front. Turn to right side tack $\frac{1}{4}$ in. turning at free edge of facing.

Tack one length of frilling under this edge, then tack facing flat to front.

Make a $\frac{1}{4}$ in. tuck parallel with facing and $\frac{3}{4}$ in. from edge of frilling.

Tack another length of frilling under the tuck, then tack flat to front.

Machine edges of facing and tuck.

Complete other side of front to match.

Make darts in back neck to fit and face back of neck. Join shoulder seams.

Hem sides and lower edges.

Make 8 buttonholes in right front $1\frac{1}{4}$ ins. apart. Sew buttons on left front.

Sew tapes to each side of front and back at waist-line.

THE LACE FRONT

MATERIALS

$\frac{1}{2}$ yd. of 36-in. wide lace.

2 yds. of contrasting satin bias binding.

2 yds. matching bias binding.

Method.—Using Diagram 1 as a guide, cut pattern shapes in paper as follows:

A. **Fronts.**—Cut an oblong 16 ins. deep by 9 ins. wide, and snip off a corner triangle, 3 ins. across the top and 6 ins. deep. This diagonal edge will be the neck edge.

B. **Back Yoke.**—Cut a semi-circle 6 ins. in radius and from it cut an inner semi-circle 3 ins. in radius.

C. **Jabot.**—Cut a semi-circle $7\frac{1}{2}$ ins. in radius and from it cut away an inner semi-circle $4\frac{1}{2}$ ins. in radius.

D. **Waistband.**—Cut a strip 12 ins. long by 2 ins. deep.

Cut the pattern shapes in the lace, reversing A shown in Diagram 1, and cutting it a second time, then make up.

Run a gathering thread along the top of the front pieces marked A and draw each piece up to 3 ins. Turn under the straight edges of the yoke marked B and set the fronts under these, keeping diagonally cut edges towards centre.

Using the contrasting binding, bind right round the straight edges and the outer curve of the jabot marked C.

LACE FRONT

BACK YOKE

6 in.

3 in.

B

3 in.

3 in.

A

FRONT

6 in.

16 in.

3 in.

3 in.

JABOT

3 in.

C

$4\frac{1}{2}$ in.

9 in.

3 in.

$4\frac{1}{2}$ in.

D—WAIST BAND

2 in.

DIAGRAM I

12 in.

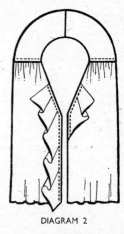

DIAGRAM 2

JABOT TACKED
IN PLACE

FOR THE SMART YOUNG MATRON. *A charming accessory for a dark suit is this lace front and jabot. It is gathered into a narrow waistband at the front, and is set into shoulder yokes which fasten at the back of the neck with press fasteners.*

Now, beginning on the left-hand side of the blouse front, tack the inner curve of the jabot to the neck edge of the front starting about 4½ ins. up on the diagonal edge and continuing right down to the waist edge. Both jabot and blouse front must be right side uppermost. Cut off the surplus portion of jabot at the waist edge and tack it to the neck edge on the right-hand side of the blouse, to match the revers on the left side. Diagram 2 shows the jabot tacked in place on both sides of the blouse.

Seam the two halves of the front to-gether, on the wrong side, with the jabot sandwiched between, and open and press the seam. Cut the yoke through at the centre back and neaten both edges to wrap over for a fastening, then bind the neck edge with the contrasting binding.

Neaten both outer edges from the back opening down to the waist edge, with a facing of matching binding. Arrange the jabot in cascade formation and tack its lower edge to the waist edge of the blouse. Gather the bottom raw edge each side of the jabot and set it into a band made from the strip marked D.

BREAKFAST-IN-BED SET

Tray Cloth, Napkin and Cosy Cover

MATERIALS

¾ yd. of 36-in. wide yellow linen.

¼ yd. of 36-in. wide blue linen.

Few strands of embroidery thread in each colour.

THE TRAY CLOTH

Method.—From the yellow linen cut an oblong 16 ins. wide by 22 ins. long and from the blue linen a square, 6 ins. each way. Cut the blue square across diagonally to make two triangles and pin these in two opposite corners of the oblong leaving an inch margin of yellow on each edge. Tack them securely in place and appliqué each along the diagonal edge with narrow satin stitch. Turn the 1 in. margin over the blue linen and make a hem all round the cloth, mitreing the corners neatly. The hem can be stitched down with ordinary hemming or with mock hemstitch.

Now cut out a heart-shape in strong paper, 2½ ins. in depth and width. Pin it diagonally in one blue corner of the cloth and work round its edge with small running stitches through both thicknesses of material. Remove the paper and using small, sharp-pointed scissors, cut the heart-shape out of the blue linen only, keeping just inside the running stitches and taking great care not to snip the yellow linen beneath. You now have a yellow heart-shape surrounded by blue linen. Appliqué the raw edges of the blue linen with narrow satin stitch in blue embroidery thread.

Work the opposite corner in the same way then take the blue heart-shapes that have been cut out and appliqué them in the two remaining corners.

THE NAPKIN

Cut a square of yellow linen, 13 ins. each way, and a triangle of blue linen, 5 ins. along its two right-angled sides. Tack the blue triangle in one corner of the yellow square, leaving a ½ in. margin of yellow on each side. Now proceed exactly as for the tray cloth but using a heart-shape measuring 1¾ ins. each way. Cut out the blue heart in the same way and appliqué it on the opposite corner, leaving the two remaining corners plain.

THE TEA COSY COVER

From the yellow linen cut two oblongs each 11 ins. deep by 13 ins. wide. Place them one on top of the other and round off the top corners in a tea cosy shape. Cut two strips of blue linen each 4½ ins. deep by 13 ins. wide and tack one along the bottom of each half of the cover so that the lower edge of the blue is ½ in. below the lower edge of the yellow. Appliqué the top edge of the blue linen to the yellow linen on both halves.

Now take the paper pattern of the larger heart, pin it on one of the blue bands about 2 ins. to the left of the centre and proceed as for the tray cloth, stitching the blue cut-out heart on the yellow linen, about 2 ins. to the right of the centre.

Complete the other half of the cover in the same way but with the yellow heart to the right and the blue heart to the left of the centre.

Place the two halves together with right sides facing and sew round the curved edges, putting a piping of blue linen in the seam. Along the bottom straight edges turn the blue linen up over the yellow linen, inside the cover, and make a narrow hem.

FOR THE OLDER WOMAN.   *The freshness of spring is brought to you early in the morning by this delightful breakfast-in-bed set in yellow and blue linen.   The tray cloth and napkin are trimmed with appliqué heart-shaped motifs at each corner, and the cosy cover has a blue piping in the seam.*

DAINTY GIFTS

Sweet Scented Sachets

MATERIALS

Scraps of satin, velvet, crepe, lace, net and ribbon.

Roll of cotton-wool.

Perfume.

N.B.—For the fillings for perfume sachets, put a few drops of perfume on a small piece of cotton-wool and wrap it well round with further layers until the perfumed piece is completely enclosed. The perfume will gradually permeate all the filling.

VELVET SACHETS

Method.—Cut two oblongs of material, velvet or satin, in each of three sizes : 5 ins. by 4 ins, 4 ins. by 3 ins., and 3 ins. by 2½ ins. Take the two largest oblongs and turn in the edges on to the wrong side. Put them together, right sides outside with perfumed cotton-

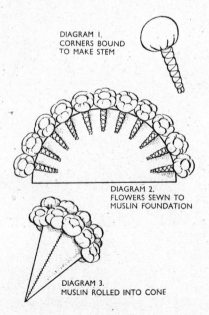

DIAGRAM I.
CORNERS BOUND
TO MAKE STEM

DIAGRAM 2.
FLOWERS SEWN TO
MUSLIN FOUNDATION

DIAGRAM 3.
MUSLIN ROLLED INTO CONE

wool filling sandwiched in between. Tack the material together along all four sides and then work narrow satin overcast stitch over the edges, with embroidery silk, to give a cord-like finish.

Make up the sachets in the other two sizes, in the same way, then place them one above the other and tie together with ribbon as shown in the illustration.

LACE SACHET

Method.—Cut a 6-in. square of piece lace and two squares of silk in the same size. Tack the lace over one square of silk, place the other square on top and seam together along three sides. Turn inside out, insert the perfumed cotton-wool filling and sew up the remaining side. Whip a frilling of narrow lace or net edging round the edges and trim the sachet with a lovers' knot bow.

BON-BON SACHET

Method.—Cut a piece of silk 4 ins. square, fold it in half and seam it on the long edges. Turn it right side out to make a tube. Turn in the raw edges at both ends with small running stitches, then fill the tube with perfumed cotton-wool and draw up the gathering threads tightly at both ends.

For the outer covering, cut a piece of net 8 ins. by 6 ins. Stitch the 6-in. sides together, then run a gathering thread right round each of the other two sides, about 1 in. in from the edges. Slip the padded roll inside the net and draw up the gathering threads tightly. Spread out the frill of net at each end and tie a bow of ribbon round the centre.

EVERY WOMAN'S GIFT. *Four sweet-scented sachets : top left is a silk cushion covered with lace, and next to it is a miniature Victorian posy made with silk flowers : bottom left is a net bon-bon sachet, and on the right three velvet sachets tied with ribbon.*

VICTORIAN POSY

Method.—For this, in addition to scraps of silk and net or lace edging, a 6-in. circle of organdie or stiff muslin will be needed, also an 8-in. silver paper doily.

To make a flower, cut a 2-in. square of silk and run a gathering thread in a circle inside it, keeping about $\frac{1}{4}$ in. within the edges. Put a small ball of perfumed cotton-wool into the centre of this circle and draw up the gathering thread. Bind the four corners of the material together with the thread to make a stem as in Diagram 1. Sew a frill of gathered net or lace round the top of the stem under the ball of silk, to complete the flower. Make ten more flowers in the same way.

Cut a 6-in. circle of organdie or stiff muslin, fold in half and turn in the raw edges. Stitch the flowers round the outer edge of this semi-circle, as shown in Diagram 2. Put a thin layer of cotton-wool over the muslin and then roll the semi-circle round into a cone shape so that the flowers are bunched together in posy formation as shown in Diagram 3.

Fold the silver paper doily in half and wrap it round the cone of muslin. Bind it firmly round with thread about half-way up the cone then spread the doily round the flowers and tie with ribbon.

DRESS ACCESSORIES

Four Detachable Collars

PETAL COLLAR

MATERIALS

  4 3-in. circles of organdie.

  1 yd. narrow lace or net edging.

  ½ yd. bias binding.

Method.—Fold a circle of organdie in half so that the fold runs diagonally across the weave of the material. Turn in the raw edges towards one another and press. Cut a 9-in. length of narrow lace or net edging and gather it up to fit the outer edge of the organdie semi-circle. Tack this frill between the turned in edges and sew all three layers together. This completes one petal.

  Make four of these petals then pin them together in a row so that the frilling overlaps a little. Sew a strip of bias binding along the folded edges, stretching the binding a little so that it pulls the petals into a slight curve.

Press collar well, with binding inside.

POINTED COLLAR

MATERIALS

  Scraps of gingham, seersucker or striped cotton.

  1 yd. of contrasting bias binding.

  12 ins. of white binding.

Method.—From the scraps of material cut four right-angled triangles, each 5 ins. deep and 3½ ins. wide and tack them together in pairs. Bind the straight edges of both with the contrasting binding, then place them side by side with the ends of their shortest sides just overlapping, as shown in Diagram 1. Bind along the diagonal raw edges of both triangles with one strip of binding, stretching the binding slightly to shrink the edges into a curve.

  Cut another strip of material about 1¼ ins. wide and 7 ins. long and bind both long edges Fold the ends over to meet in the centre at the back and draw the strip in with a few stitches to make the two loop ends of a bow. Secure the bow in the centre with a small piece of binding stitched over it, and then sew the bow where the two points of the collar overlap. Press collar well with binding inside.

BIB COLLAR

MATERIALS

  8-in. circle of linen or piqué.

  ¼ yd. of bias binding.

Method.—Fold the circle of material in half with the fold running diagonally across the weave of the material. Along the folded edge mark a point in the

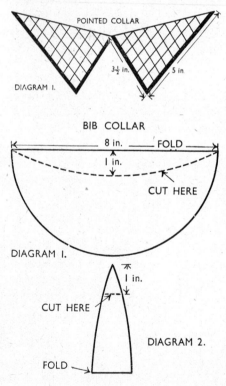

POINTED COLLAR

3¼ in. 5 in.

DIAGRAM 1.

BIB COLLAR

8 in. ——— FOLD

1 in.

CUT HERE

DIAGRAM 1.

1 in.

CUT HERE

FOLD

DIAGRAM 2.

FOR THE SMART WOMAN. *A lovely choice to be made between crisp white linen revers with button-hole stitched scalloped edges and small eyelet holes ; a petal collar made of half-circles of organdie bound with narrow gathered lace ; a gay pointed collar and bow of seersucker edged with dark bias binding, and a folded bib collar.*

centre 1 in. down and cut out a section sloping gently up towards the fold at the extreme edges on both sides as shown in Diagram 1. This leaves a bib-shaped portion for the collar itself. Seam round the outer edges, turn inside out, which is the right side, and press.

Now take the portion that has been cut out and fold it in half widthways. Cut off the top point about 1 in. down as shown in Diagram 2 ; seam the sides of

the remainder, turn right side out and press. Tack the top raw edges of this flap to the raw edges of the collar at the centre and bind along the inner curve of the collar with the bias binding. Make a tiny hem at both ends of the binding.

Make a fold across the deepest part of the bib-shape and put in a stitch or two to hold the shaped flap over the pleat. Press the collar well with a hot iron and a damp cloth, with the binding turned inside.

SCALLOPED REVERS

MATERIALS

Oblong of linen, 7 ins. by 9 ins.

Skein of linen thread, or embroidery thread.

1 yd. bias binding.

Method.—Cut the strip of linen in half diagonally to make two triangles, the shortest side of each being the top edge of the revers, and the cross-cut edge, the inside. Using a penny as a guide, pencil in scallops along the two straight edges of each triangle keeping within about 1 in. of the raw edges. Work round the pencil lines with small running stitches, then work a second row of running stitches $\frac{1}{8}$ in. inside the first line. Work over both these lines with close buttonholing then cut away the surplus material beyond the scalloping, with small, sharp-pointed scissors.

Mark a tiny circle in the centre of the first scallop and work small running stitches round it. Pierce the material in the circle with a stiletto or a steel knitting needle and work close satin stitch over the raw edges to make an eyelet hole. Work a similar eyelet hole in the centre of each scallop.

Bind the raw diagonal edge of one rever with the bias binding, leave about 8 ins. of binding between the two, and bind the raw edge of the second rever. Stitch together the two edges of the binding along the centre portion, then press the revers well, on the wrong side, with a hot iron over a damp cloth.

LEATHER BELT

With a Two-Way Fastening

MATERIALS

Piece of leather 9 ins. by 16 ins.

$1\frac{1}{2}$ yds. stiff ribbon 1 in. wide.

$\frac{1}{2}$ yd. stiff ribbon $2\frac{1}{2}$ ins. wide.

2 1-in. buckles.

Cut one leather strip $15\frac{3}{4}$ ins. by 3 ins.

Cut two leather strips 13 ins. by $1\frac{1}{2}$ ins.

Cut two leather strips 11 ins. by $1\frac{1}{2}$ ins.

Cut ribbon linings to fit.

Method.—Turn in all edges of leather about $\frac{1}{4}$ in., mitreing both ends of the longer narrow strips and one end of the shorter narrow strips.

Face with lining and stitch edges about $\frac{1}{16}$ in. from edges.

Stitch buckles to straight ends of narrow strips, piercing holes about $\frac{3}{4}$ in. from end for point of buckle.

Stitch one long and one short strip to one end of the wide strip with $\frac{1}{2}$ in. space between. Then join remaining strips to opposite end, so that each buckle meets a pointed strip.

To make belt adjustable, pierce three holes at intervals of 1 in., along the centre of the belt, beginning $3\frac{1}{2}$ ins. from pointed ends.

Work small neat buttonhole stitches round these holes.

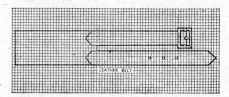

FOR THE GIRL WITH A PLAIN FROCK. *This attractive belt is in red leather and is lined with ribbon. It is a single strip three inches wide at the back, and the front is cut into four single strips which fasten in opposite directions with small buckles*

EVENING HEAD SCARF

and Bag to Match

NET EVENING SCARF

MATERIALS

1 yd. black net, 36 ins. wide.

Sequins for trimming, approximately 60 each, silver, emerald and cyclamen.

Method.—Fold the square of net in half diagonally, and run a tacking thread along the fold as far as the centre of the square. Cut a triangle of paper about 18 ins. deep by 13 ins. wide and from a centre line draw in three sets of "fronds" in diminishing sizes. Pin this paper under the net with its centre line exactly beneath the tacking thread, then run tacking threads out each side over the top of the drawn-in "fronds".

Sew on sequins singly and about 1 in. apart, along these tacking threads, using cyclamen for the top and bottom curves, and emerald for the centre ones. Finally, remove the tacking threads.

Fold each side of the net into eight and cut into scallops merging the end scallops of each side to make one large scallop right round the corner. Sew one green and two silver sequins in each of the side scallops and two green and three silver ones round the corner scallops.

EVENING BAG

MATERIALS

Black satin, approximately 13 ins. by 13 ins.

Silk for lining, approximately 12 ins. by 12 ins.

Canvas, 11 ins. by 11 ins.

Zip fastener 9 ins. long.

Sequins for trimming, approximately 125 silver, 50 emerald, 100 cyclamen.

Method.—Cut a circle of canvas, 11 ins. in diameter and fold it in half, then follow Diagram 1 to make the bag shape. Mark a point A 3 ins. along the outer edge from the fold and another point B, 2½ ins. along the bottom fold. Crease the canvas from A to B to mark the gusset and make a similar one at the other side. Cut remaining edges of semicircle into four equal-sized scallops.

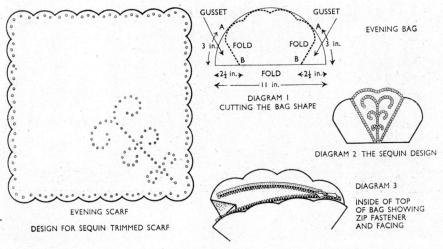

EVENING SCARF

DESIGN FOR SEQUIN TRIMMED SCARF

GUSSET   GUSSET   EVENING BAG

A   A

3 in.   FOLD   FOLD   3 in.

B   B

◄2½ in.►   FOLD   ◄2½ in.►

◄——— 11 in. ———►

DIAGRAM 1
CUTTING THE BAG SHAPE

DIAGRAM 2 THE SEQUIN DESIGN

DIAGRAM 3

INSIDE OF TOP
OF BAG SHOWING
ZIP FASTENER
AND FACING

FOR THE SMART GIRL. *A lovely gift for a lucky girl is this glamorous set for evening wear. The filmy black net head scarf has a sequin motif in one corner, and the scalloped edge is trimmed with sequins. The black satin handbag has the " frond " motif outlined in sequins to match the scarf.*

Open this canvas out and using it as a pattern, cut the shape in the black satin and the lining, allowing ¼ in. turnings all round. Keep the centre fold to the straight of the material.

Tack the canvas shape to the wrong side of the satin with rows of tacking stitches radiating out from the centre to keep the two layers firmly together. Turn the satin over on to the canvas round the edge, snipping it between the scallops, and catch-stitch it down, taking care that the stitches do not show on the right side. Remove the tackings and press well, fold the shape in half and

fold in the gussets then trim one side of the bag with sequins as shown in Diagram 2. The design should be marked in first of all in tailoring chalk or tacking threads, and then the sequins sewn on in overlapping formation with back-stitch. The outer line of sequins should be silver, the top and bottom " fronds " cyclamen and the centre ones emerald.

Open the bag out again and tack the lining in place, hemming it neatly round the outer edge. From the remaining pieces of black satin, cut facings for the top edges of the bag, about 1½ ins. deep and from gusset to gusset in width.

Turn in the inner edges of these facings and sew along both sides of the zip fastener. Turn in the outer edges of the facings and hem them to the top of the bag itself, then run a line of back-stitching about $\frac{1}{4}$ in. from the metal fastener to keep the facing in place, as in Diagram 3. The stitches should not, of course, show on the outside of the bag.

Finally, whip together the top edges of the gussets, from the inner point to within $\frac{1}{2}$ in. of the creases at the sides of the bag, making small neat stitches.

BOX FOR HATS
Shaped Like A Drum

MATERIALS

11 yds. 2-in. wide white webbing braid.
3 yds. 1$\frac{1}{2}$-in. wide red webbing braid.
4$\frac{1}{2}$ yds. red cord.
2 red tassels.
Sheet of corrugated cardboard approximately 3 yds. by 18 ins. wide.
Roll of white shelf paper.
Roll of adhesive paper, 2 ins. wide.
Glue.

Method.—To make the box foundation, cut a 16-in. circle of corrugated cardboard for the base and a 9-in. deep strip exactly long enough to go round the edge of the circle, for the sides. Join the ends of the strip with adhesive paper inside and out (ridges inside), then join the bottom edge to the outer edge of the circular base using short strips of the adhesive paper, as shown in Diagram 1. For security, use the gummed strips inside and outside the foundation.

Make a lid in exactly the same way, but cutting the circle 17 ins. wide and the strip only 1$\frac{1}{2}$ ins. deep.

Cut 9-in. long strips of the white braid and glue these up the sides of the box foundation, letting their edges just overlap. The bottom of each strip should be about 1 in. from the base of the box and the top should go over the edge and inside a little way. When the glue is quite dry arrange four crosses of red cord at regular intervals round the outside, sewing the ends of the cord to the braid just inside the top of the box and through the cardboard foundation at the bottom. Now glue a band of the red braid round the bottom of the box, covering the raw edges of the white strips and the ends of the red cord crosses, which can be unravelled a little to lie flat.

Cover the top of the box lid with strips of white braid glued across from side to side and extending a little way down the side of the lid. Glue a band of red braid round the side.

For the handle, take a piece of red cord, about 1$\frac{3}{4}$ yds. long, join the two ends and fold it in half. Stitch a red tassel at each end and sew the tassels to opposite sides of the box about half-way down and between the red cord crosses.

DRUM HAT BOX

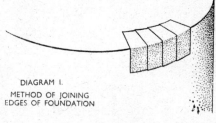

DIAGRAM I.
METHOD OF JOINING
EDGES OF FOUNDATION

FOR ANY WOMAN. *A pretty yet practical gift is this unusual and attractive hat box. It is shaped like a large drum and will hold several hats at one time. It is made of white and red braid arranged over a cardboard foundation. The lid and sides are decorated with red cord and tassels.*

To line the sides of the box, and to give it extra strength, as well as finish, paste narrow strips of white shelf paper with their edges overlapping, wallpaper style, down the inside. Cut a circle of corrugated cardboard to fit the floor of the box tightly, cover its flat side with white shelf paper, turning the edges on to the under side, and press it well down into the bottom of the box. Line and strengthen the inside of the lid, with shelf paper, in the same way.

CASE FOR NEEDLES

Trimmed with Beads

BEAD NEEDLECASE

MATERIALS

Approximately 1,200 small green beads.
Approximately 500 small pearl, or white beads.
Approximately 100 small pink beads.
Scraps of net, stiff muslin, satin and flannel.
Small sheet of thick blotting paper.
Needles—assorted sizes.

Method.—The beads are stitched in rows on to a foundation of white net, and as the work is best done in a hoop frame, the piece of net must be large enough to fit the frame. The beads chosen should be a little larger than the mesh of the net so that they will not slip through. Diagram 1 shows how the beads are sewn on diagonally across the mesh.

Begin by working the centre motif, following the chart which is keyed for the three different coloured beads. Fill in a background of pearls surrounding the motif in a diamond shape (the actual size is immaterial) and edge the centre panel with a single row of pink beads. Now put in rows of green beads round the centre panel to form a border about ¾ in. wide. Finish it with one row of pearls round the outer edge.

Take the net out of the frame and cut out the beaded section leaving a margin of ½ in. of net all round. Cut a piece of stiff muslin exactly the same size and tack muslin and net together round the edges. From the blotting paper cut a diamond shape exactly the same size as the beaded section, smear a very little glue on it, place it on the muslin backing and turn the edges of the muslin and net over on

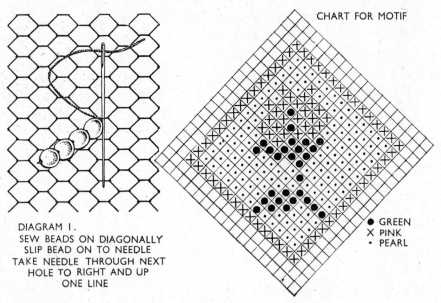

DIAGRAM 1.
SEW BEADS ON DIAGONALLY
SLIP BEAD ON TO NEEDLE
TAKE NEEDLE THROUGH NEXT
HOLE TO RIGHT AND UP
ONE LINE

CHART FOR MOTIF

● GREEN
X PINK
· PEARL

FOR THE NEEDLEWOMAN. *The interest of this enchanting little diamond shaped needlecase is focused on the beaded front. Seed pearls and beads are stitched in rows on a foundation of white net. The back is quite plain, and two pieces of flannel with pinked edges are stitched inside to hold the needles.*

to it. Mitre the corners of the net and muslin neatly and glue the raw edges down on to the blotting paper. This completes the front of the case.

For the back of the case, cut a second diamond of blotting paper and a slightly larger diamond of satin. Glue them together with the raw edges of the satin over the blotting paper. When the glue is quite dry, cut a double strip of satin a little shorter than the sides of the diamonds, turn in its edges top and bottom and stitch one long side inside the front cover and the other inside the back cover so that it acts as a hinge between the two. Cut two more diamonds of satin, turn in their raw edges and line back and front covers with them.

Cut two diamonds of flannel to fit, pink their edges and sew them inside the case at the top inside corners. Complete the case with a selection of needles.

CUSHION COVER

And Lampshade to Match

MATERIALS

1 yd. 36-in. wide check gingham.
Bias-cut strip of thin white material
suitable for lining lamp, size approximately 36 ins. by 7 ins.
3½ yds. thick white piping cord.
4 yds. thin white piping cord.
3 yds. white bias binding.
Lampshade frame, approximately
9 ins. wide at base and 6 ins. deep.

THE CUSHION COVER

Method.—Cut four squares of gingham,
10 ins. by 10 ins., two of them on the
bias and two on the straight of the
material, and join them together to make
a square with the bias-cut ones at
opposite corners, as shown in Diagram 1.
Press the seams well. Cut a 1½ yd.
length of the thick white piping cord and
tie it into a bow and ends, with the two
loops exactly the same size. Pin the knot
in the centre of the cushion and spread
the loops out into triangles along the
seams in the gingham. Flatten the centre
knot as much as possible and stitch

securely, then sew the cord to the
gingham along the loops and leave the
two ends loose.

The best method of stitching the cord
on, is to take one stitch into the gingham
then run the needle through a few
strands of the cord underneath, then
another stitch into the gingham, and so
on. In this way, no stitches will show on
the top of the cord.

For the back of the cover, cut a
piece of gingham 19 ins. by 20 ins., then
join back and front of the cover together
with the right sides facing, along three
sides only. The extra inch on the open
side will make a flap under the fastening.
Turn the cover on to the right side and
stitch thick piping cord right round the
edge on all four sides.

THE LAMPSHADE

Bind round the wires of the lampshade frame with the bias binding as
shown in Diagram 2. Cut a piece of the

GINGHAM CUSHION COVER

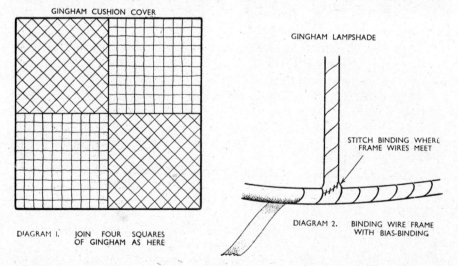

DIAGRAM 1. JOIN FOUR SQUARES
OF GINGHAM AS HERE

GINGHAM LAMPSHADE

STITCH BINDING WHERE
FRAME WIRES MEET

DIAGRAM 2. BINDING WIRE FRAME
WITH BIAS-BINDING

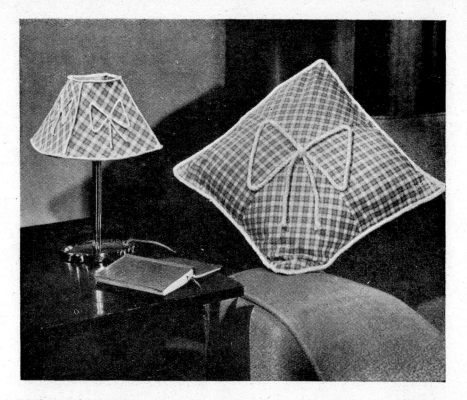

THE YOUNG-MARRIEDS' GIFT. *What could be more acceptable than this match-ing cushion cover and lampshade in check gingham? Thick white piping decorates the outside edge of the cushion, and a flat bow is stitched to the centre front. Each section of the lampshade is outlined with narrow white cord, and matching bows are stitched to the centre of the four panels.*

white fabric on the cross of the material, long enough to go round the frame at the bottom and about ½ in. deeper than the frame itself. Stitch this lining round the lower edge of the frame, with a narrow turning to the outside.

Seam the lining up on the straight of the material. Divide the top edge into quarters and ease each quarter into a quarter section of the wire frame and stitch securely to the binding, again taking a narrow turning on to the outside.

Cut pieces of gingham on the cross of the material for each section of the lamp, allowing ¼ in. turnings on each edge.

Turn in the edges and stitch the gingham on to the binding, stretching the material well over the frame so that it is quite taut.

From the narrow piping cord, cut four pieces each 18 ins. long. Tie each into bow and ends and stitch in the centre of each panel, spreading the loops out in triangular shapes similar to the bow on the cushion cover. The lines of the check will be helpful in keeping the bows to sharp angles. Stitch the loops of the cord only, leaving the ends hanging loose.

Finish the lampshade with narrow piping cord round the top and bottom edges and down each of the corner wires.

FOR BIG SISTER. *This enchanting fascinator would make a lovely gift. The original was knitted in white wool with a fringed edge. The charming little raised flowers are knitted in silk, and each flower consists of four knots in a contrast colour.*

FRINGED FASCINATOR

Trimmed with Coloured Flowers

MATERIALS

2 oz. 2-ply wool.

Some oddments of wool or silk in any number of contrasting colours (about 1⅛ yds. will be enough to make one flower).

2 No. 8 knitting needles.

A medium crochet hook.

MEASUREMENTS

36 ins. by 18 ins.

TENSION

6½ sts. to 1 in.

ABBREVIATIONS

K. knit, p. purl, st. stitch, sts. stitches, rep. repeat, sl. slip, ins. inches, t.b.l. through back of loops, con. contrasting, tog. together.

N.B.—The Fascinator is worked in the main colour with the " knots " in contrast colours, each flower consisting of 4 knots. Join in separate lengths for each flower.

With main colour cast on 243 sts. and k. 4 rows. Continue in patt. thus :—

1st row.—K. 2, * k. 7, with con. make a knot thus : winding wool twice instead of once round needle for each st. work (k. 1, p. 1) 3 times all into next st., k. 6, rep. from * to last 3 sts., k. 3. (N.B.— Always keep ends of loops on wrong side of work.)

2nd row.—K. 2, p. 2 tog., * p. 5, sl. 6 dropping extra loops, p. 8, rep. from * to last 20 sts., p. 5, sl. 6 dropping extra loops, p. 5, p. 2 tog., k. 2.

3rd row.—K. 2, k. 2 tog., k. 3, * with con. make a knot in next st., k. 6 tog. t.b.l., with con. make a knot in next st., k. 11, rep. from * to last 15 sts., with con. make a knot in next st., k. 6 tog. t.b.l.,

with con. make a knot in next st., k. 3, k. 2 tog., k. 2.

4th row.—K. 2, p. 4, * sl. 6 dropping extra loops, p. 1, sl. 6 dropping extra loops, p. 11, rep. from * to last 19 sts., sl. 6 dropping extra loops, p. 1, sl. 6 dropping extra loops, p. 4, k. 2.

5th row.—K. 2, k. 2 tog., k. 2, * k. 6 tog. t.b.l., with con. make a knot in next st., k. 6 tog. t.b.l., k. 11, rep. from * to last 19 sts., k. 6 tog. t.b.l., with con. make a knot in next st., k. 6 tog. t.b.l., k. 2, k. 2 tog., k. 2.

6th row.—K. 2, p. 2 tog., p. 2, * sl. 6 dropping extra loops, p. 13, rep. from * to last 12 sts., sl. 6 dropping extra loops, p. 2, p. 2 tog., k. 2.

7th row.—K. 5, * k. 6 tog. t.b.l., k. 13, rep. from * to last 11 sts., k. 6 tog. t.b.l., k. 5.

8th row.—K. 2, p. 2 tog., p. to last 4 sts., p. 2 tog., k. 2.

9th row.—K. 2, k. 2 tog., k. to last 4 sts., k. 2 tog., k. 2.

10th row.—K. 2, p. to last 2 sts., k. 2.

11th row.—As 9th row.

12th row.—As 8th row.

13th row.—K. to end.

14th–19th rows.—Rep. rows 8 to 13 inclusive once.

20th row.—As 8th row.

21st row.—As 9th row.

22nd row.—K. 2, p. 14, * with con. make a knot in next st., p. 13, rep. from * to last 3 sts., p. 1, k. 2.

23rd row.—K. 2, k. 2 tog., * k. 12, sl. 6 dropping extra loops, k. 1, rep. from * to last 15 sts., k. 11, k. 2 tog., k. 2.

24th row.—K. 2, p. 2 tog., * p. 10, with con. make a knot in next st., p. 6 tog., with con. make a knot in next st.,

p. 1, rep. from * to last 13 sts., p. 9, p. 2 tog., k. 2.

25th row.—K. 2, * k. 11, sl. 6 dropping extra loops, k. 1, sl. 6 dropping extra loops, rep. from * to last 13 sts., k. 13.

26th row.—K. 2, p. 2 tog., * p. 9, p. 6 tog., with con. make a knot in next st., p. 6 tog., p. 2, rep. from * to last 11 sts., p. 7, p. 2 tog., k. 2.

27th row.—K. 2, k. 2 tog., * k. 9, sl. 6 dropping extra loops, k. 4, rep. from * to last 9 sts., k. 5, k. 2 tog., k. 2.

28th row.—K. 2, * p. 10, p. 6 tog., p. 3, rep. from * to last 9 sts., p. 7, k. 2.

29th row.—As 9th row.

30th row.—As 8th row.

31st row.—K. to end.

32nd row.—As 8th row.

33rd row.—As 9th row.

34th row.—As 10th row.

Rep. rows 29 to 34 inclusive once.

41st row.—As 9th row.

42nd row.—As 8th row.

Rep. these 42 rows 3 times (19 sts. remain).

169th row.—K. 9, with con. make a knot in next st., k. 9.

170th row.—K. 2, p. 2 tog., p. 5, sl. 6 dropping extra loops, p. 5, p. 2 tog., k. 2.

171st row.—K. 2, k. 2 tog., k. 3, with con. make a knot in next st., k. 6 tog. t.b.l., with con. make a knot in next st., k. 3, k. 2 tog., k. 2.

172nd row.—K. 2, p. 4, sl. 6 dropping extra loops, p. 1, sl. 6 dropping extra loops, p. 4, k. 2.

173rd row.—K. 2, k. 2 tog., k. 2, k. 6 tog. t.b.l., with con. make a knot in next st., k. 6 tog. t.b.l., k. 2, k. 2 tog., k. 2.

174th row.—K. 2, p. 2 tog., p. 2, sl. 6 dropping extra loops, p. 2, p. 2 tog., k. 2.

175th row.—K. 5, k. 6 tog. t.b.l., k. 5.

176th row.—K. 2, p. 2 tog., p. 3, p. 2 tog., k. 2.

177th row.—K. 2, k. 2 tog., k. 1, k. 2 tog., k. 2.

178th row.—K. 2, p. 3, k. 2.

179th row.—K. 2, k. 3 tog., k. 2.

180th row.—K. 1, p. 3 tog., k. 1.

K. 3 tog. and fasten off securely.

Press work lightly with hot iron over damp cloth.

Darn in all con. ends very neatly on wrong side of flowers.

Make a fringe all round the three sides thus : cut lengths of wool 3½ ins. long, take 2 of these strands and fold double, then, using a crochet hook. Draw loop through edge, then pull both ends through the loop.

Straighten the threads of the fringe and press the knots.

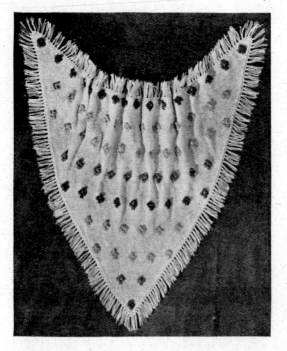

The fascinator is trimmed with raised silk knots.

LINED BEDJACKET

In Two Colours

MATERIALS

4 oz. 2 ply wool in main colour.
4 oz. 2 ply wool in contrasting colour.
2 No. 7, 2 No. 8 and 2 No. 10 knitting
   needles.
1 yd. of ribbon.

MEASUREMENTS

Length : 18 ins.
Bust size : 36 ins.
Sleeve seam : 6 ins.

TENSION

7 sts. to 1 in.

ABBREVIATIONS

K. knit, p. purl, st. stitch, sts. stitches,
rep. repeat, beg. beginning, dec.
decrease, inc. increase, patt. pattern,
wl. fwd. wool forward, wl. bk. wool
back, st.st. stocking stitch, sl. slip, ins.
inches, tog. together, mn. main colour,
con. contrast colour.

The Back of Main Part.—With No. 10
needles and mn. colour cast on 115 sts.
and k. 1 row. Continue in patt. thus :—

1st row.—P. 3, * k. 5 winding wool
twice instead of once round needle for
each st., p. 3, rep. from * to end.

2nd row.—K. 3, * wl. fwd., sl. 5
dropping extra loops, wl. bk., k. 3,
from * to end.

3rd row.—P. 3, * wl. bk., sl. 5,
wl. fwd., p. 3, rep. from * to end.

4th row.—K. 3, * (K. 1, P. 1) into
wool in front of slipped sts., P. 5 tog.
(K. 1, P. 1) into wool in front of slipped
sts., K. 3, rep. from * to end.

5th row.—P. 5, * k. 1, p. 7, rep.
from * to last 6 sts., k. 1, p. 5.

6th row.—P. 4, * k. 3, p. 5, rep.
from * to last 7 sts., k. 3, p. 4.

7th row.—K. 1, k. 3 winding wool

twice instead of once round needle for
each st., * p. 3, k. 5 winding wool
twice instead of once round needle for
each st., rep. from * to last 7 sts., p. 3,
k. 3 winding wool twice instead of once
round needle for each st., k. 1.

8th row.—K. 1, wl. fwd., sl. 3 dropping extra loops, wl. bk., * k. 3, wl. fwd.,
sl. 5 dropping extra loops, wl. bk.,
rep. from * to last 7 sts., k. 3, wl. fwd.,
sl. 3 dropping extra loops, wl. bk., k. 1.

9th row.—K. 1, sl. 3 * p. 3, wl. bk.,
sl. 5, wl. fwd., rep. from * to last 7 sts.,
p. 3, wl. bk., sl. 3, k. 1.

10th row.—K. 1, k. 1 into wool in
front of slipped sts., p. 3 tog., k. 1
into wool in front of slipped sts., * k. 3
(k. 1, p. 1) into wool in front of slipped
sts., p. 5 tog. (k. 1, p. 1) into wool in
front of slipped sts., rep. from * to last
7 sts., k. 3, k. 1 into wool in front of
slipped sts., p. 3 tog., k. 1 into wool in
front of slipped sts., k. 1.

11th row.—P. 2, k. 1, p. 6, * k. 1,
p. 7, rep. from * to last 10 sts., k. 1,
p. 6, k. 1, p. 2.

12th row.—K. 3, * p. 5, k. 3, rep.
from * to end.

These 12 rows form the patt.

Continue in patt. until work measures
3 ins., ending with a row on wrong side.

Change to No. 7 needles and continue
in patt. inc. 1 st. both ends of next row
and of every following 6th row until
there are 131 sts. on needle, working
extra sts. gradually into patt.

Continue without shaping until work
measures 11 ins., ending with a row on
wrong side of work.

Shape Armholes thus.—Keeping continuity of patt. cast off 4 sts. at beg. of

FOR THE CONVALESCENT. *A gift that will be greatly appreciated is this cosy little reversible bedjacket. Its double-thickness means warmth and protection where most bedjackets fail. The original was knitted in pale blue with a pink lining.*

the next 2 rows, then dec. 1 st. both ends of every row until 101 sts. remain.

Continue without shaping until work measures 18 ins., ending with a row on wrong side of work.

Shape Shoulders thus.—Cast off 12 sts. at beg. of the next 6 rows.

Cast off remaining sts.

The Right Front of Main Part.—With No. 10 needles and mn. colour cast on 59 sts. and k. 1 row.

Work in patt. as given for back for 3 ins., ending with a row on wrong side.

Change to No. 7 needles and continue in patt. inc. 1 st. at end of the next row and of every following 6th row until there are 67 sts. on needle, working extra sts. gradually into patt.

Continue without shaping until work measures 11 ins., ending at shaped side edge.

Shape Armhole thus.—Keeping continuity of patt. cast off 4 sts. at beg. of the next row, then dec. 1 st. at this same edge on every row until 52 sts. remain.

Continue without shaping until work measures 16 ins., ending at straight front edge.

Shape Neck thus.—Cast off 6 sts. at beg. of next row, then dec. 1 st. at this same edge on every row until 41 sts. remain, then dec. 1 st. on every alternate row at this same edge until 36 sts. remain.

Continue without shaping until work measures 18 ins., ending at armhole edge.

Shape Shoulder thus.—

Next row.—Cast off 12, patt. to end.

Next row.—Patt. to end.

Rep. last 2 rows once.

Cast off remaining sts.

The Left Front of Main Part.—With No. 10 needles and mn. colour cast on 59 sts. and k. 1 row.

Work in patt. as given for back for 3 ins., ending with a row on wrong side.

Change to No. 7 needles and continue in patt. inc. 1 st. at beg. of the next row and of every following 6th row until there

are 67 sts. on needle, working extra sts. gradually into patt.

Continue without shaping until work is 11 ins., ending at shaped side edge.

Now complete armhole, neck and shoulder shaping as given for the right front.

The Sleeves.—With No. 10 needles and mn. colour cast on 91 sts. and k. 1 row.

Continue in patt. as given for back for 1 in.

Change to No. 7 needles and continue in patt. inc. 1 st. both ends of next row and of every following 4th row until there are 107 sts. on needle, working extra sts. gradually into patt.

Continue without shaping until work measures 6 ins., ending with a row on wrong side of work.

Shape Top thus.—Keeping continuity of patt. dec. 1 st. both ends of alternate rows until 67 sts. remain.

Now dec. 1 st. both ends of every row until 47 sts. remain.

Cast off.

The Lining for Back.—With right side of main part of back facing and using No. 10 needles and contrasting wool k. up 115 sts. along cast-on edge.

Continue in st.st. (1 row k., 1 row p.) beg. with a p. row for 3 ins., ending with a p. row.

Change to No. 8 needles and continue in st.st. exactly as given for back of main part, substituting st.st. for patt. throughout.

The Lining for Right Front.—With right side of main part of right front facing and using No. 10 needles and con. wool k. up 59 sts. along cast-on edge.

Continue st.st. beg. with a p. row for 3 ins., ending with a p. row.

Change to No. 8 needles and continue in st.st. exactly as given for right front of main part substituting st.st. for patt. throughout.

The Lining for Left Front.—With

A row of double crochet decorates the neck which fastens with ribbon.

right side of main part of left front facing and using No. 10 needles and con. wool k. up 59 sts. along cast-on edge.

Continue in st.st. beg. with a p. row for 3 ins., ending with a p. row.

Change to No. 8 needles and continue in st.st. exactly as given for left front of main part substituting st.st. for patt. throughout.

The Lining for Sleeves.—With right side of main sleeve facing and using No. 10 needles and con. wool. k. up 91 sts. along lower cast-on edge.

Continue in st.st., beg. with a p. row, for 1 in., ending with a p. row.

Change to No. 8 needles and continue in st.st. exactly as given for sleeve of main part substituting st.st. for patt. throughout, until work measures 6 ins.
Shape Top thus.—Dec. 1 st. at both ends of alternate rows until 87 sts. remain.

Then dec. 1 st. at both ends of every row until 47 sts. remain. Cast off.
Make-up.—Press each piece out carefully and press lightly on wrong side with a hot iron over a damp cloth.

Join side and shoulder seams of main part. Then join side and shoulder seams of lining.

Join front edges of main part to front edges of lining and turn right side out.

Join sleeve seams of main part, then sleeve seams of lining.

Now, working through opening at neck, set in sleeve top of main part, then sleeve top of lining to corresponding armholes.

To finish neck work a row of double crochet in main colour through edges of main part and lining together.

Sew ribbons at neck edge to tie.

DAINTY KNICKERS

With Lace Stitch Leg Panels

MATERIALS

4 oz. rayon knitting yarn (about as thick as 2 ply wool).
2 No. 10 and 2 No. 12 knitting needles.
Elastic.

MEASUREMENTS

Length from lower edge of crutch to top : 14 ins.
Waist : 28 ins.

TENSION

7 sts. to 1 in. measured over st.st.

ABBREVIATIONS

K. knit, p. purl, st. stitch, tog. together, sl. slip, m. 1, make 1, p.s.s.o. pass slipped st. over, dec. decrease, st.st.

stocking st. (1 row k., 1 row p.) patt. pattern, rep. repeat, g. st. garter stitch.

The Front.—Using No. 10 needles cast on 61 sts. and work 4 rows in g.st. (every row k.).

Now work in patt. thus :—

1st row.—* k. 1, m. 1, k. 3, k. 2 tog., k. 1, k. 2 tog., k. 3, m. 1 * rep. from * to the last st., k. 1.

2nd row.—* p. 2, m. 1, p. 2, p. 2 tog., p. 1, p. 2 tog., p. 2, m. 1, p. 1 * rep. from * to the last st., p. 1.

3rd row.—* k. 3, m. 1, k. 1, k. 2

The shaped lace stitch side panels add a dainty touch. Elastic or ribbon is threaded through small holes at the waist ribbing.

tog., k. 1, k. 2 tog., k. 1, m. 1, k. 2 * rep. from * to the last st., k. 1.

4th row.—* p. 4, m. 1, p. 2 tog., p. 1, p. 2 tog., m. 1, p. 3 * rep. from * to the last st., p. 1.

5th row.—* k. 5, m. 1, sl. 1, k. 2 tog., p.s.s.o., m. 1, k. 4 * rep. from * to the last st., k. 1.

6th row.—P. to the end.

Leave these sts. on spare needle and work a second piece in the same way.

Join legs and commence gusset thus :—

7th row.—* k. 1, k. 2 tog., k. 3, m. 1, k. 1, m. 1, k. 3, k. 2 tog. * rep. from * to the last st., k. 1.

Now cast on 30 sts. for gusset, then work 7th patt. row across the second set of 61 sts. (152 sts. on needle).

8th row.—* p. 1, p. 2 tog., p. 2, m. 1, p. 3, m. 1, p. 2, p. 2 tog. * rep. from * 4 times more, p. 31, rep. from * to * 5 times, p. 1.

9th row.—* k. 1, k. 2 tog., k. 1, m. 1, k. 5, m. 1, k. 1, k. 2 tog. * rep. from * to * 4 times more, k. 1, sl. 1, k. 1, p.s.s.o., k. 26, k. 2 tog., rep. from * to * 5 times, k. 1.

10th row.—* p. 1, p. 2 tog., m. 1, p. 7, m. 1, p. 2 tog. * rep. from * to * 4 times more, p. 29, rep. from * to * 5 times, p. 1.

11th row.—K. 2 tog., * m. 1, k. 9, m. 1, sl. 1, k. 2 tog., p.s.s.o., * rep. from * to * 4 times more ending 4th rep. k. 2 tog. (instead of sl. 1, k. 2 tog., p.s.s.o.), sl. 1, k. 1, p.s.s.o., k. 24 (k. 2 tog.) twice, repeat from * to * 5 times ending 5th rep. k. 2 tog. instead of sl. 1, k. 1, p.s.s.o.

12th row.—P. to the end.

13th row.—Rep. from * to * as in 1st row 5 times, k. 1, sl. 1, k. 1, p.s.s.o., k. 22, k. 2 tog., rep. from * to * as in 1st patt. row 5 times, k. 1.

14th row.—Rep. from * to * as in 2nd row 5 times, p. 25, rep. from * to * as in 2nd row 5 times, p. 1.

15th row.—Rep. from * to * as in

3rd row 5 times, k. 1, sl. 1, k. 1, p.s.s.o., k. 20, k. 2 tog., rep. from * to * as in 3rd row 5 times, k. 1.

16th row.—Rep. from * to * as in 4th row 5 times, p. 23, rep. from * to * as in 4th row 5 times, p. 1.

17th row.—Rep. from * to * as in 5th row 5 times, k. 1, sl. 1, k. 1, p.s.s.o., k. 18, k. 2 tog., rep. from * to * as in 5th row 5 times, k. 1.

18th row.—P. to the end.

19th row.—Rep. from * to * as in 7th row 4 times, k. 1, k. 2 tog., k. 3, m. 1, k. 7, sl. 1, k. 1, p.s.s.o., k. 16, k. 2 tog., k. 7, m. 1, k. 3, k. 2 tog., rep. from * to * as in 7th row 4 times, k. 1.

20th row.—Rep. from * to * as in 8th row 4 times, p. 1, p. 2 tog., p. 2, m. 1, p. 34, m. 1, p. 2, p. 2 tog., rep. from * to * as in 8th row 4 times, p. 1.

21st row.—Rep. from * to * as in 9th row 4 times, k. 1, k. 2 tog., k. 1, m. 1, k. 9, sl. 1, k. 1, p.s.s.o., k. 14, k. 2 tog., k. 9, m. 1, k. 1, k. 2 tog., rep. from * to * as in 9th row 4 times, k. 1.

22nd row.—Rep. from * to * as in 10th row 4 times, p. 1, p. 2 tog., m. 1, p. 36, m. 1, p. 2 tog., rep. from * to * as in 10th row 4 times, p. 1.

23rd row.—K. 2 tog., rep. from * to * as in 11th row 4 times, m. 1, k. 11, sl. 1, k. 1, p.s.s.o., k. 12, k. 2 tog., k. 11, m. 1, sl. 1, k. 1, p.s.s.o., rep. from * to * as in 11th row 4 times ending last rep. k. 2 tog. instead of sl. 1, k. 1, p.s.s.o.

24th row.—P. to the end.

Beginning again with the first patt. row work the first 6 rows with only 4 complete patts. from * to * at each end of every row still dec. 1 st. at both sides of gusset in every right side row, and working all sts. between the patt. sts. in st.st.

Then, still dec. gusset sts. as before work the patt. at each end of the rows as in rows 19 to 23 but with only 3 complete patts. from * to * instead of 4 and with

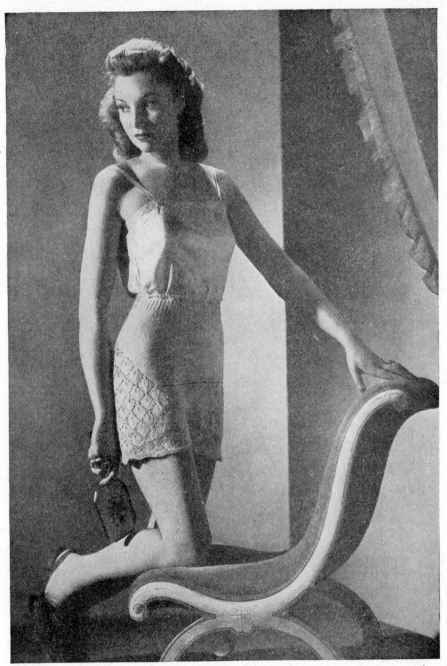

FOR ANY WOMAN. *A pair of lightweight knickers for summer wear is a practical gift that is sure to please. This attractive little garment is knitted in rayon yarn ; the main part is in stocking stitch, with diamond stitch side leg panels.*

the extra sts. in between patt. sts. in st.st.

Next row.—P. 61, p. 2 tog., p. 61.

Continue working the patt. with 3 complete patts. at each end of the next 6 rows as in rows 1 to 6, then 2½ patts. in the next 6 rows as in rows 19 to 24 and at the same time dec. 1 st. at both sides of centre st. (remaining gusset st.) in the 21st patt. row.

Dec. row.—Work to within 2 sts. of centre st., sl. 1, k. 1, p.s.s.o., k. 1, k. 2 tog., work to the end.

Continue working half a patt. less at each end of rows every 6 rows until all sts. are in st.st., at the same time dec. 1 st. each side of centre st. every 8th row until 109 sts. remain.

Now continue in st.st. without shaping until work measures 12 ins. from cast-on edge of gusset, ending on wrong side.

Next row.—K. 6, k. 2 tog., * k. 10, k. 2 tog., rep. from * to last 5 sts., k. 5 (100 sts.).

Change to No. 12 needles and work in k. 1, p. 1 rib for 1½ ins.

Next row.—* Rib 2, m. 1, work 2 tog., rep. from * to the last st. rib 1.

Now continue in k. 1, p. 1 rib until work measures 14 ins. from lower edge of gusset. Cast off loosely in rib.

The Back.—Work exactly as given for front until work measures 12 ins., ending with a row on the wrong side.

Now shape thus :—

1st row.—K. to the last 7 sts., turn.

2nd row.—P. to the last 7 sts., turn.

3rd row.—K. to the last 14 sts., turn.

4th row.—P. to the last 14 sts., turn.

5th row.—K. to the last 21 sts., turn.

6th row.—P. to the last 21 sts., turn.

7th row.—K. to the last 28 sts., turn.

8th row.—P. to the last 28 sts., turn.

Continue thus working 7 sts. less in every row until there are only 18 sts. being worked in centre of row.

Next row.—Work to the end.

Next row.—K. 6, k. 2 tog. * k. 10, k. 2 tog., rep. from * to last 5 sts., k. 5.

Change to No. 12 needles and work ribbing with holes to match front.

Make-up.—Press pieces with a hot iron. Join side and gusset seams. Thread elastic through holes at waist.

TAILORED CARDIGAN
For the Well-Dressed Woman

MATERIALS

8 oz. 3-ply wool in main colour.
1 oz. 3-ply wool in 1st contrast colour.
1 oz. 3-ply wool in 2nd contrast colour.
2 No. 10 and 2 No. 12 knitting needles.
9 buttons.

MEASUREMENTS

Length.—21 ins.
Bust size.—35 ins.
Sleeve seam.—18 ins.

TENSION

7½ sts. to 1 in. measured over st.st. worked on No. 10 needles.

ABBREVIATIONS

K. knit, p. purl, st. stitch, sts. stitches, rep. repeat, beg. beginning, dec. decrease, inc. increase, st.st. stocking stitch (1 row k., 1 row p.), ins. inches, m.st. moss stitch (K.1, p. 1 alternately), patt. pattern, tog. together.

The Back.—With No. 10 needles and main colour cast on 105 sts. and work in m.st., thus :—

1st row.—K. 1, * p. 1, k. 1, rep. from * to end.

Rep. this row for 1 in.

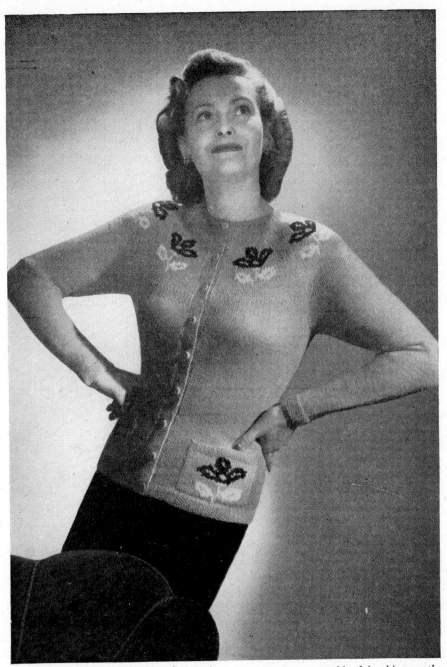

FOR THE SMART MATRON. *Grace and charm are combined in this smooth-fitting long sleeved cardigan. The deep round yoke is outlined with a narrow band of moss stitch, and the large flower motifs add a distinctive and smart touch.*

Now continue in st.st. for 4 ins. (5 ins. from cast-on edge).

Change to No. 12 needles and continue in st.st. until work measures 6½ ins. from cast-on edge, ending with a p. row.

Change to No. 10 needles and continue in st.st. inc. 1 st. both ends of next row and of every following 4th row until there are 129 sts. on the needle.

Continue without shaping until work measures 13½ ins., ending with a p. row.

Shape Armholes thus.—Cast off 2 sts. at beg. of the next 2 rows, then dec. 1 st. both ends of every row until 107 sts. remain.

Leave these sts. on a spare needle.

The pocket linings.—With No. 10 needles and main colour cast on 34 sts. and work in st.st. for 3½ ins., ending with a p. row.

Leave sts. on a spare needle.

Work a second piece in the same way.

The Right Front.—With No. 10 needles and main colour cast on 53 sts. and work in m.st. for 1 in.

Next row.—K. to end.

Next row.—P. to end.

Now continue in st.st. with patt. panel thus :—

The 26 squares in the patt. chart form the complete patt.

A guide to the colours used in the patt. will be found with the chart.

The odd rows, i.e., 1, 3, 5, and so on, will be k. rows and are worked from right to left, the even rows, i.e., rows 2, 4, 6, and so on, will be p. rows and are worked from left to right.

Thus the next 2 rows will be :—

1st row.—K. 15 main colour, work next 26 sts. from the chart (working from right to left), k. 12 main colour.

2nd row.—P. 12 main colour, work next 26 sts. from the chart (working from left to right), p. 15 main colour.

Continue in this way until the 30 patt. rows are completed.

Break off the contrast wools and continue with main colour.

Next row.—K. to end.

Next row.—P. to end.

Next row.—K. 11 (k. 1, p. 1) 17 times, k. 8.

Next row.—P. 8 (p. 1, k. 1) 17 times p. 11.

Rep. these 2 rows for ½ in. ending with a row on right side.

Next row.—P. 8, cast off 34 sts. in m.st., p. to end.

Next row.—K. 11, k. across 34 sts. of a pocket lining, k. 8.

Change to No. 12 needles and continue in st.st. until work measures 6½ ins., ending with a p. row.

Change to No. 10 needles and continue in st.st. inc. 1 st. at end of the next row and of every following 4th row until there are 65 sts. on needle.

Continue in st.st. without shaping until work measures 13½ ins., ending at shaped side edge.

Shape Armhole thus.—Cast off 2 sts. at beg. of the next row, then dec. 1 st. at this same edge on every row until 54 sts. remain.

Leave these sts. on a spare needle.

The Left Front.—With No. 10 needles and main colour cast on 53 sts. and work in m.st. for 1 in.

Next row.—K. to end.

Next row.—P. to end.

Now continue in st.st. with patt. panel to match right front, using the same method but reversing the st.st. panels on each side of the patt. panels thus :—

1st row.—K. 12 main colour, work next 26 sts. from the chart (working from left to right), k. 15 main colour.

2nd row.—P. 15 main colour, work next 26 sts. from the chart (working from right to left), p. 12 main colour.

Continue in this way until the 30 patt. rows are completed.

Break off the contrast wools and continue with main colour :—

The cardigan buttons right up to the neck, and the side fronts, neck band, wrist bands, lower edge and pocket tops are edged with a narrow band of moss stitch.

Next row.—K. to end.

Next row.—P. to end.

Next row.—K. 8 (k. 1, p. 1) 17 times, k. 11.

Next row.—P. 11 (p. 1, k. 1) 17 times, p. 8.

Rep. these 2 rows for ½ in. ending with a row on right side.

Next row.—P. 11, cast off next 34 sts. in m.st., p. to end.

Next row.—K. 8, k. across 34 sts. of a pocket lining, k. 11.

Change to No. 12 needles and continue in st.st. until work measures 6½ ins., ending with a p. row.

Change to No. 10 needles and continue in st.st. inc. 1 st. at beg. of next row and of every following 4th row until there are 65 sts. on the needle.

Continue without shaping until work measures 13½ ins., ending at the shaped side edge.

Shape Armhole and complete as given for the Right front.

The Sleeves.—With No. 12 needles and main colour cast on 59 sts. and work in m.st. for 1 in.

Continue in st.st. until work measures 3 ins., ending with a p. row.

Change to No. 10 needles and continue in st.st. inc. 1 st. both ends of the 5th row and of every following 6th row until there are 99 sts. on the needle.

Continue without shaping until work measures 18 ins., ending with a p. row.

Shape Top thus.—Cast off 2 sts. at beg. of the next 2 rows, then dec. 1 st. both ends of every row until 77 sts. remain.

Leave these sts. on a spare needle.

Work the second sleeve in the same way.

The Yoke.—Arrange sts. on a No. 10 needle in the following order with wrong side of work facing : sts. for left front, sts. for a sleeve, sts. for back, sts. for a second sleeve, sts. for right front (369 sts.)

Work in m.st. for 1 in. ending with a row on wrong side and dec. 1 st. at the end of the last row. (368 sts.)

Next row.—K. 2 tog., * k. 10, k. 2 tog., rep. from * to last 6 sts., k. 4, k. 2 tog. (336 sts.) Work 9 rows in st.st.

Now continue in st.st. with patt. panels using separate small balls of contrast wools for each motif.

1st row.—* k. 8, work across 26 sts. from the patt. chart working from right to left, k. 8, rep. from * 3 times, ** k. 8, now work across the 26 sts. from the patt. chart but work from left to right to reverse the patt. but making this a k. row as for first panel, k. 8, rep. from ** 3 times.

2nd row.—* p. 8, work across 26 sts. from the patt. chart working from right to left and making this a p. row, p. 8, rep. from * 3 times, ** p. 8, work across the 26 sts. from the patt. chart but work from left to right, p. 8, rep. from ** 3 times. Rep. these 2 rows 4 times.

Keeping continuity of the patt. shape thus :—

Next row.—* k. 2 tog., k. 6, patt. 26, k. 6, k. 2 tog., rep. from * to end.

Work 9 rows without shaping allowing for dec. sts. and keeping patt. correct throughout.

Next row.—* k. 2 tog., k. 5, patt. 26, k. 5, k. 2 tog., rep. from * to end.

Work 9 rows without shaping.

Break off contrast colours, complete with main colour.

Next row.—* k. 2 tog., k. 2, rep. from * to end. Work 9 rows in st.st.

Next row.—* k. 2 tog., k. 1, rep. from * to end. Work 9 rows in st.st.

Next row.—* k. 2 tog., k. 1, rep. from * to last 2 sts., k. 2 tog.

Change to No. 12 needles and work ½ in. in m.st. Cast off in m.st.

The Left Front Band.—With No. 12 needles and main colour cast on 9 sts. and work in m.st. until the band is long enough to fit along left front edge when slightly stretched. Cast off in m.st.

The Right Band.—Place 9 pins in the left front band to mark the position for the buttons, the first one about ½ in. from lower edge and the others at regular intervals with the top one about ¼ in. from cast-off edge.

Now work the right front band as given for left front band making button-holes at the marked places as follows :—

1st row of buttonhole.—M.st. 3, cast off 3, m.st. to end.

2nd row of buttonhole.—M.st. 3, cast on 3, m.st. 3.

Make-up.—Press work lightly on wrong side with a hot iron over a damp cloth.

Join side and sleeve seams. Sew shaped tops of sleeves to armhole edges.

Sew round pocket linings on wrong side of work. Sew front bands into position to front edges. Sew buttons to left front band. Press seams.

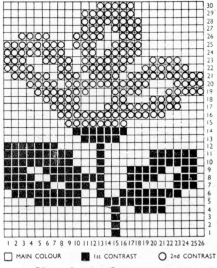

1 2 3 4 5 6 7 8 9 10 11 12 13 14 15 16 17 18 19 20 21 22 23 24 25 26

□ MAIN COLOUR   ■ 1st CONTRAST   ○ 2nd CONTRAST

Chart showing flower pattern.

ANKLE SOCKS

and Gloves to Match

MATERIALS

3 oz. 4-ply wool in dark colour.
1½ oz. 4-ply wool in light colour.
2 No. 12 knitting needles.

MEASUREMENTS

The Gloves : Length of palm, 4 ins.
Width all round, 7 ins.
The Socks : Length of leg, 4½ ins.
Length of foot, 10 ins.

TENSION

8 sts. to 1 in.

ABBREVIATIONS

K. knit, p. purl, st. stitch, tog. together,
dec. decrease, inc. increase, sl. slip,
p.s.s.o. pass slipped st. over, dk. dark,
lt. light, patt. pattern, rep. repeat,
st.st. stocking stitch.
N.B.—When working the 2 colour
patt. the wools should be stranded
loosely on the wrong side to ensure
elasticity.

THE SOCKS

Using dk. wool cast on 56 sts. and work
in k. 2, p. 2 rib for 1¾ ins. inc. 1 st. at the
end of the last row (57 sts.).

Now work in patt. thus :—

1st row.—K. 1 lt., * 7 dk., 1 lt., rep.
from * to the end.

2nd row.—P. * 2 lt., 2 dk., 1 lt., 2 dk.,
1 lt., rep. from * to the last st., 1 lt.

3rd row.—K. 1 dk., * 2 lt., 3 dk.,
2 lt., 1 dk., rep. from * to the end.

4th row.—P. * 4 lt., 1 dk., 3 lt., rep.
from * to the last st., 1 lt.

These 4 rows form the patt.

Continue in patt. until work measures
4½ ins. from commencement, ending
with a row on the wrong side.

Divide for Instep thus.—Keeping the
continuity of the patt. work thus :—

1st row.—Patt. 43 sts., turn, and
leave remaining sts. on a safety pin.

2nd row.—Patt. 29 sts., turn and
leave remaining sts. on a safety pin.

Now continue in patt. on these 29 sts.
until work measures 7 ins. from beginning
of instep, ending with a row on the
wrong side.

Break off lt. wool and continue with dk.

Shape Toe thus.—

Next row.—K. 1, sl. 1, k. 1, p.s.s.o.,
k. to the last 3 sts., k. 2 tog., k. 1.

Next row.—P. to the end.

Rep. these 2 rows until 11 sts. remain
ending with a k. row.

Next row.—P. 1, p. 2 tog., p. to the
end (10 sts.).

Return to the 2 sets of sts. on safety
pins and slip these 28 sts. on to a No. 12
needle so that leg seam will be in the
centre and right side of work facing when
working first row.

Using dk. wool work in st.st. (1 row k.,
1 row p.) on these 28 sts. for 1½ ins.
ending with a row on the wrong side.

The Heel.—Now turn heel thus :—

1st row.—K. 16, sl. 1, k. 1, p.s.s.o.,
turn.

2nd row.—P. 5, p. 2 tog., turn.

3rd row.—K. 6, sl. 1, k. 1, p.s.s.o.,
turn.

4th row.—P. 7, p. 2 tog., turn.

5th row.—K. 8, sl. 1, k. 1, p.s.s.o., turn.

6th row.—P. 9, p. 2 tog., turn.

Continue thus working 1 st. more on
every row before dec. until 16 sts. remain,
thus ending with p. 15, p. 2 tog.

With wrong side of work facing continue from the last row of heel turning
and pick up and p. 16 sts. evenly down
side of heel flap, turn, k. to the end, then
pick up and k. 16 sts. evenly down other
side of heel flap (48 sts.).

Shape for Instep thus.—

1st row.—K. 1, sl. 1, k. 1, p.s.s.o., k. to the last 3 sts., k. 2 tog., k. 1.

2nd row.—P. to the end.

Rep. these 2 rows until 28 sts. remain. Now work in st.st. on these 28 sts. until work measures 7 ins. from beginning of instep, measured at side edge, ending with a row on the wrong side.

Shape toe as given for top of foot omitting final dec. on p. row.

Graft tog. the 2 sets of 10 sts., join foot and leg seams. Press.

Work second sock in the same way.

THE GLOVES

Using dk. wool cast on 73 sts. and work in patt. as given for socks until work is 2½ ins. ending with a 4th patt. row.

Continue with dk. wool thus :—

Next row.—* k. 2 tog., k. 2, k. 2 tog., k. 3, rep. from * to the last 10 sts. (k. 2 tog., k. 2) twice, k. 2 tog. (56 sts.).

Now work in k. 2, p. 2 rib for 1 in., inc. 1 st. at the end of the last row (57 sts.).

Continue in 2 colour patt. as before until work measures 2½ ins. from end of ribbing at wrist, ending on wrong side.

Thumb row for Right Hand Glove

Next row.—Patt. 28 sts., k. the next 11 sts. with an odd length of wool in a different colour, slip the 11 sts. back on to left hand needle, k. 11, and work in patt. to the end.

Thumb row for Left Hand Glove

Next row.—Patt. 18 sts., k. the next 11 sts. with an odd length of wool in a different colour, slip the 11 sts. back on to left hand needle and work in patt. to the end.

Next row.—Work in patt. across all sts., including sts. worked with odd wool.

Now continue in patt. until work measures 3¾ ins. from end of ribbing, ending with a 4th patt. row.

Next row.—Patt. 7 sts., slip these sts. on to a safety pin, cast on 1 st., work in patt. to the last 6 sts., and slip these 6 sts.

on to a safety pin, turn, and cast on 1 st.

Keeping the continuity of the patt. work 3 more rows on these 46 sts., thus ending with a 4th patt. row.

Break off lt. wool and continue with dk.

First Finger.—

1st row.—K. 31, turn, cast on 1 st.

2nd row.—P. 17, turn, cast on 1 st.

Continue in st.st. on these 18 sts. until finger measures 2½ ins. or required length, ending on wrong side.

Shape Top thus.—

1st row.—* k. 1, k. 2 tog., rep. from * to the end.

2nd row.—P.

3rd row.—* k. 2 tog., rep. from * to the end.

Break off wool and thread through remaining sts., draw up and fasten off. Then sew down to base of finger.

Second Finger.—With right side of work facing and using dk. wool pick up and k. 2 sts. at base of 1st finger, k. 7, turn, and cast on 1 st.

Next row.—P. 17, turn, cast on 1 st.

Work in st.st. on these 18 sts. until work measures 2¾ ins. or required length. Shape top and complete as for first finger.

Third Finger.—With right side of work facing and using dk. wool pick up and k. 2 sts. at base of 2nd finger, k. to the end.

2nd row.—P. to the end. Now work on these 18 sts. as for 1st finger.

Fourth Finger.—With right side of work facing and using dk. wool pick up and k. 1 st. at base of 3rd finger, k. the 6 sts. from 2nd safety pin.

Next row.—P. to the end, including the 7 sts. from 1st safety pin.

Work in st.st. on these 14 sts. until work measures 2¼ ins. ending with a row on the wrong side.

Shape top thus.—

Next row.—* k. 1, k. 2 tog., rep. from * to the last 2 sts., k. 2 tog.

Next row.—P. to the end.

Next row.— (k. 2 tog.) 4 times, k. 1. Thread wool through remaining sts.

FOR THE 21-YEAR-OLD. *Ankle socks and gloves that will delight the eye and comfort cold toes and fingers throughout the autumn and winter. The set is knitted in a two-colour design, with the fingers of the gauntlet gloves in plain wool, and plain ribbing at the wrists so that they fit snugly.*

and fasten off then sew down side of hand to within 2 ins. of top of gauntlet.

The Thumb.—Unpick the piece of odd wool worked over 11 sts. in hand and pick up the 2 sets of 11 sts. thus formed.

With dk. wool work in st.st. on one of these sets of 11 sts. until work measures $2\frac{1}{4}$ ins., ending with p. row.

Shape Top thus.—

Next row.—* k. 1, k. 2 tog., rep. from * to the last 2 sts., k. 2 tog.

Next row.—P.

Next row.—(K. 2 tog.) 3 times, k. 1.

Break off wool and thread through remaining sts. Draw up and fasten off.

Work on the 2nd set of 11 sts. in the same way. Sew edges tog.

The Glove Border.—With right side of work facing and using dk. wool begin at top of wrist ribbing and pick up and k. 24 sts. evenly along side edge of gauntlet, 73 sts. round top of glove and 24 sts. down second side of gauntlet.

1st row.—K. to the end.

2nd row.—P. to the end.

Rep. these 2 rows until work measures $\frac{3}{4}$ in. Cast off.

Make-up.—Press with a hot iron.

Turn in binding round top of glove and hem on the wrong side.

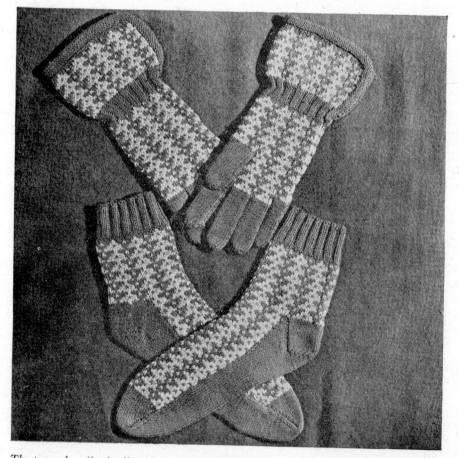

The two-colour " wing " pattern of this sock and glove set was knitted in red and grey.

HOOD AND MITTS

For Winter Weather

MATERIALS

7 ozs. 4-ply wool in navy.
1 oz. 4-ply wool in red.
5 ozs. 3-ply wool in light blue.
2 No. 12 and 2 No. 14 knitting needles.
A crochet hook.

MEASUREMENTS

Hood : To fit average size head.
Mittens : Width all round 7 ins.
Length of hand 7½ ins.

TENSION

8 sts. to 1 in. on No. 12 needles.

ABBREVIATIONS

K. knit, p. purl, rep. repeat, st. sitch, st.st. stocking stitch, patt. pattern, dec. decrease, inc. increase, tog. together, r. red, n. navy, sl. slip, p.s.s.o. pass slipped st. over, lt. bl. light blue. *N.B.*—When working the two-colour pattern strand wool not in use loosely at back of work.

THE MITTENS

The Left Hand.—Using n. wool and No. 12 needles cast on 75 sts. and work in st.st. for 5 ins., ending with a k. row.

Next row.—* P. 3, p. 2 tog., rep. from * to the last 5 sts., p. 5 (61 sts.).

Change to No. 14 needles and continue thus :—

1st row.—P. 1, * slip the next 2 sts., on to a spare needle and leave at front of work, k. next 2 sts., now k. 2 sts. from spare needle, p. 1, rep. from * to the end.

2nd row.—K. 1, * p. 4, k. 1, rep. from * to the end.

3rd row.—P. 1, * k. 4, p. 1, rep. from * to the end.

4th row.—As 2nd row.

Rep. these 4 rows until work measures 6½ ins., ending with a row on the wrong side.

Change to No. 12 needles and keeping the first 30 sts. in st.st. in navy for the palm, work 2 colour patt. in the last 31 sts. for back of hand thus :—

1st row.—K. 30 n. K. 6 n., * 1 r., 3 n., rep. from * to the last st., 1 n.

2nd row.—P. 2 n., * 3 n., 1 r., rep. from * 5 times more, 5 n. P. 30 n.

3rd row.—K. 30 n. K. 1 n., * 3 n., 1 r., rep. from * to the last 6 sts., 6 n.

4th row.—P. 1 n., * 3 n., 1 r., rep. from * 6 times more, 2 n. P. 30 n.

5th row.—K. 30 n. K. 3 n., * 1 r., 3 n., rep. from * to the end.

6th row.—P. 2 n., * 1 r., 3 n., rep. from * 6 times more, 1 n. P. 30 n.

Rep. these 6 rows twice, more. Work should now measure about 2 ins. from end of cable patt. at wrist.

25th row.—K. n. to the end.

26th row.—P. n. to the end.

27th row.—K. 30 n. K. 6 n., 1 r., 1 n., 1 r., 4 n., 1 r., 1 n., 1 r., 1 n., 1 r., 4 n., 1 r., 1 n., 1 r., 6 n.

28th row.—P. 7 n., 1 r., 4 n., 1 r., 2 n., 1 r., 2 n., 1 r., 4 n., 1 r., 7 n. P. 30 n.

29th row.—K. 30 n. K. 7 n. (1 r., 3 n.) 4 times, 1 r., 7 n.

30th row.—P. (7 n., 1 r.) 3 times, 7 n. P. 30 n.

31st row.—K. 19 n., k. the next 11 sts. with an odd length of wool in a different colour for thumb. Slip these 11 sts. back on left hand needle and k. 11 n. K. 4 n., 5 r., 5 n., 3 r., 5 n., 5 r., 4 n.

32nd row.—P. 3 n., 7 r., 3 n., 1 r., 1 n., 1 r., 1 n., 1 r., 3 n., 7 r., 3 n. P. 30 n.

Back view of set showing clearly the patterned design of the gloves and hood.

33rd row.—K. 30 n. K. 3 n., 1 r., 2 n., 5 r., 1 n., 1 r., 2 n., 1 r., 2 n., 1 r., 1 n., 5 r., 2 n., 1 r., 3 n.

34th row.—P. 5 n., 6 r., 4 n., 1 r., 4 n., 6 r., 5 n., p. 30 n.

35th row.—K. 30 n. K. 4 n., 3 r., 1 n., 2 r., 2 n., 7 r., 2 n., 2 r., 1 n., 3 r., 4 n.

36th row.—P. 4 n., 1 r., 3 n., 2 r., 3 n., 5 r., 3 n., 2 r., 3 n., 1 r., 4 n. P. 30 n.

37th row.—K. 30 n. K. 7 n., 2 r., 1 n., 1 r., 3 n., 3 r., 3 n., 1 r., 1 n., 2 r., 7 n.

38th row.—P. 8 n., 2 r., 5 n., 1 r., 5 n., 2 r., 8 n. P. 30 n.

39th row.—K. n. to the end.

40th row.—P. n. to the end.

41st row.—K. 30 n. K. 2 n., * 1 r., 3 n., rep. from * to the last st. 1 n.

42nd row.—P. * 3 n., 1 r., rep. from * 6 times more, 3 n. P. 30 n.

43rd row.—K. 30 n. K. 1 n., * 3 n., 1 r., rep. from * to the last 2 sts. 2 n.

44th row.—P. 4 n., * 1 r., 3 n., rep. from * 5 times more, 3 n. P. 30 n.

45th row.—K. 30 n. K. 5 n., * 1 r., 3 n., rep. from * to the last 2 sts., 2 n.

46th row.—P. 6 n., * 1 r., 3 n., rep. from * 5 times more, 1 n., p. 30 n.

Rep. from the 41st to the 46th rows twice more, dec. 1 st at end of 64th row. Work should now measure about 5¾ ins. Break off r. wool and continue with n. wool.
Shape Top thus.—

1st row.—K. 1, sl. 1, k. 1, p.s.s.o., k. 24, k. 2 tog., k. 2, sl. 1, k. 1, p.s.s.o., k. 24, k. 2 tog., k. 1.

2nd row.—P. to the end.

3rd row.—K. 1, sl. 1, k. 1, p.s.s.o., k. 22, k. 2 tog., k. 2, sl. 1, k. 1, p.s.s.o., k. 22, k. 2 tog., k. 1.

4th row.—P. to the end.

5th row.—K. 1, sl. 1, k. 1, p.s.s.o., k. 20, k. 2 tog., k. 2, sl. 1, k. 1, p.s.s.o., k. 20, k. 2 tog., k. 1.

6th row.—P. to the end.

Continue thus dec. 1 st. at both ends and each side of centre 2 sts. in every k. row until 20 sts. remain, ending with a k. row.

FOR THE SPORTS GIRL. *An intriguing and unusual winter set consisting of a monk's hood and deep gauntlet mitts. The set is lined throughout and can be worn reverse ways. The original was knitted in navy with red motifs and blue lining.*

Next row.—P. 10.

Now graft these 2 sets of 10 sts. tog., fasten off.

The Thumb.—Unpick the odd piece of wool worked across 11 sts. in palm and pick up the 2 sets of 11 sts. thus formed on 2 needles.

With right side of work facing and using n. wool work in st. st. on one of these sets of sts. until work measures 2¼ ins. or required length, ending with a p. row.

Shape Top thus.—

Next row.—K. 2 tog., * k. 1, k. 2 tog., rep. from * to the end.

Next row.—P. to the end.

Next row.—K. 1, * k. 2 tog., rep. from * to the end.

Break off wool, thread through remaining sts., draw up and fasten off.

Work on the second set of sts. in the same way.

The Right Hand.—Work exactly as given for the left hand until cable patt. at wrist is completed, and work measures 6½ ins., ending with a row on the wrong side, and 61 sts.

Change to No. 12 needles and continue, working the patt. as in left hand mitten but working the first 31 sts. in 2 colour pattern and last 30 sts. plain for palm, thus the first 2 rows will be as follows :—

1st row.—K. 6 n., * 1 r., 3 n., rep. from * 5 times more, 1 n. K. 30 n.

2nd row.—P. 30 n., p. 2 n., * 3 n., 1 r., rep. from * to the last 5 sts., 5 n.

Continue thus until the 30th patt. row has been completed.

31st row.—Patt. the first 31 sts., k. the next 11 sts., with an odd piece of wool in a different colour, slip the 11 sts. on to left hand needle and k. n. to end.

Complete mitten as for left hand, reversing plain and patt. sts. as before.

THE HOOD

The Back.—Using No. 12 needles and n. wool cast on 31 sts. and work in st.st. for ½ in., ending with a p. row.

Now work the 2 colour patt. exactly as in mittens, inc. 1 st. at both ends of the 7th and every following 14th row, working all increasings in n. wool, until there are 39 sts., then complete patt. without further shaping until the 64 patt. rows have been completed.

Break off r. wool and continue in st. st. with n. wool until work measures 6½ ins. from lower edge.

Shape Top thus.—

Dec. 1 st. at both ends of every row until 19 sts. remain.

Cast off.

The Front.—Using No. 12 needles and n. wool cast on 62 sts.

1st row.—K. to the last 16 sts. (p. 1, k. 4) 3 times, p. 1.

2nd row.—(K. 1, p. 4) 3 times, k. 1, p. to the end.

3rd row.—K. to the last 16 sts. (p. 1, slip the next 2 sts. on to a spare needle and leave at front of work, k. 2, k. 2 from spare needle) 3 times, p. 1.

4th row.—As 2nd row.

Rep. these 4 rows until work measures 23 ins. from commencement.

Cast off.

The Collar.—Join st.st. edge of front of hood to back, sewing along the two long edges of back of hood and shaped top, easing in fullness.

With right side of work facing and using No. 14 needles and n. wool pick up and k. 148 sts. evenly all round neck edge of hood, and work in k. 1, p. 1 rib for 2 ins., ending with a row on wrong side.

Next row.—* k. twice in the first st., p. 1., rep. from * to the end (222 sts.).

Next row.—* k. 1, p. 2, rep. from * to the end.

Continue in k. 2, p. 1 rib for 1 in.

Change to No. 12 needles and continue in k. 2, p. 1 rib for a further in., ending with a row on the wrong side.

This view shows the ribbed cowl shape of the hood which fits snugly round the neck and fastens at the front with two looped " frogs ".

Next row.—* k. 2, p. twice in the next st., rep. from * to the end.

Now work in k. 2, p. 2 rib until collar measures 6 ins. from commencement.

Cast off loosely in rib.

THE LININGS

The Mittens.—Work linings for mitters by using 3-ply lt. bl. wool and working with the same number of sts. and to the same measurements as before but omitting cable patt. at wrist and 2-colour patt. and working in k. 1, p. 1 rib throughout. Do not forget to change to No. 14 needles at wrist, for 1½ ins.

Work linings for front and back of hood in same way in lt. bl. wool and working in k. 1, p. 1 rib throughout, making both pieces slightly shorter than before.

Sew front and back together and work

collar lining in lt. bl. wool, as for main part.

Make-up.—Press work lightly with a hot iron and damp cloth.

Join the cast off edges of collar and lining together by working a picot edge through both thicknesses as follows :—

Using navy wool 1 single crochet into edge * 3 chain, 1 double crochet into the first of these chain, miss a small space, 1 single crochet into edge, rep. from *. (Take care not to draw the edge in when working the picot.)

Work the same picot edge round front of hood, also all round gauntlet, hand and thumb of mitts.

Work a length of crochet chain in r. wool, make into two looped " frogs " and stitch at neck of hood.

Fasten with right hand loop over a button on left side to correspond.

BLOUSE FRONT

In Openwork Crochet

MATERIALS

2 ozs. No. 20 crochet cotton.
No. 3 steel crochet hook.
Muslin, 12 by 20 for back.

MEASUREMENTS

12 ins. wide, 20 ins. long.
Ribbon.

ABBREVIATIONS

Ch. chain, d.c. double crochet, tr. treble, rep. repeat, ins. inches, patt. pattern.
Make 180 ch.

1st row.—* 5 ch., 1 d.c. into 3rd ch. from hook, forming a picot, 5 ch., 1 d.c. into 3rd ch. from hook, 2 ch. miss 5 of foundation ch., 1 dc. into next foundation ch., rep. from * to end.

2nd row.—* 5 ch., 1 d.c. into 3rd ch., 5 ch., 1 d.c. into 3rd ch., 2 ch. 1 d.c. into loop of previous row between the 2 picots, rep. from * to end.

Rep. 2nd row until work measures 13 ins.

Shape for Neck thus.—

Next row.—Work to 1 loop before centre of row, 8 ch., 1 d.c. into centre of row, turn.

Next row.—3 ch., 11 tr. into the 8 ch. loop, work in picot patt. to end of row.

Next row.—Work in picot patt. to 1st tr., * tr. into tr., 2 ch., miss 1 tr., rep. from * 5 times, 2 ch., 1 tr. into 3 ch. turn.

Next row.—* 5 ch., 1 d.c. into 4th ch. from hook, 1 ch., 1 d.c. into 2 ch., rep. from * 5 times, 5 ch., 1 d.c. into 3rd ch., 2 ch., 1 d.c. into loop between 2 picots. Work in picot patt. to end of row.

Rep. last 4 rows, working the 8 ch. loop into the 7th picot from end, then, when turning on 3rd row, working 1 d.c. into the 6th picot from end before working the row of picots edging the scallop.

Continue until 6 scallops have been worked along opening then work 1 in. in picot patt. working only 3 ins. from side edge to form shoulder. Break off.

Work other half of front opening and shoulder to match. Starch and press work.

Hem round back, making darts at centre back to fit.

Join shoulders of back to shoulders of front, turn back revers. Sew narrow ribbon to both sides of front and back at waistline, to tie.

The blouse front is edged with picot.

FOR THE BUSINESS WOMAN.   *This crochet blouse front is a charming gift that will brighten a plain suit. It is in an openwork stitch, and the revers are edged with shell pattern. The front has a muslin back and it ties at each side with ribbon.*

BEDSPREAD

Or Knee Rug Knitted in Sections

MATERIALS

Odd amounts of wool.
4 No. 12 knitting needles with points both ends.

FOR EACH TRIANGLE

Cast on 96 sts. (32 on each of 3 needles).

1st round.—K.

2nd round.—* k. to last 2 sts. of needle, k. 2 tog., rep. from * twice more.

Rep. last round 3 times more.

6th round.—* p. 2 tog., p. to end of needle, rep. from * twice.

Rep. last round 3 times more.

Rep. last 8 rounds until 6 sts. remain.

Break the wool, thread the end through the remaining sts., draw it up and fasten off.

Section to fill in at sides to make a straight edge.—Cast on 48 sts.

1st row.—K.

2nd row.—K. 2 tog., k. to end.

3rd row.—P. 2 tog., p. to end.

Rep. last 2 rows once.

6th row.—P. 2 tog., p. to end.

7th row.—K. 2 tog., k. to end.

Rep. last 2 rows once.

Rep. last 8 rows until 2 sts. remain.

Fasten off.

Cast on 36 sts.

1st row.—K. to end.

2nd row.—P. 28 turn.

3rd row.—K. 28.

Rep. last 2 rows once.

6th row.—K. to end.

7th row.—K. 8, p. 28.

This sectional rug can be used for more than one purpose. It looks most attractive shown above as a bedspread. The original is about one hundred years old and has been handed down and known as " Joseph " from the dozens of colours used in making it.

FOR GRANNY. *An ingenious idea for using up oddments of coloured wool, this delightfully warm knee rug will make a most acceptable gift. It is quite simple to knit in sections of plain and purl which form ridged triangles ; these are joined together and will make any size rug. It is edged with a deep pleated border knitted in plain wool.*

8th row.—K. 28 turn.

9th row.—P. 28.

Rep. last 2 rows once.

12th row.—K. to end.

Rep. these 12 rows as required.

No extra shaping is worked at the corners but, when sewing on the border, the inner edge should be gathered sufficiently to allow it to lie flat.

As the kilted border would take a great deal of wool, all in one colour, a crochet shell edging could be substituted.

First work a row of double crochet all round evenly into the edge of the knitting, then work a second row thus :—
*1 single-crochet into double crochet, 2 chain, 3 treble into same double crochet, miss 2 double crochet, rep. from * ending with 1 single crochet.

A larger shell may be worked 4 chain instead of 2 chain and 5 double treble instead of 3 treble, then 4 double crochet.

OPEN-RIB BED SOCKS

Cosy and Warm

MATERIALS

4 oz. 3-ply wool.
2 No. 6 knitting needles.
1 yd. ribbon.

MEASUREMENTS

Length of leg, 8 ins.
Length of foot, 9 ins.
Width all round, 8 ins.

TENSION

$5\frac{1}{2}$ sts. to 1 in.

ABBREVIATIONS

K. knit, p. purl, m. make, sl. slip, tog. together, p.w. purlwise, p.s.s.o. pass slipped st. over, rep. repeat, patt. pattern.

N.B.—Use double wool throughout.

Using double wool cast on 44 sts. and work in k. 1, p. 1 rib for $\frac{1}{2}$ in.

Now continue in patt. thus :—

1st row.—P. 2, * m. 1, k. 2 tog., m. 1, sl. 1, k. 1, p.s.s.o., m. 1, p. 2, rep. from * to the end.

2nd row.—K. 2, * k. into the back of the next st., p. 1, m. 1, sl. 1 p.w., p. 1, k. into back of next st., k. 2, rep. from * to the end.

3rd row.—P. 2, * k. 2 tog. (k. into the back of the next st.) twice, sl. 1, k. 1, p.s.s.o., p. 2, rep. from * to the end.

4th row.—K. 2, * p. 4, k. 2, rep. from * to the end.

These 4 rows form the patt.

Continue in patt. until work measures 5 ins. from commencement, ending with a 4th patt. row.

Work 3 rows in k. 1, p. 1 rib.

Next row.—* k. 1, m. 1, k. 2 tog., p. 1, rep. from * to the end.

Work 4 more rows in k. 1, p. 1 rib.

Next row.—K. 12, p. 2, * m. 1, k. 2 tog., m. 1, sl. 1, k. 1, p.s.s.o., m. 1, p. 2,

rep. from * to the last 12 sts., k. 1, turn, and leave the remaining sts. on a large safety pin.

Next row.—K. 3, * k. into back of next st., p. 1, m. 1, sl. 1 p.w., p. 1, k. into the back of next st., k. 2, rep. from * to the last 12 sts., k. 1, turn and leave remaining sts. on a safety pin.

Next row.—K. 1, p. 2, * k. 2 tog., (k. into back of next st.) twice, sl. 1, k. 1, p.s.s.o. p. 2, rep. from * to the last st., k. 1.

Next row.—K. 3, * p. 4, k. 2, rep. from * to the last st., k. 1.

Continue in patt. on these 22 sts., as given for the leg but with an extra k. st. at both ends of every row until work measures 6 ins. from end of ankle ribbing, ending with a 4th patt. row.

Shape Toe thus.—

Next row.—K. 1, sl. 1, k. 1, p.s.s.o., k. to the last 3 sts., k. 2 tog., k. 1.

Next row.—P. to the end.

Rep. these 2 rows until 10 sts. remain. Break off wool and place these sts. on a safety pin.

Return to the 2 sets of sts. at leg ribbing and place these on to a No. 6 needle so that leg seam will be in the centre and right side of work facing when working the first row.

1st row.—K.

2nd row.—P.

Rep. these 2 rows 4 times more.

Shape Heel thus.—

Next row.—K. 14, sl. 1, k. 1, p.s.s.o., turn.

Next row.—P. 7, p. 2 tog., turn.

Next row.—K. 8, sl. 1, k. 1, p.s.s.o., turn.

Next row.—P. 9, p. 2 tog., turn.

FOR GRANNY AGAIN. *Cosy and warm, these bed socks do not take long to knit and will make a very charming gift. The socks are knitted in double wool throughout in an open-rib stitch with plain heels and toes. They fit snugly round the ankles and ribbon is threaded through holes then tied in a bow at the front of the leg.*

Next row.—K. 10, sl. 1, k. 1, p.s.s.o., turn.

Continue thus working 1 st. extra in every row before dec. and turn, until all sts. are worked, thus ending with a p. row and 14 sts.

Next row.—K. to the end.

Now pick up and k. 10 sts. evenly down side edge of heel flap, turn and p. back, then pick up and p. 10 sts. from other side of heel flap (34 sts.).

Next row.—K. 1, sl. 1, k. 1, p.s.s.o., k. to the last 3 sts., k. 2 tog., k. 1.

Next row.—P. to the end.

Rep. these 2 rows until 22 sts. remain, then continue in st.st. (1 row k., 1 row p.)

until work measures 6 ins. at side edge from end of ankle ribbing, ending with a row on the wrong side.

Shape the toe as given for the front of the foot.

Graft the 2 sets of sts. at top of toe shaping.

Work a second sock in the same way.

Make-up.—Press work with a hot iron and damp cloth.

Join seams at sides of foot and centre back of leg.

Press seams.

Cut the ribbon into two and thread one piece into the ankle of each sock through the line of holes.

FOR THE CONVALESCENT. *A gift that will be greatly appreciated is this practical bed reading- or writing-table. The table is supported by folding legs and an adjuster is fitted to the back so that the height can be altered. It folds quite flat when not in use.*

MATERIALS

The Table : 9 ins. by 20 ins. by $\frac{1}{2}$ in. (hardwood).
Or 9 ins. by 20 ins. by $\frac{5}{8}$ in. or $\frac{3}{4}$ in. (softwood).

The Frame : 2 pieces, 20 ins. by $1\frac{1}{2}$ ins., by $\frac{3}{4}$ in.
2 pieces, 6 ins. by $1\frac{1}{2}$ ins. by $\frac{3}{4}$ in.

The Legs : 4 pieces, $9\frac{3}{4}$ ins. by 1 in. by $\frac{1}{2}$ in.
4 pieces, 10 ins. by $\frac{1}{2}$ in. by $\frac{1}{4}$ in.

The Adjuster : $8\frac{1}{2}$ ins. by $1\frac{1}{4}$ ins. by $\frac{1}{4}$ in. (hardwood).

1 $1\frac{1}{4}$-in. hinge.
2 2-in. hinges.
5 1-in. roundhead screws No. 5.
12 ins. of $\frac{3}{8}$ in. dowel.

Method :

The Frame.—The four pieces of wood are joined by dowels. On one end of a 6 in. piece, gauge a line AB $\frac{3}{8}$ in. from one edge. Keeping the gauge at the same width, mark a line CD on the $\frac{3}{4}$ in. side of a 20 in. piece, Diagram 1. Make this line $1\frac{1}{4}$ ins. long. Now set the gauge to $\frac{7}{16}$ in. and cut across the lines AB and CD at right angles, Diagram 1. Alter the gauge to $1\frac{1}{16}$ ins. and cut lines AB and CD again, Diagram 1, still working from the same side as that from which the first intersections were gauged. These intersections mark the positions of the holes for the dowels.

Grip the short piece in the vice and bore two holes $\frac{3}{4}$ in. deep with a $\frac{3}{8}$ in. twist bit. In boring, it is essential to keep the bit dead upright. Now bore the two holes on line CD. Cut pieces of $\frac{3}{8}$ in. dowel stick long enough to join the ends, slightly round the outer edges of

the dowel ends. Repeat the process for the other three corners and when all dowels have been fitted glue the frame together leaving in a cramp to dry. When dry, clean up the corners with a finely set plane.

The Legs.—Round all corners of the four $9\frac{3}{4}$ in. pieces. 1 in. from an end of one of these pieces mark a groove, $\frac{1}{4}$ in. deep and $\frac{1}{2}$ in. wide on the narrow side. Mark a similar groove $2\frac{1}{4}$ ins. from the other end, Diagram 2. Cut out these grooves, remembering to saw inside the lines. Repeat process for the other 3

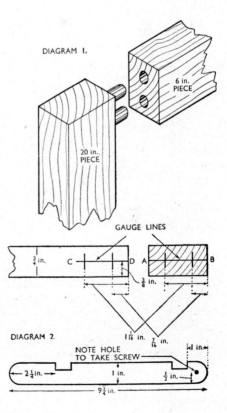

DIAGRAM 1.

6 in. PIECE

20 in. PIECE

GAUGE LINES

$\frac{3}{4}$ in. C D A B

$\frac{3}{8}$ in.

DIAGRAM 2. $1\frac{1}{16}$ in. $\frac{7}{16}$ in. 1 in.

NOTE HOLE TO TAKE SCREW

$2\frac{1}{4}$ in. 1 in. $\frac{1}{2}$ in.

$9\frac{3}{4}$ in.

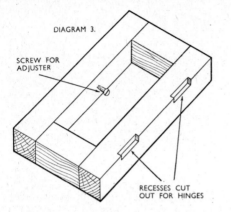

DIAGRAM 3.

SCREW FOR ADJUSTER

RECESSES CUT OUT FOR HINGES

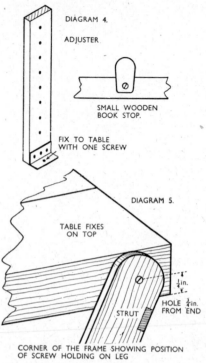

DIAGRAM 4.

ADJUSTER

SMALL WOODEN BOOK STOP.

FIX TO TABLE WITH ONE SCREW

DIAGRAM 5.

TABLE FIXES ON TOP

STRUT

HOLE $\frac{1}{4}$ in. FROM END

$\frac{1}{4}$ in.

CORNER OF THE FRAME SHOWING POSITION OF SCREW HOLDING ON LEG

leg pieces. At this stage, holes to take the screws fixing the legs on to the frame may be made, see Diagram 2.

Now fix in the cross struts, adjusting them so that when the legs fold over they will lie outside the frame, i.e., the distance between the two sides of the legs will be about $9\frac{1}{8}$ ins. Glue in the struts, fixing each with a $\frac{5}{8}$-in. veneer pin. When dry, clean up the grooves (remember to punch in the pins first).

To Fix Table to the Frame.—3 ins. from each end of the frame, cut a recess to take the closed hinge. Screw the hinges to frame and then fix on the table. **The Adjuster.**—Bore $\frac{3}{8}$-in. holes at inch intervals, screw one side of the hinge to the adjuster, and the other side to the underneath of the table, fixing with one screw in the centre. This enables the adjuster to swivel round and lie flat when the table is folded. The pivot screw is $2\frac{3}{4}$ ins. from the edge farthest away from the hinges and equidistant from each end. A 1 in. roundhead screw, projecting $\frac{3}{4}$ in., Diagram 3, serves as a stop for the adjuster.

Two small book stops are made from pieces of 1 in. by $\frac{1}{2}$ in. by $\frac{1}{4}$ in., Diagram 4. They are screwed into the front edge of table with $\frac{1}{2}$ in. by 3 ins. roundhead screws and used very much like door buttons, and are vertical when needed as book stops.

Fixing Legs to Frame.—Holes in the legs having been already made, corresponding marks in the frame are made $\frac{3}{4}$ in. from the ends and $\frac{1}{4}$ in. from the underneath edge of the frame. The legs are not screwed centrally on the side of the frame, as they would not fold properly, Diagram 5.

Finish.—Hardwood is obviously the choice of wood for this model, but softwood may be used. If using the latter, finish by painting (size the wood first) or varnishing or by varnish staining (bought ready to use). Whichever method be adopted, deal with the individual parts, re-assembling when all are dry. With hardwood, finish with french polish or wax, staining the wood first. A good quality wax polish should be used, and, as before, polish each part, and then re-assemble.

WOOL-WINDER

And Knitting Bag

MATERIALS for WOOL-WINDER

Base 7 ins. by 7 ins. by $\frac{3}{4}$ in.
Upright 7 ins. by $1\frac{3}{8}$ ins. by $1\frac{3}{8}$ ins.
4 arms each 12 ins. of $\frac{3}{8}$ in. dowel.
$2\frac{1}{4}$ ins. of $\frac{5}{8}$ in. dowel.
4 2-in. pieces of knitting needle.
Bag to contain all above pieces, about 9 ins. by 14 ins.
Baize to cover base, 7 ins. by 7 ins. (Finished sizes).

N.B.—The whole of this wool-winder may be taken to pieces and packed into a bag. It may also be fixed together permanently if desired.

Method.

The Upright.—Chamfer each long edge with a chisel, starting $\frac{3}{4}$ in. from one end of the upright. Curve the chamfer at the beginning (use the chisel bevel-face downwards here) as in Diagram 1, and take off $\frac{1}{4}$ in. of wood. Next, cut off $1\frac{3}{8}$ ins. from the other end of the upright; this top piece is fitted with arms and made to rotate on top of the upright (which now measures $5\frac{5}{8}$ ins.). This is done as follows :—

Carefully bore a $\frac{5}{8}$ in. hole 1 in. deep, dead centre in the top of the upright, and a similar hole in the smaller top as in Diagram 2. Fit the $2\frac{1}{4}$ ins. piece of dowel into the top and rasp off enough wood to enable the top to rotate in the hole of the upright. There should be $\frac{1}{4}$ in. separating the two pieces of wood. When all is satisfactory, glue in the dowel to the top unit. After the glue has set, bore a $\frac{7}{16}$-in. hole in the centre of each of the four faces of the top, about $\frac{1}{2}$ in. deep (or two holes right through two faces at right angles); the arms will fit in when the ends have been slightly tapered. Finally chamfer the top edges of the rotating piece.

The Base.—Find the centre of the base by drawing the diagonals, then cut out a $1\frac{3}{8}$-in. square hole as in Diagram 3, by boring out as much wood as possible, then finishing off the edges with a chisel, so that the upright fits nicely into this hole.

Next, saw out a $1\frac{1}{4}$ in. square from each corner of the base and round the corners with a chisel and glasspaper. Finally chamfer the edges, using a chisel for the corners. Take off $\frac{1}{4}$ in. wood.

Assemble the model and if a candle is

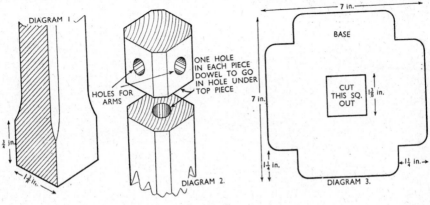

DIAGRAM 1.
$\frac{3}{4}$ in.
$1\frac{3}{8}$ in.

HOLES FOR ARMS
ONE HOLE IN EACH PIECE
DOWEL TO GO IN HOLE UNDER TOP PIECE
DIAGRAM 2.

7 in.
BASE
7 in.
CUT THIS SQ. OUT
$1\frac{3}{8}$ in.
$1\frac{1}{4}$ in.
$1\frac{1}{4}$ in.
DIAGRAM 3.

rubbed over the dowel pin it will rotate

may be kept in a suitable bag as this model is rather awkward to store if it is glued together. The base is covered with a piece of baize, so that the winder may be used at table level, and a G cramp will hold the winder secure when in use.

KNITTING BAG

MATERIALS

Leather, 21½ ins. by 19 ins.
Zip-fastener, 10 ins.

Polish pieces with leather polish.
Make the handles first. Punch holes down the centre of the handle pieces making the first hole 1½ ins. from the end then alternate spaces of ½ in. and ¼ in. as in Diagram 1. Starting from the wrong side, thread thonging through holes finishing with the end on the wrong side. Place the rope as in Diagram 2 and machine edges close to the rope. Trim edges if necessary. Fix handles to the side panels as in Diagram 3.

Place the zip-fastener carefully in

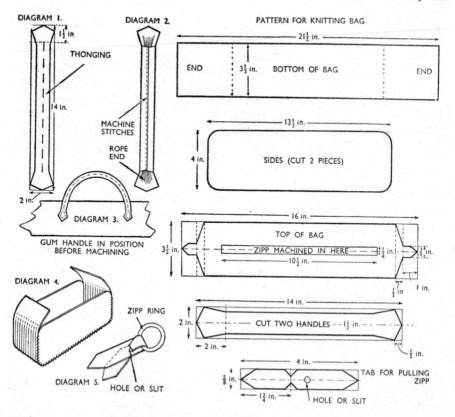

DIAGRAM 1.

1½ in

THONGING

14 in.

2 in.

DIAGRAM 2

MACHINE STITCHES

ROPE END

DIAGRAM 3.

GUM HANDLE IN POSITION BEFORE MACHINING

DIAGRAM 4.

ZIPP RING

DIAGRAM 5.   HOLE OR SLIT

PATTERN FOR KNITTING BAG

21½ in.

END   3½ in.   BOTTOM OF BAG   END

13½ in.

4 in.   SIDES (CUT 2 PIECES)

16 in.

TOP OF BAG

3½ in.   ZIPP MACHINED IN HERE   1½ in.   ¾ in.
10½ in.

½ in   1 in.

14 in.

2 in.   CUT TWO HANDLES   1½ in.

2 in.   ½ in.

4 in.

⅝ in.   TAB FOR PULLING ZIPP

1¼ in.   HOLE OR SLIT

FOR THE KNITTER. *An extremely useful rotating wool-winder which can be taken apart and stored in a suitable bag, and a compact little knitting bag with thonged seams.*

position on the correct piece of leather (see pattern) and machine with two rows of stitching.

Making the Bag.—Clip one panel to the long gusset strip and gum the edges, clipping them together with spring clips. When the edges have stuck, punch the holes carefully, then thong, starting half-way down the short side, and ending at the same place on the other end. For method of starting and ending thonging, see Mirror and Comb Case instructions given on page 176.

Repeat the whole process for the other side. Now place the top piece in position, and machine the ½-in. overlap from the sides under it, with a double row of stitching. Gum the sides and corners, punch the holes, and complete the thonging. Two stitches should be made in each hole at the corners for extra strength. **The Tab for Zip-Fastener.**—Cut out the tab as in Diagram 5. With wrong side uppermost, pass short end through the ring of the zip-fastener then through a punched hole in long end.

Piece of lining, paper or cloth, 9 ins. by 9 ins.

2 eyelets, optional.

N.B.—This case was made to fit a pad 8½ ins. by 4 ins. Other pads can, of course, be used in this case so long as they are not larger than the measurements already given.

Method.—Cut the skiver 10 ins. by 10¾ ins. and mark out, on the wrong side, as in Diagram 1. Paste the skiver and lay

...indicated. Turn over the edges (opposites first) and press them well down with a ruler. Now cut a piece of skiver 8½ ins. by 1¾ ins. and paste it over the gap between the cards leaving a ¼ in. border top and bottom, Diagram 2. Press well down. Next turn the case over and, with a sharp knife, cut three slits through the skiver and card, Diagram 3. One is for the tongue and the other two for the loop, both forming the case fastener.

The Tongue.—Is a piece of skiver (two thicknesses pasted together) 4 ins. by ¾ in.

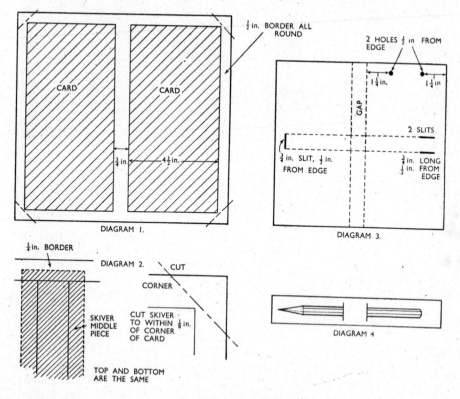

DIAGRAM 1.

½ in. BORDER ALL ROUND

2 HOLES ½ in FROM EDGE

1¼ in. 1¼ in

GAP

2 SLITS

¾ in. SLIT, ¼ in. FROM EDGE

¾ in. LONG ½ in. FROM EDGE

DIAGRAM 3.

¼ in. BORDER

DIAGRAM 2. CUT CORNER

SKIVER MIDDLE PIECE

CUT SKIVER TO WITHIN ⅛ in. OF CORNER OF CARD

TOP AND BOTTOM ARE THE SAME

DIAGRAM 4

FOR THE BRIDGE PLAYER. *A neat little bridge scoring pad in a leather case.*
The pad is fixed with cord, and the case is fastened with a leather tongue.

and is taken through the slit and the end pasted inside the card, about ¾ in.

The Loop.—Is 2½ ins. by ¾ in., the ends of which, after going through the slit, are pasted inside the card.

Now line each card, and the pasted down ends, with a piece of coloured paper or cloth measuring 8½ ins. by 4 ins. It will be noticed that a ¼ in. border is left all round. Leave under a weight (not *too* heavy) to dry.

Fixing the Pad.—The pad is fixed by paper fasteners or cord through two holes

made at the top of one card, Diagram 3. Eyelets may be put in these holes. Corresponding holes are made on the top of the pad. Fasteners may now be inserted or cord passed through and tied, as shown in the illustration above.

A pencil-holder is made by carefully cutting two ¾ in. slits in the middle strip of skiver, Diagram 4. The slits should be done with a sharp knife and great care taken not to cut the outside skiver. Prise up the skiver between the two cuts, and this forms a loop for the pencil.

FOR THE BRIDE. *A gift that will always prove useful and cannot fail to please is this attractive tray. The sides are attractively finished with a rounded moulding and the two handles are shaped to match. The original was painted in cream enamel.*

A PRACTICAL GIFT

Decorated Tray with Handles

MATERIALS

Ply base 18 ins. by 14 ins.
4 sides—2 pieces 18 ins. by 1 in. by
$\frac{3}{4}$ in.
2 pieces 12$\frac{1}{2}$ ins. by 1 in. by $\frac{3}{4}$ in.
2 handles, 3 ins. by 1 in. by $\frac{7}{8}$ in.
6 ins. of $\frac{1}{4}$ in. dowel.

Method.—Mark out the ends of the
two long sides as in Diagram 1a, and
the two short sides as in Diagram 1b.
Remove waste wood with a tenon saw,
sawing *outside* the lines. Clean the rough
saw cuts with a broad chisel and round
off the corners with a chisel and medium
glasspaper.

The sides at each corner are joined
with a $\frac{1}{4}$ in. dowel. Mark out the faces
to be joined as in Diagram 2. Bore $\frac{1}{4}$ in.
holes, about $\frac{1}{2}$ in. deep, gripping the
wood in the vice and keeping the bit
upright. Fit one corner at a time and
when all four are satisfactory, glue and
pin the base and sides, using $\frac{5}{8}$ in. pins
from underneath. Set aside to dry, and

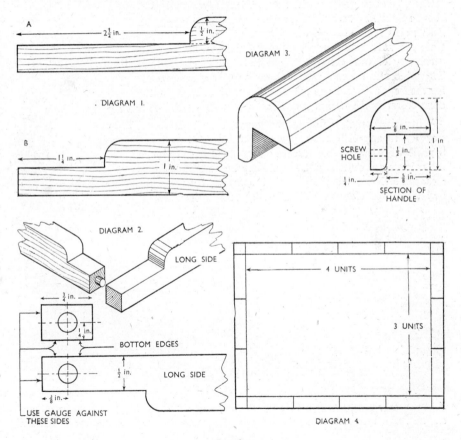

A

DIAGRAM 1.

2$\frac{1}{2}$ in.

$\frac{1}{2}$ in.

DIAGRAM 3.

B

1$\frac{1}{4}$ in.

1 in.

$\frac{7}{8}$ in.

1 in

SCREW HOLE

$\frac{1}{2}$ in.

$\frac{1}{4}$ in.

$\frac{3}{8}$ in.

SECTION OF HANDLE

DIAGRAM 2.

LONG SIDE

$\frac{3}{4}$ in.

1$\frac{1}{4}$ in.

BOTTOM EDGES

$\frac{1}{2}$ in.

LONG SIDE

$\frac{3}{8}$ in.

USE GAUGE AGAINST THESE SIDES

4 UNITS

3 UNITS

DIAGRAM 4

smooth plane, round them off with a chisel and spokeshave (if unavailable use medium glasspaper). Also round the edges of the plywood.

Finish.—Glasspaper well, rub all over with a filler (plaster of paris or any similar filler) and, when dry, rub down well with medium, then fine, paper. Next give a coat of glue size to render the wood non-porous. When this has dried paint with two coats of good enamel.

The Design.—Draw this on paper first, transferring by means of carbon paper to the tray. The design is a border about $13\frac{1}{4}$ ins. by 10 ins. First make a tracing of the corner design shown on this page, and, by means of carbon paper, trace the units round as a continuous pattern, keeping the continuity of the leaf design and the rabbits equidistant. There should be two rabbits between the corner motifs for the long side and one for the short. If the pattern is done correctly the design should be continuous.

When the design is finished on paper, transfer it to the tray by means of carbon paper. Students' oil colours, applied with small sable brushes, should be used. When the colours are quite dry, clean off any traces of carbon by means of a clean rag and a drop of turpentine, then give the tray a coat of clear varnish. Finally attach the handles.

This delightful little animal border looks most attractive round the inside of the tray. A complete corner is shown here which should be traced, by means of carbon paper, on to the tray, then painted. Repeat the units to form a complete pattern.

TRAY CLOTH

To Match Painted Tray

MATERIALS.

Piece of suitable fabric to fit tray.
Stranded cotton in three colours, for embroidery.

Method.—Using a piece of transparent paper, trace off the design from the pattern on page 68. The portion given is for one corner only, but the sides can be extended to any length by repeating the curved sections. Place the tracing on top of the material in the required position and pin firmly along one side. Now slip a sheet of well-worn typing carbon under the tracing, carbon side downwards, and pin the remaining sides of the tracing so that it cannot slip out of place.

Work over every line of the design with a sharp pointed pencil or a steel knitting needle, avoiding heavy pressure on the other parts of the carbon as much as possible. Remove the tracing and carbon paper and the design is ready for embroidering.

For the trailing leaf spray, use lazy daisy stitch for the leaves and stem stitch for the centre stem, working them with three strands of thread.

Outline the rabbits with fine stem stitch or outline stitch, using two strands of thread, and work the flowers in buttonhole stitch, also with two strands of thread.

Buttonhole stitch, worked in groups of three, would make a suitable edging.

Above is shown a corner of a tray cloth embroidered to match the tray on page 66. The design is traced from the pattern on the facing page, and it can be embroidered at one corner only, or continued all the way round. The original was in green linen.

MATERIALS
Wild flowers, leaves and grasses.
Small picture frame
Piece of self-coloured wallpaper
Small bottle of spirit gum.

as soon as possible after gathering them
and keep them pressed until they are dry.
Now arrange them on the background
of wallpaper, in an attractive bouquet.
Stick them down, one at a time, using
good spirit gum economically. Press

Method.—The wild flowers, leaves and grasses should be colourful.

Press them separately in a heavy book the whole picture again under a heavy weight, protecting it with tissue paper, then frame it in a suitable frame.

FOR ANY WOMAN. *This enchanting picture is made of pressed wild flowers. They are stuck down, one at a time, on a background of wallpaper, with the colours and shapes balanced to make a bouquet as shown above, with the tallest flowers at the back and continuing so that the smaller ones are in the centre front.*

HAND-PRINTED GIFTS

Made with Lino Blocks

TOOLS

Cutting knife.
2 V-tools.
2 round-ended gouges.
Hammer.
Roller.
Tile.
Palette knife or old table knife.
2 or 3 tubes of fabric printing ink.
Pieces of plain linoleum.

Method.—The design is first drawn out on cartridge drawing paper; the parts which are to print are painted in with indian ink to distinguish them from the white parts which represent the cut-out parts on the lino block.

The outline of the design is then traced on tracing paper and transferred, in reverse, to the lino block. This is quite easily done by placing a piece of carbon paper face down on the lino, pinning the tracing on it and marking

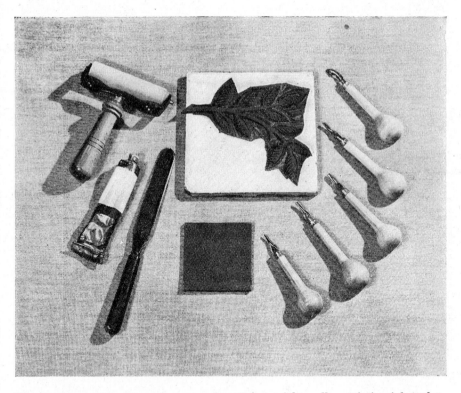

The lino block tools shown above are, from left to right, roller, printing ink, palette knife, lino, 2 V-tools, 2 round-ended gouges, and cutting knife. On the tile in the centre is shown a piece of lino with the design cut ready for printing.

over the outline with a pencil. As a safeguard, and to prevent cutting out a wrong part, it is advisable to paint the design on the block just as it was painted in the design. With the lino tools cut away the parts which are not to print.

When the design has been transferred to the piece of lino the block is ready for cutting, which means that the parts of the design which are not painted have to be cut away with the knife or the gouges. Consequently, when cut, the surfaces of these parts are lower than the other parts of the block and will not receive the printing ink when it is rolled over the face of the block. Some parts of a design are cut more easily with a knife, others with either the small or large V-gouge and any larger spaces between these cuts removed with the round-ended gouges.

When cutting with a knife, the point is inserted into the lino and drawn along the edge of the inked part towards the worker and sloping away from the line. Turn the block round, insert the point of the knife into the lino and make a sloping cut towards the first cut so that a triangular piece of lino is removed, leaving a V-shaped cut on one side of the black part of the design.

The same result is obtained in one operation with the V-tools. In this case the tool is pushed away from the worker following the outline of the part to be removed. A few experiments with the tools and an odd piece of lino will demonstrate the process quite clearly.

When everything is ready for printing spread several sheets of newspaper over the table and on these sheets place the tile, roller, printing ink and so on.

Squeeze some colour from the tube on to the tile and spread it over the surface with the palette knife. Next take the roller and roll it backwards and forwards several times over the colour thus charging the roller with ink.

The block is then placed face upwards on the newspaper and the inked roller rolled over the surface in several directions, so inking the block.

Pick the block up very carefully, by its edges if possible, and lay it face downwards on the fabric against the pencilled guide line. Press it down with the fingers and give it several sharp blows with the hammer, keeping the head of the hammer as flat

HEAD SCARF

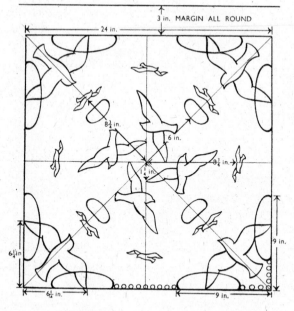

Diagram showing layout of the design and disposition of the lino blocks.

FOR ANY GIRL FRIEND. *This attractive head scarf will make a charming gift. The original was in white, lino-printed in a delightful flying gull and cloud design. The large gulls were printed in soft grey, the clouds in salmon pink, and the flying gulls and border dots were in sapphire blue.*

as possible on the back of the block. By this means the colour from the block is discharged evenly on to the fabric and the first impression of the design is made.

This operation is repeated and the block is carefully inked afresh every time the design is printed until the whole work is completed.

The printed fabric should be put on one side to dry and later on pressed, by placing a damp cloth over the printed parts, and ironing very carefully with a warm iron.

The fabric should have an old blanket, or several sheets of newspaper, placed under the parts which are to be printed to form a soft padding. This helps to keep the distribution of the ink on the fabric uniform.

HEAD SCARF

MATERIALS

A piece of silk or other material suitable for a scarf, 30 ins. to 36 ins. square. 7 pieces of lino to take the various blocks shown on Diagram. Fabric printing ink.

Method.—Pin the fabric on a table, or a board, with the pad of newspapers, or the folded blanket, underneath, and with a piece of tailor's chalk mark out the structural lines as shown in the Diagram on page 72.

On these lines indicate the various positions where the blocks are to be placed and proceed to print.

Full size details of lino blocks are given on the pattern sheet at the back of the book.

Print the cloud forms first, the two large ones at each corner and the smaller ones on the diagonal lines, followed by the four gulls in the centre of the scarf. The large gulls, at the corners, are the next to be printed, the position being fixed by the mark on the structural border line.

It is quite in order to print the wings over the clouds; the latter, being in a pale tint, will hardly affect the colour of the wings. The hollow flying gull is the next block to be used, and it is repeated eight times in the positions shown on the horizontal, vertical, and diagonal lines; when this is dry the small block, which fits inside, is printed in the cloud

T A B L E   C L O T H

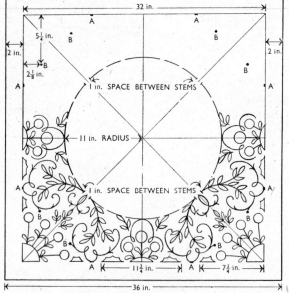

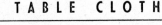

Diagram showing layout of design and disposition of the lino blocks. The design is 32 ins. square. The centre is 22 ins. diameter. The centre loop of scrolls must touch the border line at A. The points B are 2⅛ ins. from one side and 5¼ ins. from the other.

FOR THE HOUSEWIFE. *Charming gifts for the home. The table-cloth was lino-printed in an intriguing scroll design ; the curtain motif on the left was hand-printed in crimson on natural coloured cotton, and the fabric hanging on the right was block printed in black ink on green cotton material.*

colour. Finally the dotted borders at the centre of each side and at the corners are printed, thus binding the whole design together and completing the scarf.

Let the fabric ink dry for two or three days and then place a damp cloth over the work and press with a warm iron.

The french chalk lines are easily removed by lightly rubbing with a clean duster.

The large gulls on the scarf shown in the illustration on page 73 were printed in soft grey, the clouds in salmon pink and the small flying gulls and border dots in sapphire blue. The centres of the flying gulls were printed in the cloud colour.

Black and white fabric ink were mixed together for the grey, and white with a very small touch of scarlet for the salmon-pink.

SMALL TABLE CLOTH

MATERIALS

1 sq. yd. of cotton fabric.

8 pieces of lino to take the various blocks shown on the pattern sheet.

Fabric printing ink.

Method.—Trace the drawings given on the pattern sheet at the back of the book, and trace on to the lino and cut the blocks. Pin the material on a kitchen table, or a large drawing board, with a pad of newspapers, or the folded blanket, underneath and mark out the structural lines of the design with tailor's chalk.

If two colours are mixed to get the desired tone then see that enough is made to finish that part of the design, otherwise it will be almost impossible to match the colour by a later mixing.

Print the four corner blocks first, then the centre ones at each side. The right- and left-hand leaf sprays come next and when these have been printed that will complete one colour.

The scrolls are in the second colour. Choose the one which fits above the flowers of the centre block and print that first. It will be found to fit in between the flowers and the two small leaf sprays.

The small scroll which fits on the diagonal line above the corner block should be done next. When this has been printed in each corner it only remains for the large right- and left-hand scrolls to be fitted in, the loop touching the border line at A and the other part touching the point C which has already been marked on the fabric in the position shown on the Diagram on page 74.

Let the printing dry for two or three days and finish by pressing the work with a damp cloth and a warm iron. If possible print all the blocks of the same colour at the same time.

The second colour can be printed on another day, although it is an advantage to complete the cloth at one sitting.

The blocks, roller, tile, and palette knife can be cleaned with paraffin, thoroughly dried with a piece of rag and stored for further use.

FABRIC HANGINGS

MATERIALS

A length of cotton fabric suitable for hangings.

1 piece of lino.

Fabric printing ink.

Method.—Pin the fabric on a board, or table, with several layers of newspaper, or a piece of old blanket folded into two or three thicknesses, under the part to be printed. Rule a line along the top across the whole width of the fabric and on this line mark out the width of the block as many times as it will go into the width of the fabric. This is very necessary before starting to print an "all over" design, like the specimens illustrated on page 75, because the block must touch each printed impression to give the continuous pattern. The design can be traced from the pattern sheet at the back of the book.

Start printing from the left-hand selvedge and work across to the right, so completing the first printed row. When printing the second row the top of the lino block should just touch the bottom of the printed impression in the row above. Great care should be taken to place the block in the exact position to obtain a close fitting and continuous all over pattern both horizontally and vertically.

If a spare piece of material is obtainable make a trial print on it first because it is difficult to judge the exact amount of ink required for a good impression on each particular fabric.

Some fabrics require the block to be rather heavily charged with colour while others, especially silk, can have a thinner film of ink rolled over the block.

GIFTS IN PLASTIC

Decorative and Useful

TOOLS

A fretsaw and fretsaw board.

A small vice.

A hand drill and three drills $\frac{1}{16}$ in., $\frac{1}{8}$ in. and $\frac{1}{4}$ in.

1 or 2 files and needle files.

A fair sized wire nail driven into a wooden handle and filed to a point to make a scriber.

A set-square, or preferably a small metal try-square.

A metal ruler.

Medium and fine sandpaper.

Pumice powder and metal polish.

Perspex.—Is a synthetic material which looks like glass, is very light in weight, and is practically unbreakable ; it can be purchased in sheets, or small pieces, by the pound and is $\frac{1}{8}$ in. or $\frac{3}{16}$ in. in thickness.

Lactoid.—Is a casein product; it is obtainable in sheets measuring 10 ins. by 8 ins. and about $\frac{1}{8}$ in. or $\frac{3}{16}$ in. in thickness. It is made in several colours and is hard and opaque.

Both these materials can be sawn, filed, and drilled and by immersion in boiling water can be bent, or moulded, to the shape required. Finally they can be smoothed and finished with sandpaper and pumice powder, and polished with metal polish.

Perspex is covered on each side with white paper to protect the polished surface. This paper must not be removed but can be used for drawing out the pattern before cutting.

With Lactoid, a paper pattern is placed on the surface and the outline marked round with the scriber. Cutting is done with the fretsaw leaving a small margin all round.

PERSPEX CIGARETTE BOX

MATERIALS

2 pieces Perspex, $4\frac{3}{4}$ ins. long by $2\frac{1}{4}$ ins. deep for sides.

2 pieces Perspex, 3 ins. long by $2\frac{1}{4}$ ins. deep for ends.

1 piece Perspex, $6\frac{1}{2}$ ins. long by 3 ins. deep for curve.

1 piece Perspex, $4\frac{1}{2}$ ins. long by 3 ins. deep for lid.

1 piece Perspex, $2\frac{1}{8}$ ins. long by $\frac{7}{8}$ in. deep for handle plate.

1 piece Perspex, $2\frac{3}{8}$ ins. long by $\frac{1}{2}$ in. deep for handle.

Perspex cement.

All these pieces can be set out on one sheet of Perspex, leaving just enough space between the pieces for sawing and filing.

Method.—Cut out all the shapes with the fretsaw and file away the margins to the correct size. Carefully test every angle and edge with the try-square to see that they are square and true. The ends of the box fit in between the sides. The curved piece, to hold the cigarettes, just fits the inside of the box with edges $\frac{1}{8}$ in. below the top of each end. These edges form the supports on which the lid rests when it is dropped into the box as shown by dotted lines on the Diagram on page 78.

To assemble the box, cement the $2\frac{1}{4}$ in. edge of one end and stick it to the side-piece. Do the same to the other end. Now take the $6\frac{1}{2}$ in. piece and place it in a pan of boiling water. After immersion for about a minute it will be plastic enough to bend. Take it out of the boiling water and quickly wipe both sides with a piece of cotton wool and

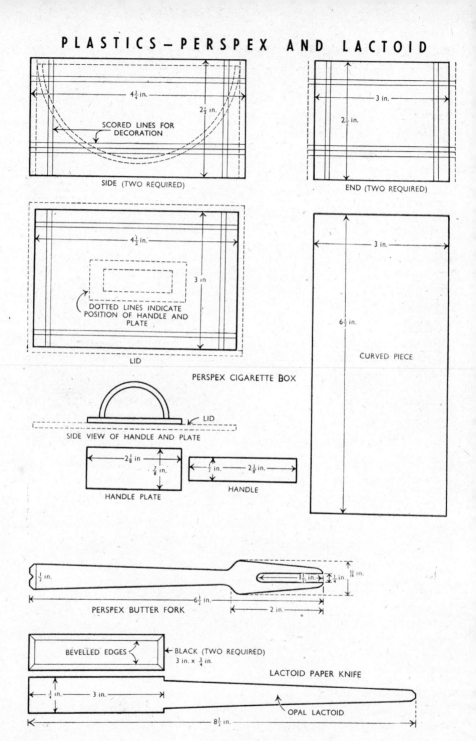

SCORED LINES FOR DECORATION

$4\frac{1}{4}$ in.

$2\frac{1}{2}$ in.

SIDE (TWO REQUIRED)

3 in.

$2\frac{1}{2}$ in.

END (TWO REQUIRED)

$4\frac{1}{2}$ in.

3 in

DOTTED LINES INDICATE POSITION OF HANDLE AND PLATE

LID

PERSPEX CIGARETTE BOX

3 in.

$6\frac{1}{2}$ in.

CURVED PIECE

LID

SIDE VIEW OF HANDLE AND PLATE

$2\frac{1}{8}$ in

$\frac{7}{8}$ in.

HANDLE PLATE

$\frac{1}{2}$ in.

$2\frac{3}{8}$ in.

HANDLE

$\frac{1}{2}$ in.

$1\frac{1}{2}$ in.

$\frac{1}{4}$ in.

$\frac{11}{16}$ in.

$6\frac{1}{2}$ in.

2 in.

PERSPEX BUTTER FORK

BEVELLED EDGES

BLACK (TWO REQUIRED)
3 in. x $\frac{3}{4}$ in.

LACTOID PAPER KNIFE

$\frac{1}{4}$ in.

3 in.

OPAL LACTOID

$8\frac{1}{2}$ in.

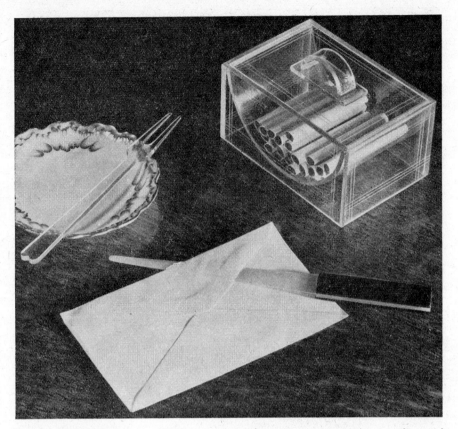

FOR THE HOUSEWIFE. *Three practical gifts ; a transparent cigarette box with a curved piece inside to hold cigarettes and finished with simple engraving on sides and lid ; a neat little pronged butter fork ; and a useful paper knife in Lactoid.*

bend it round a tin or similar article. It was found that a tin measuring 4¾ ins. in diameter gives the proper curve to fit the box. Test the curve to see that it fits inside the portion of the box already made. If not quite correct re-heat and bend again. The edges on which the lid rests must be filed flat to enable the lid to fit on them properly. When the curved piece is quite ready apply a little cement along the two straight edges, which touch the ends, and fit it into position taking care that it comes to within ⅛ in. of the top of the ends. The cement is like liquid Perspex

and sticks in a few minutes. When doing this the box should be placed on its side with the two ends standing up, it is then quite easy to fit in the curved piece.

Now cement the 2½ in. edges of the upright ends and place the remaining side in position. Test the lid and see that there is a little play between the opening of the box and the lid itself.

The next thing to do is to score, or engrave, the lines on the sides, ends, and lid.

Mark the position of the handle plate on top of the lid, four tiny dots made with the scriber will be sufficient, apply

TO PLEASE ANY WOMAN. *Decorative and original, these attractive silhouette ornaments will make delightful gifts. The swan and cat are in Perspex, and the wee Scottie dog is cut out of black Lactoid glued on to a red base.*

a line of cement on the underside of each end of the plate and stick it in position as shown by the dots. Place the handle in boiling water and when ready bend it to a curve. A broom handle, or the handle of a chisel, will probably give the correct curve when bending this piece of Perspex. File the ends quite flat and see that they sit nicely on the handle plate. Cement the ends and stick into position.

Finish.—Clean the edges with fine sandpaper and pumice powder, wet and dry, and finally polish with metal polish. Polishing by hand requires a certain amount of care and patience, but if wet pumice powder is smeared on a piece of felt or thick cloth and the article rubbed on it, that will be found very effective.

PERSPEX BUTTER FORK

MATERIALS

1 piece Perspex 6¾ ins. long by ⅞ ins. wide.

Method.—Draw out the shape shown in the Diagram on page 78 on the paper covering of the Perspex. Cut out with the fret-saw, but before cutting out the 1½-in. piece, which forms the inside of the prongs, drill a $\frac{3}{16}$-in. hole at the base. This will give a good curve and each side cut can then be sawn down to the hole.

The ends of the prongs are filed down until they taper gradually from the thickness of the material to about $\frac{1}{16}$-in.

This charming and distinctive table accessory is illustrated on page 79.

LACTOID PAPER KNIFE

MATERIALS

1 piece opal Lactoid 8¾ ins. long by 1 in. wide.

2 pieces black Lactoid 3¼ ins. long by 1 in. wide.

Method.—Cut the paper patterns as shown in Diagrams on page 78, and mark around the shapes with the scriber.

Cut out with the fretsaw, leaving a small margin which is carefully filed away up to the marginal lines but only of the blade at present.

File the edges of the blade to make them thin enough to cut folded paper and also taper the blade so that it is reduced in thickness as it approaches the tip.

File and sandpaper both surfaces of the opal handle, also the under surfaces of the black pieces. Place them together to see that the surfaces are quite smooth and make good joints.

Cover the surfaces with liquid glue and, when tacky, stick them together. To make a perfect joint the handle should be placed in the vice, screwed up tightly, and left for several hours.

To prevent the two black pieces from shifting wrap a short length of paper tightly around the handle before screwing up in the vice.

When dry the margins of the handle can be filed to the correct shape and the edges of the black pieces bevelled. Finish with sandpaper, pumice powder and metal polish.

PERSPEX AND LACTOID ORNAMENTS

The Diagrams with sizes shown on page 82 are for ornaments.

The Dog.—Is cut out of black Lactoid and is glued on to a red Lactoid base. The underside of the paws and their position on the base must be roughened to enable the glue to adhere properly and, if possible, should be kept under pressure for a short time.

The Cat—and base are in Perspex. After cutting out and filing up to the outline the sharp edges should be taken off with fine sandpaper and all the edges well polished. To give a realistic touch to the cat it should be slightly curved. To do this place it in a pan of boiling water for about a minute, or a minute and a half, take it out and wipe it quickly, hold the neck in the left hand, and the back, just under the tail, in the right hand and bend slightly. Cement the underside of the paws and stick the cat to the base.

The Swan.—Shows a method of building up which gives a more substantial appearance than the simple silhouette.

The swan consists of five pieces and the base of two pieces. Cut out all the pieces, well round the outer edges of the four wing pieces and the upper edges of the base plates. The feather marks on the wings and tail are made with the triangular file. The beak is frosted by sandpapering and the eye is made by two or three turns of the drill on each side in exactly the same position.

It is easier to polish each piece separately rather than attempt a high finish when all the parts are assembled.

To put together, lay the swan on a flat surface, put one or two dabs of cement on the back of the large wing and stick it to the swan ; turn over and cement the other large wing in a similar position. Now the small wings are cemented on to the large ones, fitting them into the position shown on the Diagram.

Cement the two pieces of the base together and then cement the underside of the swan and stick it to the base.

Perspex cement dries very quickly and it is almost impossible to cover a large surface and get it to adhere nicely to the other piece, so it will be found that dabs of cement are quite enough to hold the parts in position.

PLASTICS-PERSPEX AND LACTOID ORNAMENTS

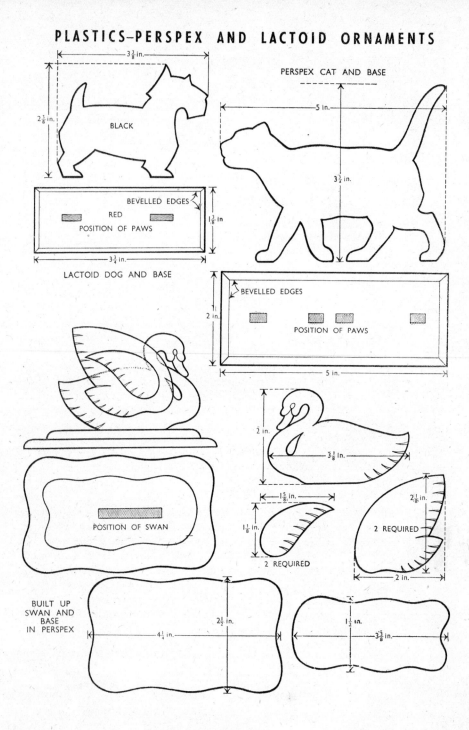

3 3/8 in.

2 3/8 in.

BLACK

PERSPEX CAT AND BASE

5 in.

3 1/4 in.

BEVELLED EDGES

RED

POSITION OF PAWS

1 3/8 in.

3 3/4 in.

LACTOID DOG AND BASE

BEVELLED EDGES

2 in.

POSITION OF PAWS

5 in.

2 in.

3 1/8 in.

POSITION OF SWAN

1 5/8 in.

1 1/8 in.

2 REQUIRED

2 1/8 in.

2 REQUIRED

2 in.

BUILT UP
SWAN AND
BASE
IN PERSPEX

2 1/2 in.

4 1/4 in.

1 1/2 in.

3 5/8 in.

[82]

LEATHER BAGS

Week-end Bag and Child's Sling Bag

SMALL WEEK-END BAG
WITH ZIP-FASTENER

MATERIALS

A strong sheepskin, seal, crocodile or llama grain or thin hide if obtainable.
1 piece, 25 ins. deep by 15 ins. wide for bag.
1 piece, 31½ ins. deep by 5 ins. wide for gusset.
2 pieces, 18 ins. deep by 1½ ins. wide for handles.
2 pieces, 2½ ins. deep by 2½ ins. wide for tabs.
4 pieces, 3 ins. deep by 1¼ ins. wide for "D" ring tabs.
1 piece stiff paper, 25 ins. by 15 ins.

1 piece stiff paper, 31½ ins, by 5 ins.
Skiver lining to suit above.
1 piece, 25 ins. deep by 15 ins. wide.
1 piece, 31½ ins. deep by 5 ins. wide.
2 pieces, 18 ins. deep by 1½ ins. wide.
2 pieces, 2½ ins. deep by 2½ ins. wide.
4 pieces, 3 ins. deep by 1¼ ins. wide.
1 piece, 8 ins. deep by 6 ins. wide for small pocket.
1 piece, 10 ins. deep by 15 ins. wide for large pocket.
4 metal "D" rings.
4 metal studs for base of bag.
1 zip-fastener, 16 ins. long.
1 yard medium sash cord.
1 piece thick cardboard, 14⅜ ins. deep by 4¾ ins. wide.

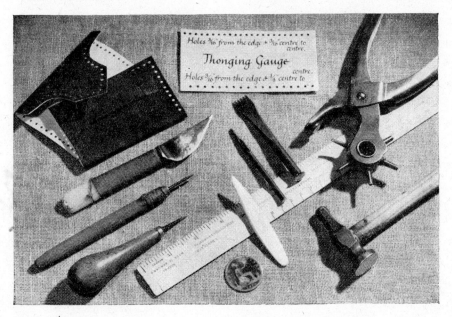

Tools used for leather work shown above are, from top left, purse punched for thonging, knife, tracing tool, awl, metal-edged ruler, smooth penny, bone folder, single hammer punch, stitch-spacer, cardboard thonging gauge, six-way punch and hammer.

FOR MOTHER AND DAUGHTER. *This small week-end bag will prove a most acceptable gift. The original was made in a light tan leather with thonged seams, and the lining was thick skiver dyed in variegated colours. The charming little sling bag for schoolgirl daughter was made from tan wessex grain sheepskin.*

Thonging and thread for stitching.

N.B.—All the above measurements are net and $\frac{1}{8}$ to $\frac{1}{4}$ in. extra all round should be allowed for margins.

Method.—Out of a stiff piece of cartridge drawing paper cut a pattern as shown in the Diagram on page 87, for the bag, gussets and handles. The other small pieces can be marked out on the skin. Place patterns on the leather, mark round the edge with a pencil and cut out with scissors leaving a small margin all round.

Cut skiver lining for each piece of leather.

Line the leather for the bag and gusset with drawing paper. This strengthens the leather and helps to keep the bag in shape.

To prepare the pockets, fold each piece of skiver in half and cut two pieces of paper, one measuring $5\frac{1}{4}$ ins. deep by $15\frac{1}{2}$ ins. wide and the other $4\frac{1}{4}$ ins. deep and $6\frac{1}{2}$ ins. wide. Paste the whole of the inside of the skiver and place the appropriate sized paper on one half, fold over the remaining half and press well together. Put under a weight to dry.

When dry cut the small pocket to measure 4 ins. deep by 6 ins. wide and the large pocket to 5 ins. deep, but keep the margins at the side. Put an edging of glue on two sides and the bottom of each pocket and stick into position on the skiver. The small pocket should be $1\frac{1}{2}$ ins. up from the bottom gusset fold and the large one 1 in. up.

With the stitch spacer and hammer prick the stitching holes and stitch pockets to skiver. This is done by back stitching, which gives a very even effect on the right side, the long stitches on the back being hidden when the skiver is pasted to the leather.

Cut the " D " ring tabs to size, thread through the rings and glue the folded pieces together. Mark and punch five holes along each side and four or five along the bottom ; glue into position on sides of bag. When dry, punch through the holes already in the tabs using the single hammer punch, and make corresponding holes in the bag itself opposite those in the tabs. These are necessary to enable the tabs to be laced on the bag as shown in the illustration.

When the leather has been lined with paper, lay the pattern on it and mark round indicating where the bottom gusset comes. Do the same on the skiver lining.

Now take the $14\frac{3}{8}$ ins. by $4\frac{3}{4}$ ins. piece of cardboard, bevel the edges on one side and glue the other side in the space which forms the bottom gusset.

Punch four holes through the leather and cardboard, using the single hammer punch, and insert four studs, one at each corner, bend the prongs down on to the cardboard and hammer flat. Cut four small pieces of skiver, pare down the edges and stick them over the prongs of the studs.

Cut four small V pieces out of the skiver margin where the bottom gusset comes, and see that they fit over the markings of the bottom gusset of the bag as shown on the diagram.

The lining can now be pasted to the leather in the following way. Paste the centre piece of lining a little beyond each side of the V cuts and stick this part to the leather, covering the cardboard. Rub down well then turn one side of the lining back on to newspaper and paste it all over. Fold back and stick it to the leather. Do the same to the other side and dry under a weight.

The next step is to prepare the long gusset. Mark and cut out the $16\frac{1}{4}$ ins. by $\frac{3}{8}$ in. slot to take the zip fastener and cut a corresponding slot in the gusset lining. Mark position of pulling tabs, 1 in. from each end of cut. Cut tabs to shape, damp and fold over the $\frac{3}{4}$ in. ends, mark and punch holes, thong front edges of tabs and glue folded portion in position. Punch holes in gusset, as described for " D " ring tabs, and lace in position.

Lay the zip fastener flat on a table, glue along each side of the fabric and place the slot in the leather over it, taking care that the teeth of the zip are exactly in the centre of the slot. Next paste the back of the gusset lining and stick it to the leather ; the slot in the lining should be immediately under the slot in the leather. Rub well to ensure sticking. If care is exercised in getting this right the appearance of the bag is much improved.

On the leather mark a line $\frac{1}{16}$ in. from edges of the slot, stitch space the holes and fasten the leather, zip and lining together with back stitching.

Cut the bag and the gusset to the correct size according to the pattern, using a sharp knife and metal edged ruler. A saucer $5\frac{1}{2}$ ins. or 6 ins. in diameter is a good guide for cutting the curves on the sides of the bag. Damp and fold up the sides on each side of the bottom gusset.

It is a good plan to find the centre of each side and punch a lacing hole on that spot and a corresponding hole in the centre of each side of the gusset. Tie a piece of thread in these four holes, thus enabling the correct number of holes to be punched on each side of the centre hole on both bag and gusset. The holes on the gusset at the bottom of the bag must be identical in number with the holes at the bottom of the gusset.

It must be remembered that in counting the holes on the gusset the four corner ones are included in the sides as well as the bottom, thus the corner hole must have two thonging stitches in it to account for this.

When bag and gusset are punched, tie the gusset to the bag and the general appearance can then be judged.

Choose a soft and pliable length of thonging, start in the centre of one end of the bottom gusset, work right and left up the side, along the top and down the other side, finishing in the centre of the opposite gusset.

The best way to join the thonging is to thread the end back under the last three or four stitches and pull it tight. The new length of thonging is threaded through the hole containing the last stitch and the end laid down on the opposite side and laced over for three or four stitches.

The handles are now cut to the correct size and shape and punched as shown in the Diagram. Each piece of sash cord should be 14 ins. long and have the ends frayed out and thinned down. Start lacing the handles in the centre and work to right and left fixing the ends to the " D " rings as shown.

Finally a small leather tassel is attached to the metal tag of the zip fastener. Cut a narrow strip of leather and thread it through the hole in the tag. Cut another piece of leather about $1\frac{3}{4}$ ins. long by $1\frac{1}{2}$ ins. deep, stitch one end to the narrow strip of leather, fringe the bottom edge, roll it round on the strip and stick the edge. Bind it round with thread as shown in the Diagram. Lightly hammer the thonging and polish the bag if necessary.

SLING BAG

MATERIALS

Sheep skin, any grain such as Wessex, crocodile, hog or seal would be suitable.

1 piece 18 ins. deep by 8 ins. wide for bag.

2 pieces 6 ins. deep by $3\frac{1}{2}$ ins. wide for gussets.

2 pieces 36 to 40 ins. deep by $\frac{7}{8}$ ins. wide for sling. (Shorter pieces could be joined together to obtain the required length.)

SMALL WEEK-END BAG WITH ZIP FASTENER

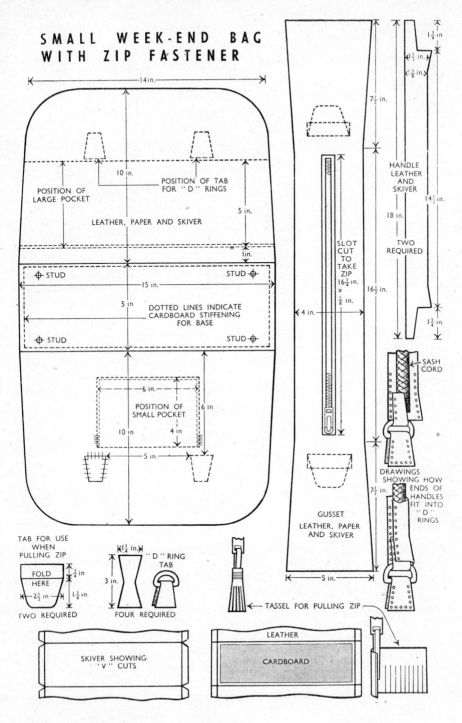

14 in.

POSITION OF LARGE POCKET

10 in.

POSITION OF TAB FOR "D" RINGS

5 in.

LEATHER, PAPER AND SKIVER

1 in.

⊕ STUD   STUD ⊕

15 in.

5 in.   DOTTED LINES INDICATE CARDBOARD STIFFENING FOR BASE

⊕ STUD   STUD ⊕

6 in.

POSITION OF SMALL POCKET   6 in

10 in   4 in

5 in.

TAB FOR USE WHEN PULLING ZIP

FOLD HERE   3/4 in

2 1/2 in   1 3/4 in

TWO REQUIRED

1 1/4 in.

3 in

"D" RING TAB

FOUR REQUIRED

SKIVER SHOWING "V" CUTS

LEATHER

CARDBOARD

← TASSEL FOR PULLING ZIP →

SLOT CUT TO TAKE ZIP 16 1/4 in. x 5/8 in.

4 in.

16 1/2 in.

GUSSET LEATHER, PAPER AND SKIVER

7 1/2 in.

5 in.

7 1/2 in.

1 3/4 in.

1 1/2 in.

1 3/8 in.

HANDLE LEATHER AND SKIVER

TWO REQUIRED

14 1/2 in.

18 in.

1 3/4 in.

SASH CORD

DRAWINGS SHOWING HOW ENDS OF HANDLES FIT INTO "D" RINGS

SLING BAG

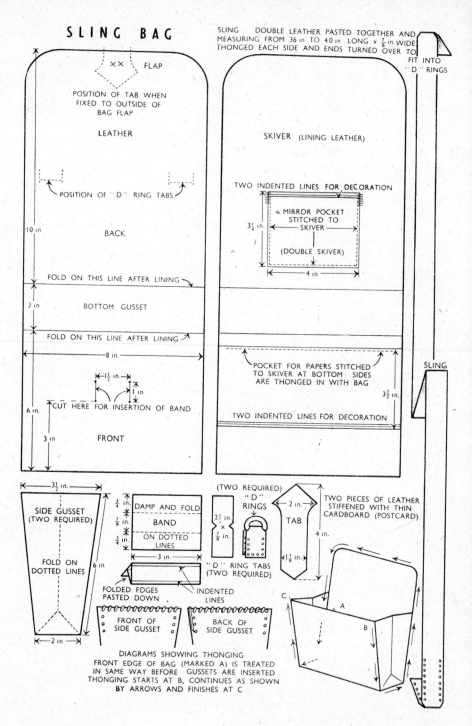

SLING DOUBLE LEATHER PASTED TOGETHER AND MEASURING FROM 36 in TO 40 in LONG × $\frac{7}{8}$ in. WIDE THONGED EACH SIDE AND ENDS TURNED OVER TO FIT INTO "D" RINGS

×× FLAP

POSITION OF TAB WHEN FIXED TO OUTSIDE OF BAG FLAP

LEATHER

POSITION OF "D" RING TABS

10 in

BACK

SKIVER (LINING LEATHER)

TWO INDENTED LINES FOR DECORATION

MIRROR POCKET STITCHED TO SKIVER

$3\frac{1}{4}$ in.

(DOUBLE SKIVER)

4 in.

FOLD ON THIS LINE AFTER LINING

2 in

BOTTOM GUSSET

FOLD ON THIS LINE AFTER LINING

8 in.

POCKET FOR PAPERS STITCHED TO SKIVER AT BOTTOM SIDES ARE THONGED IN WITH BAG

$3\frac{1}{2}$ in.

$1\frac{1}{2}$ in.

1 in

CUT HERE FOR INSERTION OF BAND

6 in.

3 in

FRONT

TWO INDENTED LINES FOR DECORATION

SLING

$3\frac{1}{2}$ in.

SIDE GUSSET (TWO REQUIRED)

FOLD ON DOTTED LINES

6 in.

2 in.

$\frac{3}{4}$ in.

DAMP AND FOLD

$\frac{7}{8}$

BAND

$\frac{3}{4}$

ON DOTTED LINES

3 in.

FOLDED EDGES PASTED DOWN

INDENTED LINES

FRONT OF SIDE GUSSET

BACK OF SIDE GUSSET

(TWO REQUIRED)

"D" RINGS

$2\frac{1}{2}$ in. × $\frac{7}{8}$ in.

"D" RING TABS (TWO REQUIRED)

2 in.

TAB

$1\frac{1}{8}$ in.

TWO PIECES OF LEATHER STIFFENED WITH THIN CARDBOARD (POSTCARD)

4 in.

C

A

B

DIAGRAMS SHOWING THONGING
FRONT EDGE OF BAG (MARKED A) IS TREATED
IN SAME WAY BEFORE GUSSETS ARE INSERTED
THONGING STARTS AT B, CONTINUES AS SHOWN
BY ARROWS AND FINISHES AT C

2 pieces 4 ins. deep by 2 ins. wide
for tab.

1 piece 2¾ ins. deep by 3 ins. wide
for band.

2 pieces 2½ ins. deep by ⅞ in. wide
for " D " ring tabs.

Skiver lining to suit above.

1 piece 18 ins. deep by 8 ins. wide.

2 pieces 6 ins. deep by 3½ ins. wide.

2 pieces 2½ ins. deep by ⅞ in. wide.

1 piece 6½ ins. deep by 4 ins. wide for
mirror pocket.

1 piece 7 ins. deep by 8 ins. wide for
large pocket.

Two metal " D " rings.

Thonging and thread for stitching.

N.B.—All the above measurements
are net and ⅛ to ¼ in. extra all round
should be allowed for margins.

Method.—Cut a paper pattern for the
bag, gusset and tab as shown in the
Diagrams on page 88. The sling and
other small pieces can be marked out on
the leather. Place patterns on the
leather, mark round the edge with a
pencil and cut out with scissors leaving a
small margin all round. Cut the skiver
lining to the size of the leather pieces
which are to be lined, also the pieces
for the pockets.

To prepare the pockets fold each
piece of skiver in half and cut two pieces
of paper, one measuring 4½ ins. by 3½ ins.
and the other 8½ ins. by 3¼ ins. Paste
the whole of the inside of the skiver and
place the appropriate sized paper on
one half, fold over the remaining half and
press well together. Put under a weight
to dry. When ready cut the mirror
pocket to the size shown in Diagram, and
the large pocket to 3½ ins. deep, but keep
the margins at the sides. Put an edging
of glue on the sides and bottom of each
pocket and stick into position on the skiver.

With the stitch spacer and hammer
prick the stitching holes as shown in the
Diagram and stitch pockets to lining.

The next step is to line the gussets
and " D " ring tabs with skiver. The
bag tab is made of two pieces of leather
stiffened in between with thin card. An
old postcard is quite suitable. Then the
two lengths of leather forming the sling
are pasted together.

Cut the " D " ring tabs to size, thread
through the rings and glue the folded
pieces together. Mark out the position
of the tabs on the back of the bag and
glue the tabs in place. These can be
either stitched or thonged to the leather
as desired.

Cut two slits, each 1 in. deep and 1½
ins. apart in the front of the bag.
Make the band by paring the 3-in.
edges, folding over and sticking down as
shown in the Diagram. When this is
dry pare down the ends and insert them
in the cuts ; glue the ends to the inside
of the leather.

The large piece of leather forming the
bag can now be lined with the skiver
with the pockets attached. With a
metal-edged ruler and a sharp knife
cut away the margins on all the
pieces.

With the thonging gauge mark corresponding holes on the edges of the bag
and the gussets, and punch with care and
accuracy. The importance of this operation cannot be stressed too much because
the whole appearance of the finished
article depends upon it.

Thong the tops of the side gussets
and the edge of the bag marked A in the
Diagram, starting and finishing as shown.
Tie the gussets into position, start
thonging at B, continue according to
arrow marks and finish at C. Close the
bag by folding over the flap, insert the
pointed tab under the band, mark the
position on the flap and fix to the bag by
thonging or stitching.

Thong the sling and fasten the ends
into the " D " rings. Lightly hammer
the thonging and folds.

SHOPPING BAG

In Leather, with Handles and Purse Pocket

MATERIALS

Suede leather using the skin side for the outside of the bag, or Persian sheep.

2 pieces 12 ins. deep by 10 ins. wide for bag.

1 piece 6 ins. deep by 5 ins. wide for pocket.

1 piece 35 ins. deep by 2½ ins. wide for gusset (shorter pieces can be joined together to obtain the required length).

4 pieces 18 ins. long by ⅞ in. wide for handles.

Skiver lining to suit above.

2 pieces 12 ins. deep by 10 ins. wide.

1 piece 6 ins. deep by 5 ins. wide.

1 piece 35 ins. deep by 2½ ins. wide.

N.B.—All the above measurements are net and ⅛ to ¼ in. extra all round should be allowed for margins.

Method.—Cut a paper pattern for one side of the bag, the pocket and the handle, as shown in the Diagram below; the gusset can be marked out on the skin. Place patterns on the leather, mark round the edge with a pencil and cut out with scissors, leaving a small margin all round. Cut the skiver lining to correspond with the pieces of leather and paste the skiver on to the leather.

Prepare the handles in the same way only in this case they are made of two thicknesses of leather. When dry cut

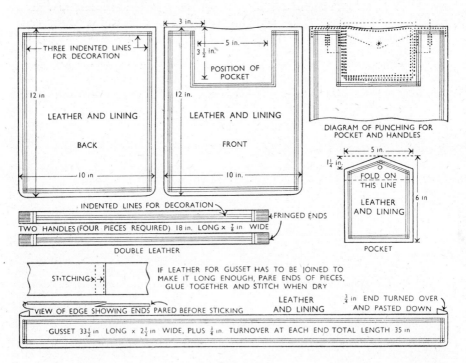

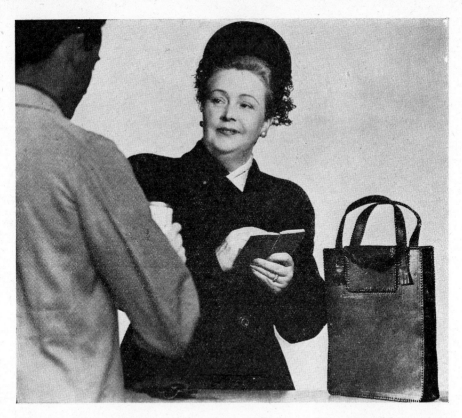

FOR THE HOUSEWIFE. *A shopping bag that is capacious without being cumbersome will prove a welcome gift. The original was made from black suede with the skin side outside. The seams are thonged and it has a purse pocket in the front.*

away all the margins on all the pieces using a metal-edged ruler and a knife.

If the leather is smooth, or has a fine grain, then the indented lines can be put on, as shown in the diagram.

With the thonging gauge mark the holes on the edges of the bag and gusset to correspond, and punch with care and accuracy. The punching holes on the side of the bag which take the handles and purse pocket must be made with the single punch and hammer.

Thong the two top edges of the bag first, also the pointed flap of the purse pocket, starting and finishing the latter below the fold at the back.

Insert the pocket piece into the bag, lining facing lining, and thong it in position. To do this thong from hole to hole horizontally at the sides and vertically at the bottom. Fix a press stud to keep the flap closed.

The handles come next. Indent the lines, fringe the ends and punch the edges, stopping at the two cross lines just above the fringe. Thong the edges, starting and finishing five holes from each end. Now attach the ends of the handles to the front and back of the bag using the five holes left for that purpose.

Tie gusset in position and thong the front and back of the bag to the gusset.

GIFTS IN RAFFIA

Work Basket, Mat and Pet Basket

SMALL WORK BASKET WITH LID IN COILED RAFFIA

MATERIALS

Approximately 16 yds. white sash cord.
Raffia, natural and coloured.
Oval wooden bead.
Raffia needle (large eye and blunt point).

The simplest stitch in raffia basketry is known as the Lazy Squaw and is the stitch used for this basket and lid.

Pulp cane, when obtainable, and strands of raffia can be used as the foundation material, but in this case fine white sash cord is used. Natural raffia can be purchased in small hanks but the cheapest way is to buy it by the pound. As only a small quantity of coloured raffia is used in proportion to the natural it is more satisfactory to dye it yourself.

A good powder dye, dissolved in boiling water, to which is added one or two tablespoons full of non-brewed vinegar will be found quite effective. Immerse the raffia in the hot dye and keep stirring it with a piece of stick, leave it in the solution for ten minutes or a quarter of an hour, according to the depth of colour required, then take it out and hang it up to drain.

If this cannot be done out of doors, spread newspapers on the floor to catch the dye which drops from the raffia.

Raffia is more easily worked if it has been damped but it is unnecessary to damp dyed raffia.

Method.—The basket measures 7¾ ins. across the top and is 2½ ins. deep. The lid is raised slightly in the centre.

Take a length of sash cord, fray out and bind one end with raffia as shown in the Diagram on page 95.

The Lazy Squaw stitch is quite easy to work, the raffia is bound round one row of sash cord and stitched over two, and so on ; the work always proceeds from right to left and the stitch is always brought over and downwards.

After the end of the sash cord has been bound with raffia bend it into as tight a coil as possible and hold it together with a long stitch (over two cords); gradually work it round, binding one cord and stitching two, until a firm coil begins to form. Keep on like this for three or four rows and it will then be noticed that the space between the long stitches is getting wider, owing to the increasing circumference of the rows, so in the next row round make two long stitches in the space instead of one and the coil will be strengthened.

When the coil is 5 ins. across introduce two rows of coloured raffia and begin to turn up to form the side after the first coloured row has been worked. As the side is built on a curved slope it is as well to cut a cardboard template of the shape required, and as the basket grows, test each row against the template. There is a small sketch on the Diagram showing how the side fits the template. When building up a sloping side each succeeding row of sash cord must project slightly beyond the previous one. When the side reaches 2¼ ins. deep, finish off with one row of coloured raffia. Tapering cord as Diagram on page 95.

The lid is made in the same way as the base of the basket but with a slight

FOR MOTHER. *A lightweight needlework basket in coiled raffia to delight the heart of every needlewoman. A ring is fitted to the centre of the lid to make it easy to carry about. The original was in natural and red raffia. The oval table mat on the right in coiled raffia will also make a very useful gift.*

rise in the centre. In other words start the coil by keeping it flat for three or four rows then begin by depressing the sash cord until about eight rows have been completed when it should be worked flat again until the dimension of 7¾ ins. across has been reached. It must be understood that this depression is the inside of the lid. Finish the last row in colour and introduce three rows of colour as shown in the reproduction at the head of this page.

When working try to select strands of raffia of the same thickness, one is bound to find finer strands in the bundle. These need not be wasted, but can be used double to preserve the even appearance of the rows.

Make a small ring of sash cord, bind it round with coloured raffia and fix it to the centre of the lid. For the fastening loop make a ring of raffia (the sash cord would be too thick) and bind that tightly with coloured raffia fixing it firmly to the edge of the basket. Thread a short length of coloured raffia through the hole in the wooden bead, bind the two ends together so that they form a shank, and fix it to the basket in a position which corresponds with the fastening loop.

Fix the lid to the basket by several figure-of-eight stitches, exactly opposite the fastening loop. This method of fastening is preferable to oversewing which is inclined to bind the lid too tightly to the basket and prevent it opening freely.

To join two lengths of sash cord, fray and thin out each end, overlap them and bind with a fine strand of raffia. If properly done there should be no difference in the thickness of the sash cord at the join.

The basket shown in the illustration was stitched in natural and scarlet raffia.

TABLE MAT
IN COILED RAFFIA

MATERIALS

Approximately 8 yds. of medium waxed sash cord.

Raffia, natural and coloured.

Raffia needle (large eye and blunt point).

Method.—For this oval mat measuring 11 ins. long and 7½ ins. wide the Navajo or figure-of-eight stitch is used and waxed sash cord, instead of the ordinary kind, because it makes the mat so much firmer when finished.

The Navajo stitch is simple and built up on the figure eight. Bring the raffia up over the lower cord, between the two cords, and behind and over the top cord, then between the two cords and down behind the lower cord thus completing the figure eight and one stitch. Keep on like this and it will be found that each row is covered twice, which, of course, takes longer than the Lazy Squaw stitch but gives a firmer foundation. The stitch is shown on the Diagram on the facing page.

To start the oval coil, measure 4 ins. along one end of the sash cord and fold it tightly on itself. Take a length of fine raffia and bind the curved part of the fold, then start working the stitch as described. The interlacing movement of the figure eight will hold the two cords firmly together. Continue until the required size is attained and finish off as shown on the Diagram.

When making a join, pare one side of each end of the waxed sash cord and splice together, like cane, instead of fraying out, which is the method of joining the unwaxed cord.

The end of a new strand of raffia together with the end of the old strand are wrapped round the sash cord and the stitching is continued. Any ends which are showing after three or four stitches have been made can be cut away with a pair of scissors.

The mat shown in the illustration has six rows of natural raffia in the centre, two rows of turquoise blue, one row of natural, one row each of navy, purple and green, and is finished with four rows of natural.

If desired, the mat can be worked entirely in natural raffia and the proportions altered to suit one's requirement. The length of the straight piece of cord at the beginning of the mat governs the proportions. A short distance will give a broad oval and a long distance a correspondingly narrow one.

It is a good plan to experiment with paper patterns, testing the size and shape on the table where the mat is to be used. The ends of an oval mat are really half circles, so if the measurements of the half circles are added together and deducted from the length of the oval pattern, the remainder is the length of cord required to start the oval mat.

STITCHES USED IN COILED BASKETRY

RAFFIA

SASH CORD

LAZY SQUAW

BIND ONE CORD,
STITCH TWO CORDS
TOGETHER

RAFFIA

SASH CORD

NAVAJO

STITCH TWO CORDS
TOGETHER WITH
FIGURE OF 8

RAFFIA

MARIPOSA

AS LAZY SQUAW
ONLY EACH LONG
STITCH IS KNOTTED

STARTING A COIL

END OF CORD FRAYED OUT

CUT AND TAPERED

BOUND WITH RAFFIA

COIL

CIRCULAR

OVAL

CIRCULAR

COIL CONTINUED

LAZY SQUAW

MARIPOSA

TO FINISH A COIL
TAPER END OF CORD
AND OVERSEW TO
UNDER ROW

NAVAJO

CARDBOARD TEMPLATE
FOR SIDE OF BASKET

PET BASKET IN COILED RAFFIA

MATERIALS

Approximately 28 to 30 yds. of medium sash cord.

Approximately $1\frac{1}{2}$ lbs. of natural raffia.

Raffia needle (large eye and blunt point).

Method.—This basket takes rather a long time to make but is very effective when finished. The stitch employed is called Mariposa or knot stitch. It is similar to the stitch known as the Lazy Squaw, only in this case each long stitch is knotted which gives a firmer structure to the basket. These stitches are shown in detail in the working diagram on page 95.

The base of the basket is $12\frac{1}{2}$ ins. in diameter and the side 4 ins. deep.

It has an opening $8\frac{1}{2}$ ins. wide in the front, for an entrance, and the top is 14 ins. in diameter.

Take a length of sash cord, fray out and bind one end with raffia as shown in the Diagram on page 95. Bend the end into as tight a coil as possible and secure it with one row of Lazy Squaw stitching (bind one cord, stitch two cords together) then proceed with the Mariposa stitch. Make a Lazy Squaw stitch (over two cords) and the binding stitch to the left of it, bring the needle through from the back between the two cords and on the right of the long stitch, over it, and round again if necessary, thus knotting the long stitch, passing it through to the back between the two cords. Make one or two new binding stitches, then the long stitch, followed by the binder to the left, through from the back to the right of the long stitch and knot it in the same way as the first stitch.

Always work from right to left and from the back over and downwards. The knotted stitches are arranged midway between the stitches of the rows already worked, except when the spaces on the coil become too wide and two knotted stitches have to be made instead of the single one.

When twenty coils have been worked, or forty rows right across, the base of the basket should be complete, but as sash cord varies slightly in thickness it is as well to measure it and see that the $12\frac{1}{2}$ ins. diameter required has been fully completed.

The turning up of the side can now be started. In this case the outward slope of the basket is very slight, so each succeeding row of cord must only project a very little beyond the one just worked.

Care must be taken with this part of the basket, to ensure a good shape, and keep on testing the slope of the side with the cardboard template. There is a small sketch on page 95 showing how the side of a coiled basket is checked with the cardboard template.

There should be twelve rows of cord in the full depth of each side, but the opening must be allowed for in the following way.

Complete three side rows all round, then mark the opening. Each side row must now be turned back on itself on each side of the opening, gradually building up the side until eleven rows have been completed, then continue with the twelfth row, taking it down past the folded end on one side of the opening and along the bottom (making four rows) up past the folded ends of the other side of the opening and finish about 6 or 7 ins. along the top row, tapering off as shown in the Diagram.

It will be noticed that one side of the opening has more rows than the other; that cannot be avoided and is accounted for by the base being constructed on a coil.

Larger baskets can be made by increasing the size of the base and sides.

FOR THE PET LOVER. *A delightful gift for the owner of a pet puppy or kitten is this attractive pet basket in natural coiled raffia. Even if you have not attempted raffia work before you will find this very simple to make from the instructions and diagram given on the preceding pages.*

D

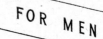

MONOGRAM SCARF

And Initialled Handkerchiefs

EVENING SCARF

MATERIALS

¾ yd. of 36-in. wide white silk.

Suitable foundation initials.

Few strands of black and white embroidery thread.

¾ yd. ready-made black and white fringe or 6 white and 3 black spools of buttonhole twist.

Method.—Fold the material in half, right side inside, to make a strip 36 ins. long by 13½ ins. wide, with the selvedge edges at the narrow ends. Tack, but do not seam the raw edges together on the long side, turn right side out and press the scarf lightly.

About 2½ ins. up from one end of the scarf, mark a centre point and arrange the foundation initials over it, interlacing them through one another to. make a pleasing monogram. Tack the initials on firmly through the top layer of material only; unpick the tacked seam for a few inches to facilitate this. Work close satin-stitch over the padding in white embroidery silk then work a narrow black line round the edges, in outline stitch.

Press the monogram well, first on the wrong side, then on the right side. Turn the scarf inside out, seam the long side then turn back again to the right side and press well.

The Fringe.—If ready-made fringe is to be used, turn in the selvedge ends, sandwich the braid edge of the fringe between the two layers of material and hem along both sides.

For hand-made fringe, first turn in the selvedge edges and whip them together with small stitches. Cut the buttonhole twist into 5-in. lengths, take three strands of black and three of white and fold them together in half. Now, working with the whipped edges to the top, pierce the material just below the edge with a small steel crochet hook, and pull the folded strands through to the front of the material. Still keeping the hook through the loop, pick up the cut ends of the strands and draw them over the whipped edge and through the loop, to make a knot on the edge of the material. Pull this knot tight.

For the next knot use six strands of white and continue along the scarf ends with alternate white and black-and-white knots. When the fringe is finished, brush the strands lightly with a clean brush and trim off any uneven ends. Press the scarf well.

HANDKERCHIEFS

MATERIALS

Large white linen or fine lawn handkerchiefs (or square of suitable material, 22 ins. by 22 ins.).

Few strands of white embroidery thread, linen or stranded cotton.

Scrap of fabric matching handkerchief material.

Method.—If the handkerchief is to be made, draw a few threads along each

FOR ANY MAN. *This white silk monogram evening scarf will make a delightful gift. The original was trimmed with black and white silk fringe and the monogram was worked in white satin-stitch, outlined in black. The H initial on the handkerchief shown above was appliquéd, and the C initial was worked in satin-stitch.*

side of the square of fabric, 1¾ ins. from the raw edges. Turn in the edges and fold down again just on to the drawn threads, squaring the corners neatly. This will give a hem about ¾ in. wide, which can then be sewn down with hemstitching through the drawn threads.

To Work the Initials.—For the script initial (the " C " on handkerchief in illustration shown above), a transfer, a foundation initial or your own handwriting can be used. On a transfer or handwriting, work over the lines with chain-stitch, putting in two or more rows where the lines are thickest, then work over the chain-stitch with close satin-stitch. If a foundation initial is used, tack this on firmly in the corner of

the handkerchief and embroider over the padding with close satin-stitch. Press well, back and front.

For the appliqué initial (the " H " on handkerchief shown above), take a scrap of material, as nearly as possible matching the texture of the hankie itself, and draw or trace on to it a block capital letter with its strokes about ¼ in. wide. Tack the piece on to the corner of the handkerchief then stitch the two layers together with very small running stitches along the outlines of the initial. Using small, sharp-pointed scissors, snip away the top fabric just beyond the running stitches and sew the raw edges down with narrow satin overcast stitch. Press the initial well first on the right and then on the wrong sides.

SPECTACLE CASE

And Library Book Cover

SPECTACLE CASE

MATERIALS

Leather, 15 ins. long by 5 ins. wide.
Lining, 15 ins. long by 5 ins. wide.
Canvas, 11 ins. long by 5 ins. wide.
2 pieces of cardboard, each 5 ins. long
by $2\frac{1}{4}$ ins. wide.
Contrasting thread.
Small quantity of cotton-wool.

Method.—Make a paper pattern, as shown in Diagram 1, for the case, and cut the shape in both leather and lining material, then cut the same shape, but without the flap, in canvas. Make up the case foundation in the following way.

Place the lining on a table or flat surface, right side downwards, with the two pieces of cardboard lying down the centre of back and front with $\frac{1}{2}$ in. space between them. In the front portion put a layer of cotton-wool underneath and on top of the cardboard : in the back portion, a layer under the cardboard only. Now put the canvas shape on top and pin canvas and lining together along the sides of the cardboard. Stitch the two layers together with small running stitches as close to the cardboard as possible then fold the foundation at the space between the two pieces of cardboard, keeping the lining to the inside. Stitch up the gussets at each side as shown in Diagram 2.

To make the outer covering, first cut a small strip of leather and stitch it on the front of the cover about an inch from the top edge, to make a loop through which the flap can be threaded.

Fold the leather shape, right side inside, and whip the edges of the gussets together with small stitches. Turn the cover right side out and with the contrasting thread work running stitches round top edge and along edges of flap.

Slip the foundation inside the leather cover, turn in the edge of the lining and slip-stitch it to the outer cover right round the top and along the edges of the flap. The point of the flap can be stiffened slightly with several layers of gummed paper cut to shape and stuck on before the lining is stitched in place.

Work the corners of the gussets into place at the bottom of the case then pinch together the fold of leather along the edges of the cardboard, back and front, and stitch through with running stitches in the contrasting thread, to keep the gussets folded inwards.

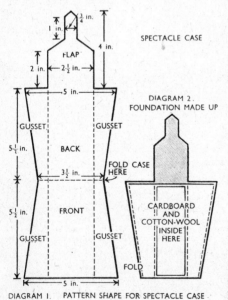

DIAGRAM 1. PATTERN SHAPE FOR SPECTACLE CASE

FOR FATHER. *A leather library book cover with his initial in the corner and a spectacle case to match are gifts that are bound to meet with his approval. Wide flaps each side of the cover keep the book in place. The spectacle case is padded with cotton-wool and lined with satin.*

LIBRARY BOOK COVER

MATERIALS

Piece of leather, 18 ins. long by 9 ins. deep.

Few strands of strong thread.

Few stud paper fasteners.

Method.—From the strip of leather cut a piece 14 ins. long for the cover itself, then cut the remaining piece into four, each 4 ins. by 2¼ ins. for the corner flaps.

Using strong, contrasting thread, stitch round two adjacent sides of each flap with even running stitches then place a flap lengthways in each corner of the cover so that the unstitched edges lie along the edges of the cover. Now stitch round the cover in the same way, working through the two thicknesses of leather at the corners. Apart from its decorative use, this stitching will prevent the leather from stretching out of shape.

Finish the cover with an initial made with stud paper fasteners.

SPILL HOLDER

Trimmed with Coloured Leather

MATERIALS

1 deep, round tin such as used for cocoa.

Strip of skiver to cover tin.

Scraps of skiver in two or three contrasting colours.

Glue.

Method.—Any suitable colour scheme can be used for this spill holder, but club colours on a neutral ground of grey or fawn are suggested.

Cut the skiver to the shape shown in Diagram 1, the top and bottom edges being the exact circumference of the tin and the depth $\frac{1}{4}$ in. more than that of the tin. The sides must be parallel, but the angle of the slope is immaterial.

See that the tin is perfectly clean, inside and out, then glue the skiver shape round it so that the sloping edges just meet in a diagonal line and the lower edge is level with the bottom of the tin. Turn the extra $\frac{1}{4}$ in. over the top of the tin and glue down inside.

From scraps of contrasting leather, skiver or suede, cut strips of material $\frac{1}{4}$ in. longer than the diagonal join and from $\frac{1}{8}$ in. to $\frac{1}{4}$ in. in width. Glue three or four of these strips in an attractive colour arrangement over the diagonal join in the skiver cover, turning the extra $\frac{1}{4}$ in. over at the top. Glue two or three more of these strips at regular intervals round the holder, keeping them parallel with the first one.

FOR THE SMOKER. *This useful spill holder is in leather with contrasting strips of coloured leather glued at regular intervals round the holder.*

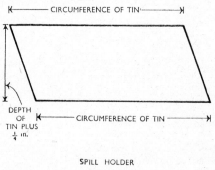

CIRCUMFERENCE OF TIN

DEPTH OF TIN PLUS $\frac{1}{4}$ in.

CIRCUMFERENCE OF TIN

SPILL HOLDER

DIAGRAM 1.

SHAPE FOR HOLDER COVER

SHAVING PACK

And Small Razor Towels

SHAVING PACK

MATERIALS

¼ yd. of 36-in. wide brown plastic material.

12-in. zip fastener.

Shaving equipment, such as razor in case, soap in container, shaving brush in container.

Method.—To make a pattern for the shaving pack, place the three articles to be contained in it flat on a sheet of paper with their lower ends level. Draw a line immediately beneath them and a circular line over the top of them to enclose them with a small margin to spare.

For average-sized articles this shape will be about 8 ins. wide at the base and 5 ins. deep from the top centre of the curve.

Leave a space beneath the base equal to the depth of the thickest article, then duplicate the top curved shape beneath this, joining the two shapes at the sides.

Cut out the paper pattern and test it for size by standing the three articles upright along its centre. The curved tops should just meet over the articles.

Cut the pattern shape twice in plastic, then take one plastic shape and pencil on it the position of the base strip as on the paper pattern. Place the three articles flat down just above this base strip, see Diagram I on this page.

Cut a strip of plastic about I in. wide and approximately 13 ins. long and lay this across each article in turn to make loops through which they can be slipped. Mark between each article where the strip is to be stitched down then remove the equipment and stitch the strip at both ends and at the marked points as shown in Diagram I at the foot of this page.

This plastic shape with the loops on it is the lining and the next step is to sew its outer curved edge to the tape of the zip-fastener.

Mark the top centre of each curve and the centre of the fastener on each braid. Turn the fastener on to the wrong side and machine the edge of the plastic over the edge of the braid, beginning at the top centre and working towards the ends of the fastener on both sides. Stitch

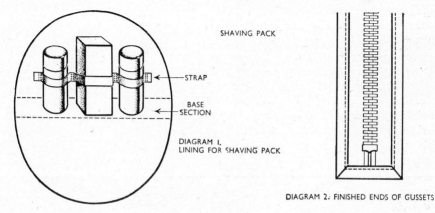

STRAP

BASE SECTION

DIAGRAM I.
LINING FOR SHAVING PACK

SHAVING PACK

DIAGRAM 2. FINISHED ENDS OF GUSSETS

FOR THE TRAVELLER. *Two useful gifts : an easily carried and compact plastic shaving pack to hold all his shaving equipment, and neat little razor towels held together with a loop of tape at one corner.*

the plastic to the braid for about ¾ in. beyond the ends of the metal, leaving the base portion of the plastic un-stitched between the two braids to form a gusset.

Now take the second plastic shape and stitch it to the right side of the fastener in the same way, working outwards from the top centre.

The fastener itself now forms a gusset between back and front of the pack. To close this gusset, at the bottom of each side, fold the unstitched plastic edges up over the braids, securely enclosing the raw edges of the braids between the lining and the outer cover.

Mitre the folded corners neatly and backstitch the plastic and braid together as shown in Diagram 2 on previous page.

RAZOR TOWELS

MATERIALS

Square of terry towelling, 12 ins. by 12 ins.

6 ins. white tape, ½ in. wide.

Few strands of coloured wool.

Method.—Fold the square of towelling into four and then cut along the folds to within 1 in. of the centre point. This gives you four square leaves, held together at one corner. Work button-hole stitch along the cut edges of each towel in coloured wool (the original used red), then sew a tape loop on the folded corner.

Work the word " Razor " across the corner of the top towel, in chain-stitch outline, as shown above.

LEATHER MITTS

For the Cyclist

MATERIALS

Chamois leather, approximately 12 ins. by 16 ins.

Piece of soft brown leather, approximately 8 ins. by 5 ins.

Strong sewing thread in brown and natural.

Size to fit average hand.

Method.—Take the pattern for the left-hand mitt from the loose pattern sheet in the back of the book, and pin the pieces on the right side of the chamois leather, as follows :—

Front, Back, Outside Thumb, Inside Thumb, Finger Gussets 1, 1A, 2, 2A, 3 and 3A.

From the brown leather cut the reinforcement for the palm and inside thumb.

When stitching the glove put the pieces together right sides outside (except in the case of the gussets) and sew through both thicknesses about $\frac{1}{8}$ in. from the edges, using small running stitches of even size back and front of the work, as shown in Diagram 1.

Begin with the thumb, sewing the two long edges A to B together, right sides outside, then the two shorter edges, C to D. Sew the thumb into place on the front of the mitt with the thumb points B, D and E coinciding with the same points on the thumb opening. Now take the brown palm reinforcement and sew it in place with the light coloured thread, putting points D and E to the same points on the chamois leather and letting the extension run up the thumb.

Join back and front of the mitt together down the outside seam. Take the

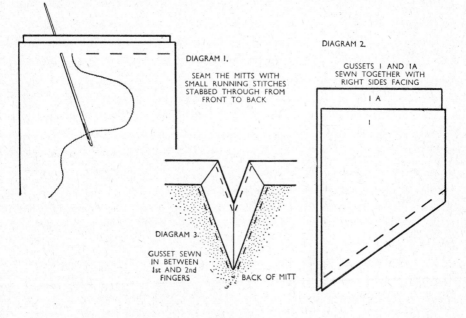

DIAGRAM 1.

SEAM THE MITTS WITH SMALL RUNNING STITCHES STABBED THROUGH FROM FRONT TO BACK

DIAGRAM 2.

GUSSETS 1 AND 1A SEWN TOGETHER WITH RIGHT SIDES FACING

1 A

1

DIAGRAM 3.

GUSSET SEWN IN BETWEEN 1st AND 2nd FINGERS

BACK OF MITT

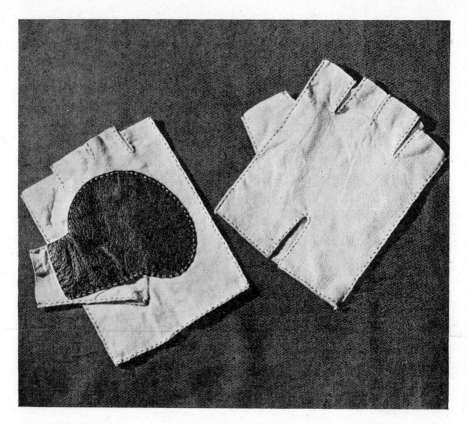

FOR THE CYCLIST. *An unusual gift that is sure to please are these cycling track mitts in chamois leather. They give the fingers the maximum amount of freedom, and the palm is reinforced with dark brown leather. The seams are saddle-stitched with brown thread, and the brown leather is stitched with light thread.*

finger gussets 1 and 1A, place them together with right sides *facing* and stitch the bottom sloping seam, Diagram 2. Insert these gussets between the first and second fingers, the shorter sides to the front of the mitt, the longer ones to the back. Stitch No. 1 to the edges of the first finger, No. 1A to the edges of the second finger as in Diagram 3. Work upwards from the lowest point of the seam in each case.

In the same way stitch together gussets 2 and 2A and sew them between the second and third fingers, then gussets 3 and 3A between the third and fourth fingers. When the gussets are all carefully stitched in sew the back and the front of the mitt together along the inside seam.

Make a narrow turning on to the wrong side along the wrist edge of the mitt and up the centre back slit, as can be clearly seen on the right-hand mitt in the illustration above, and sew with running stitches. The cut edges can be left round the tops of the fingers and thumb.

For the right-hand mitt, reverse the patterns before cutting out, then make it up in exactly the same way.

KNITTED GLOVES

In Three-Colour Fair-Isle

MATERIALS

1½ ozs. 4-ply wool in dark colour.
1 oz. 4-ply wool in light colour.
1 oz. 4-ply wool in medium colour.
2 No. 12 knitting needles.

MEASUREMENTS

To fit an average size hand.

TENSION

8½ sts. to 1 in.

ABBREVIATIONS

K. knit, p. purl, st. stitch, sts. stitches, rep. repeat, inc. increase, tog. together, ins. inches, patt. pattern, dk. dark, lt. light, md. medium.

THE RIGHT-HAND GLOVE

With dk. wool cast on 60 sts. and work 3 ins. in k. 2, p. 2 rib.

Next row.—* rib 11, inc. in next st., rep. from * to end (65 sts.).

Join in md. wool and continue in patt. :—

1st row.—K. 1 md., * 1 dk., 1 md., rep. from * to end.

2nd row.—P. 1 dk., * 1 md., 1 dk., rep. from * to end.

3rd row.—K. 1 dk., * 1 md., 1 dk., rep. from * to end.

4th row.—P. 1 md., * 1 dk., 1 md., rep. from * to end.

Join in lt. wool.

5th row.—* k. 1 lt., 4 md., rep. from * to end.

6th row.—* p. 1 lt., 2 md., 1 lt., 1 md., rep. from * to end.

7th row.—* k. 2 dk., 2 lt., 1 dk., rep. from * to end.

8th row.—* p. 1 dk., 2 lt., 2 dk., rep. from * to end.

9th row.—* k. 1 md., 1 lt., 2 md., 1 lt., rep. from * to end.

10th row.—* p. 4 md., 1 lt., rep. from * to end.

These 10 rows form the patt.

Continuing in patt. until work measures 6 ins. approximately from cast-on edge, ending with a 10th patt. row.

Work for Thumb thus.—

Next row.—Patt. 45, turn, cast on 6 sts.

Next row.—Patt. 18, turn, cast on 6 sts.

Work in patt. on these 24 sts. for 2½ ins., ending with a 4th patt. row.

Break off lt. wool and md. wool, shape top with dk. wool thus :—

Next row.—* k. 2 tog., k. 1, rep. from * to end.

Next row.—P. to end.

Next row.—* k. 2 tog., rep. from * to end.

Break off wool, thread end through remaining sts., draw up and fasten off, then sew down the side of the thumb to the base.

With right side of work facing rejoin wools and k. up 12 sts. at base of thumb, work in patt. to end.

Work in patt. for 2 ins., ending with a 10th patt. row (approximately 8 ins. from cast-on edge).

Shape for Fingers thus.—
First Finger.—

Next row.—Patt. 41 sts., turn, cast on 1 st.

Next row.—Patt. 18, turn, cast on 2 sts.

Continuing in patt. on these 20 sts. for 2¾ ins., ending with a p. row.

Break off lt. and md. wools, shape top in dk. wool thus :—

Next row.—* k. 1, k. 2 tog., rep. from * to last 2 sts., k. 2.

FOR FATHER. *These cosy winter gloves will make a welcome gift for cold winter days. They are knitted in a neat three-colour fair-isle, with finger tips in plain wool. A deep band of ribbing in plain wool allows the gloves to fit the wrists comfortably.*

Next row.—P. to end.

Next row.—* k. 2 tog., rep. from * to end.

Break off wool, thread end through remaining sts., draw up and fasten off then sew down side edges to base.

Second Finger.—With right side of work facing, rejoin wools and k. up 2 sts. at base of first finger, patt. 8, turn, cast on 2 sts.

Next row.—Patt. 20, turn, cast on 1 st.

Continue in patt. on these 21 sts. for 3 ins., ending with a p. row.

Break off lt. and md. wools, shape top in dk. wool thus :—

Next row.—* k. 1, k. 2 tog., rep. from * to end.

Next row.—P. to end.

Next row.—* k. 2 tog., rep. from * to end.

Now complete to match first finger.

Third Finger.—With right side of work facing, rejoin wools and k. up 3 sts. at base of second finger, patt. 8, turn, cast on 1 st.

Next row.—Patt. 20, turn, cast on 1 st.

Continue in patt. on these 21 sts. for 2¾ ins., ending with a p. row.

Break off lt. and md. wools, then shape the top in dk. wool as given for the second finger.

Fourth Finger.—With right side of work facing, rejoin wools and k. up 4 sts. at base of third finger, patt. to end.

Continue in patt. on these 20 sts. for 2½ ins., ending with a p. row.

Break off lt. and md. wools, shape the top in dk. wool as given for the first finger, sewing down side of hand to wrist edge and matching the patt. very carefully.

THE LEFT-HAND GLOVE

Continue as given for the right hand glove until work measures 6 ins., ending with a 10th patt. row.

Work for Thumb thus.—

Next row.—Patt. 32, turn, cast on 6 sts.

Next row.—Patt. 18, turn, cast on 6 sts.

Now complete the thumb, rest of hand and the fingers as given for the right-hand glove.

Make-up.—Press work lightly on wrong side using a hot iron over a damp cloth.

Simple to knit on two needles, the main part of these gloves is in fair-isle bands.

SLEEVELESS PULLOVER

Designed with a V-Neck

MATERIALS

5 oz. 3-ply wool in main colour.
4 oz. 3-ply wool in contrasting colour.
2 No. 12 knitting needles.

MEASUREMENTS

Length 23½ ins.
Chest 38 ins.

N.B.—For a 40-in. chest use No. 11 needles for patt. (keeping No. 12 for ribbing). For a 42-in. chest use No. 10 needles for patt. (keeping No. 12 for ribbing).

TENSION

9 sts. to 1 in. measured over the patt. on No. 12 needles.
8½ sts. to 1 in. on No. 11 needles,
8 sts. to 1 in. on No. 10 needles.

ABBREVIATIONS

k. knit, p. purl, st. stitch, sts. stitches, inc. increase, dec. decrease, patt. pattern, beg. beginning, ins. inches, mn. main colour, con. contrasting colour, tog. together, st.st. stocking stitch.

The Back.—With No. 12 needles and mn. colour cast on 120 sts. and work 4 ins. in k. 1, p. 1 rib.

Next row.—Work twice into 1st st., * rib 4, work twice into next st., rep. from * to last 4 sts., rib 2, work twice into next st., rib 1. (145 sts.)

Join in con. colour and continue in patt. thus : (Change needles here for larger sizes.)

1st row.—* k. 2 mn., 2 con. (1 mn., 1 con.) 5 times, 1 con., 1 mn., rep. from * to last st., k. 1 mn.

2nd row.—* p. 1 con., 2 mn., 2 con. (1 mn., 1 con.) 4 times, 1 con., 2 mn., rep. from * to last st., 1 con.

3rd row.—* k. 2 con., 2 mn., 2 con. (1 mn., 1 con.) 3 times, 1 con., 2 mn., 1 con., rep. from * to last st., 1 con.

4th row.—* p. 1 mn., 2 con., 2 mn., 2 con., 1 mn., 1 con., 1 mn., 2 con., 2 mn., 2 con., rep. from * to last st., 1 mn.

5th row.—* k. 1 con., 1 mn., 2 con., 2 mn., 2 con., 1 mn., 2 con., 2 mn., 2 con., 1 mn., rep. from * to last st., k. 1 con.

6th row.—* p. 1 mn., 1 con., 1 mn., 2 con., 2 mn., 3 con., 2 mn., 2 con., 1 mn., 1 con., rep. from * to last st., p. 1 mn.

7th row.—* k. (1 con., 1 mn.) twice, 2 con., 2 mn., 1 con., 2 mn., 2 con., 1 mn., 1 con., 1 mn., rep. from * to last st., k. 1 con.

8th row.—* p. (1 mn., 1 con.) 3 times, 1 con., 3 mn., 2 con. (1 mn., 1 con.) twice, rep. from * to last st., p. 1 mn.

9th row.—As 7th row.
10th row.—As 6th row.
11th row.—As 5th row.
12th row.—As 4th row.
13th row.—As 3rd row.
14th row.—As 2nd row.

These 14 rows form the patt.

Continue in patt. inc. 1 st. both ends of next row and of every following 6th row until there are 171 sts. on needle, working the extra sts. gradually into patt.

Continue without shaping until work measures 14½ ins., ending with a p. row.
Shape Armholes thus.—Keeping continuity of patt. cast off 6 sts. at beg. of the next 2 rows, then dec. 1 st. both ends of every row until 125 sts. remain.

Continue without shaping until work

FOR BIG BROTHER. *This classic V-neck sleeveless pullover is a gift that cannot help but be popular. Neat and smart in a two-colour chequered design, it is an informal garment, ideal for slipping on over a sports shirt in the home, yet not bulky when worn under a jacket out of doors.*

measures 23½ ins., ending with a p. row.

Shape Shoulders thus.—Cast off 10 sts. at beg. of the next 4 rows, then cast off 12 sts. at beg. of the next 2 rows.

Change to No. 12 needles for neck band, and, using con. wool, work 6 rows in k. 1, p. 1 rib dec. 1 st. at the beg. of each row.

Change to mn. wool and work 6 more rows in the k. 1, p. 1 rib still dec. 1 st. at the beg. of each row.

Cast off very loosely in rib with mn. wool.

The Front.—Work as given for the back until work measures 14½ ins., ending with a p. row.

Divide for Neck opening and shape Armholes thus.—

Next row.—Patt. 84, k. 2 tog., turn, leave remaining sts. on a spare needle.

Continue on these sts. only thus :—

Next row.—Patt. to end.

Next row.—Cast off 6, patt. to last 2 sts., k. 2 tog.

Next row.—Patt. to last 2 sts., p. 2 tog.

Next row.—K. 2 tog., patt. to last 2 sts., k. 2 tog.

Rep. the last 2 rows until 53 sts. remain.

This completes the armhole shaping.

Now continue in patt. with armhole edge straight, still dec. on every alternate row at the neck edge until 32 sts. remain.

Continue in patt. without shaping until work measures 23½ ins., ending at armhole edge.

Shape Shoulder thus.—

Next row.—Cast off 10, patt. to end.

Next row.—Patt. to end.

Rep. last 2 rows once.

Cast off remaining sts.

Rejoin wools to remaining 85 sts. at neck edge, work 1 row in patt. to side edge.

Next row.—Cast off 6, patt. to last 2 sts., p. 2 tog.

Next row.—Patt. to last 2 sts., k. 2 tog.

Detail of two-colour chequered pattern showing exact size of stitch.

Knitted in 3-ply wool, this sleeveless pullover is lightweight and comfortably loose fitting. The V-neckline and armhole bands are edged with two bands of ribbing.

Next row.—P. 2 tog., patt. to last 2 sts., p. 2 tog.

Rep. the last 2 rows until 53 sts. remain.

This completes the armhole shaping.

Now complete this side as given for the first side.

The Front Neck Band.—With No. 12 needles and con. wool and with the right side of the work facing, k. up 80 sts. along the neck edge, 1 st. at centre front, 80 sts. along other side of neck edge (161 sts.).

Work thus :—

1st row.—P. 1, * k. 1, p. 1, rep. from * to end.

2nd row.—Rib 79, work 3 tog., rib 79.

3rd row.—Rib 78, work 3 tog., rib 78.

4th row.—Rib 77, work 3 tog., rib 77.

5th row.—Rib 76, work 3 tog., rib 76.

6th row.—Rib 75, work 3 tog., rib 75.

Change to mn. wool and work 6 rows in rib, always taking 3 sts. tog. at centre front on each row as in previous rows.

Cast off loosely in rib with mn. wool.

The Armhole Bands.—Join shoulder seams with very narrow backstitch.

With No. 12 needles and con. wool, and with right side of work facing k. up 160 sts. evenly along armhole edge (80 sts. on each side of shoulder seams).

Work 6 rows in k. 1, p. 1 rib.

Change to mn. wool and work 6 rows in k. 1, p. 1 rib.

Cast off very loosely in rib with mn. wool.

Make-up.—Press work lightly on the wrong side, using a hot iron over a damp cloth.

Join side seams matching patt. carefully. Press the seams.

GOLF STOCKINGS

With Fair-Isle Tops

MATERIALS

6 oz. 4-ply wool in main colour.
Small balls of 4-ply wool in 2 contrasting colours.
4 No. 10 and 4 No. 12 needles with points both ends.

MEASUREMENTS

Length of leg to bottom of heel 18½ ins. (Top turned down 4½ ins.)
Length of foot 11½ ins.

TENSION

9 sts. to 1 in., using No. 12 needles.

ABBREVIATIONS

k. knit, p. purl, st. stitch, rep. repeat, inc. increase, p.s.s.o. pass slip stitch over, sl. slip, tog. together, m. 1. make one (wool forward), ins. inches. dec. decrease, patt. pattern, beg. beginning, mn. main colour, c. contrast.

With No. 10 needles and mn. colour cast on 80 sts. loosely (28, 28, 24). K. 2 rounds.

Next round.—* k. 2 tog., m. 1, rep. from * all round.

K. 2 rounds.

Next round.—Fold the work on to the wrong side and * k. tog. 1 st from needle and 1 st from cast-on edge, rep. from * to the end of round.

Begin the patt., working from the chart. Each square represents a stitch, and there are 16 sts. in each patt., so these will be repeated 4 times. Begin each round at right hand side of chart. When the 31 rounds of patt. are completed, continue thus :—

K. 2 rounds.

Next round.—* k. 2 tog., m. 1, rep. from * to the end.

Next round.—* inc. in 1st st., k. 19, rep. from * to the end (84 sts.).

Turn work inside out to reverse the top.

Change to No. 12 needles. Work in k. 1, p. 1, rib for 2 ins., then continue in k. 4, p. 2, rib thus :—

Next round.—* p. 1, k. 4, p. 1, rep. from * to the end.

Rep. this round until the work measures 15 ins. from beg., finishing at the end of round.

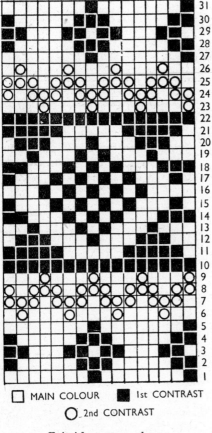

☐ MAIN COLOUR   ■ 1st CONTRAST
◯ 2nd CONTRAST

Fair-isle pattern chart.

FOR THE OUTDOOR MAN. *A pair of well-fitting ribbed stockings with fair-isle turn-over tops will make an ideal gift for the walking enthusiast or the golfer.*

Shape the Leg thus.—

1st round.—K. 2 tog., rib to the last 2 sts., sl. 1, k. 1, p.s.s.o.

Work 5 rounds without shaping. Rep. these last 6 rounds until 72 sts. remain.

Continue without shaping until the work measures 19 ins. from the beg. finishing at end of round.

Divide for Heel and Instep thus.—

Rib 54 turn, rib 36 turn, work in rib in rows on these 36 sts. for instep for 1 in., ending with row on the wrong side.

Leave these sts. and return to heel sts.

With the wrong side of the work facing, p. to end.

Continue thus :—

1st row.—* sl. 1, k. 1, rep. from * to the end.

2nd row.—P.

Rep. these 2 rows until the heel measures 3 ins., ending with a p. row.

To turn the Heel.—

1st row.—K. 24, k. 2 tog., turn.

2nd row.—P. 13, p. 2 tog., turn.

3rd row.—K. 14, k. 2 tog., turn.

4th row.—P. 15, p. 2 tog., turn.

Detail of fair-isle stocking turn-over showing exact size of stitch.

5th row.—K. 16, k. 2 tog., turn.
6th row.—P. 17, p. 2 tog., turn.
7th row.—K. 18, k. 2 tog., turn.
8th row.—P. 19, p. 2 tog., turn.
9th row.—K. 20, k. 2 tog., turn.
10th row.—P. 21, p. 2 tog., turn.
11th row.—K. 22, k. 2 tog., turn.
12th row.—P. 23, p. 2 tog., turn.
13th row.—K. 24.

Knit up 14 sts. along the side of heel flap, leaving the last in. free to be sewn to the side of instep.

Now rib across the instep sts. with the 2nd needle, then with the 3rd needle leave the first in. of the heel flap free to be sewn to the sides of the instep.

Then knit up 14 sts. along the heel flap, k. 12 from heel sts. (88 sts.).

Shape Instep thus.—

1st round.—*1st needle.* K. to the last 3 sts., k. 2 tog., k. 1.

2nd needle. Rib to the end.

3rd needle. K. 1, sl. 1, k. 1, p.s.s.o., k. to the end.

2nd round.—*1st needle.* K.

2nd needle. Rib to the end.

3rd needle. K.

Rep. these 2 rounds until 72 sts. remain.

Continue without shaping, working in rib on the 2nd needle and k. on 1st and 3rd needles until the foot measures 9½ ins. from the back of heel, finishing at end of round.

Shape Top thus.—

1st round.—*1st needle.* K. to the last 3 sts., k. 2 tog., k. 1.

2nd needle. K. 1, sl. 1, k. 1, p.s.s.o., k. to the last 3 sts., k. 2 tog., k. 1.

3rd needle. K. 1, sl. 1, p.s.s.o., k. to the end.

2nd round.—K. to the end.

Rep. these 2 rounds until 24 sts. remain. K. 6, then graft the 2 sets of 12 sts. together.

Work another sock to match.

Make-up.—Press work under a damp cloth with a hot iron. Join the sides of heel to instep neatly.

Turn down the top at the second row of holes, and press lightly.

TIE AND SOCKS

Knitted in Wool and Cotton

SHAPED TIE

MATERIALS

1 oz. 2-ply wool.
A spool of No. 20 cotton in a contrasting colour.
2 No. 14 knitting needles.

MEASUREMENTS

Length about 44 ins.
Width at widest part before making up, 8 ins.

ABBREVIATIONS

K. knit, p. purl, st. stitch, in. inch, inc. increase, dec. decrease, sl. slip, p.s.s.o. pass the slipped stitch over, rep. repeat, tog. together, st.st. stocking stitch, patt. pattern.

TENSION

10 sts. to 1 in.

Using wool, cast on 1 st., then k. 3 times into this st.

Next row.—P. twice into 1st st., p. to the end. Change to cotton.

1st row.—K. twice into 1st st., drop next st. down 1 row and sl. this st. and dropped loop, k. to the end.

2nd row.—P. twice into 1st st., p. 1, sl. the 2 wool loops, p. to the end. Change to wool.

3rd row.—K. twice into 1st st., k. to the end.

4th row.—P. twice into 1st st., p. to the end. Change to cotton.

5th row.—K. twice into 1st st., drop next st. down 1 row and sl. this st. and dropped loop, k. 3, drop next st. down 1 row and sl. this st. and dropped loop (this will now be referred to as " drop sl."), k. to the end.

6th row.—P. twice into 1st st., p. 1, sl. 2 loops, p. 3, sl. 2 loops, p. to the end. Change to wool.

7th row.—K. twice into 1st st., k. to the end.

8th row.—P. twice into 1st st., p. to the end. Change to cotton.

9th row.—K. twice into 1st st., * drop sl. next st., k. 3. Rep. from * to the last 3 sts., drop sl. next st., k. 2.

10th row.—P. twice into 1st st., p. 1, * sl. 2 loops, p. 3. Rep. from * to last 3 sts., sl. 2 loops, p. 2. Change to wool.

11th row.—K. twice into 1st st., k. to the end.

12th row.—P. twice into 1st st., p. to the end. Change to cotton.

Rep. the last 4 rows, *i.e.*, rows 9 to 12 inclusive until 60 sts. are on needle.

Keeping the continuity of the pattern, inc. 1 st. at both ends of every row until there are 80 sts. on the needle, then continue in patt. without shaping until work measures 7 ins. from commencement, ending with row on wrong side.

Now work in patt., dec. 1 st. at both ends of the next row and every following 8th row until 20 sts. remain.

Then continue without shaping until work measures 36 ins. from commencement, ending on the wrong side.

Now inc. 1 st. at both ends of the next row and every following 20th row until there are 30 sts. on needle.

Dec. 1 st. at the beginning of every row until 2 sts. remain. Work 2 tog. Fasten off.

Make-up.—Press work lightly on wrong side with a hot iron and damp cloth, taking care not to stretch fabric.

Stitch centre back seam, and press.

FOR ANY MAN. *A gift that is sure to please is this smart and neat looking tie in two colours. The original was in lime green wool and red cotton.*

SOCKS

MATERIALS

2 ozs. 2-ply wool.

A 2-oz. ball of No. 20 cotton or silk of a similar thickness.

4 No. 12 needles pointed both ends.

MEASUREMENTS

Leg, 10 ins. Length of foot, 11 ins.

TENSION

9 sts. to 1 in.

N.B.—Use the wool and cotton or wool and silk together throughout.

Cast on 80 sts. (26, 26, 28,) and work in rounds of k. 1, p. 1 rib for 4 ins.

Then continue in st.st. (every round k.) for 2½ ins. finishing at end of round.

Shape Leg thus.—

1st round.—K. 1, sl. 1, k. 1, p.s.s.o., k. to last 3 sts., k. 2 tog., k. 1.

Work 3 rounds without shaping. Rep. these 4 rounds until 62 sts. remain.

Continue without shaping until work measures 9 ins. from lower edge finishing at end of round.

Divide for Heel and Instep thus.—

Next row.—K. 16 turn, p. 32 turn, leave remaining 30 sts. on two needles.

Work on 32 heel sts. thus.—

1st row.—* sl. 1, k. 1, rep. from * to end. 2nd row.—P.

Rep. these 2 rows until heel measures 3 ins. ending with a p. row.

Turn the Heel thus.—

1st row.—K. 20, k. 2 tog., turn.

2nd row.—P. 9, p. 2 tog., turn.

3rd row.—K. 10, k. 2 tog., turn.

4th row.—P. 11, p. 2 tog., turn.

5th row.—K. 12, k. 2 tog., turn.

6th row.—P. 13, p. 2 tog., turn.

7th row.—K. 14, k. 2 tog., turn.

8th row.—P. 15, p. 2 tog., turn.

9th row.—K. 16, k. 2 tog., turn.

10th row.—P. 17, p. 2 tog., turn.

11th row.—K. 18, k. 2 tog., turn.

12th row.—P. 19, p. 2 tog., turn.

Break off wool, rejoin wool to instep sts. and work in st.st. in rows (1 row k., 1 row p.) for 1 in. ending with a p. row. Sew this in. to sides of heel.

Now with right side of work facing k. up 12 sts. at side of heel then 10 sts. from heel. With 2nd needle k. across the remaining 10 sts. then k. up 12 sts. along side of heel. With 3rd needle k. across instep sts., then shape instep.

1st round.—

1st needle. K. 1, sl. 1, k. 1, p.s.s.o., k. to end.

2nd needle. K. to last 3 sts., k. 2 tog. k. 1.

3rd needle. K. to end.

2nd round.—K. to end.

Rep. these 2 rounds until 60 sts. remain, then continue without shaping until work measures 9 ins. from back of heel finishing at 3rd needle.

Shape Toe thus.—

1st round.—

1st needle. K. 1, sl. 1, k. 1, p.s.s.o., k. to end.

2nd needle. K. to last 3 sts., k. 2 tog., k. 1.

3rd needle. K. 1, sl. 1, k. 1, p.s.s.o., k. to last 3 sts., k. 2 tog., k. 1.

2nd round.—K. to end.

Rep. these 2 rounds until 20 sts. remain. Graft the 2 sets of 10 sts. tog.

Work another sock in the same way.

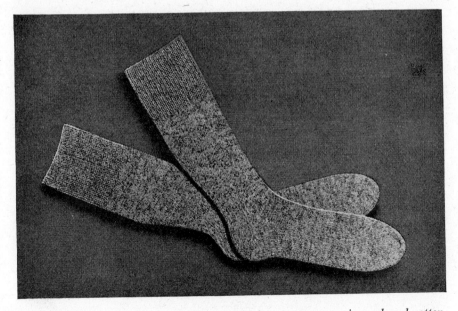

FOR FATHER. *A pair of well-fitting socks for summer wear in wool and cotton. They are knitted on four needles in stocking stitch with ribbed tops.*

CARVED BOOK-ENDS

And Holder for Matches

BOOK-ENDS

MATERIALS

Scrap lead.

Small piece of baize.

2 pieces of hardwood approximately
$5\frac{1}{2}$ ins. by $3\frac{1}{2}$ ins. by 2 ins.

Method.—Plane up all four sides of the
wood. Square off one end with try-
square and knife and saw off to the mark.
Clean up the end with a smoothing
plane set very finely.

The Diagram shows a suggested shape
for the ends set out on a grid of $\frac{1}{2}$ in.
squares. The simplest way is to cut
out a cardboard or stiff paper template
and use this to mark out the wood. Saw
just outside your line with a bow or
coping saw, or alternatively saw as much
as possible off with a hand or tenon
saw and chisel to shape. Finish off the
surface with a spokeshave.

Bore a large hole (say 1 in.) in the
base about $1\frac{1}{4}$ ins. deep as indicated on
the Diagram and another smaller hole
meeting the first at an angle. Melt
some lead in a ladle or an old kitchen
spoon and gently pour into the hole
and allow it to set.

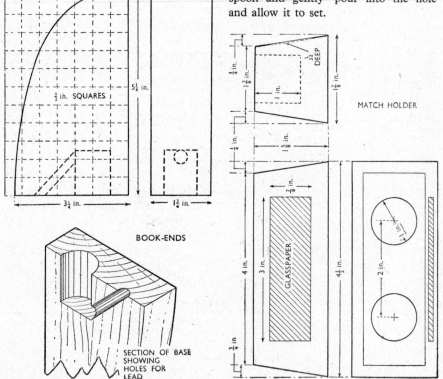

BOOK-ENDS

SECTION OF BASE
SHOWING
HOLES FOR
LEAD

MATCH HOLDER

FOR THE MAN OF THE HOME. *Gifts that cannot fail to please. A choice between two pairs of carved wood book-ends with felt bases ; and a very useful little match holder with a strip of glasspaper on the front to be used when striking matches.*

The surfaces can now be carved if desired or left plain. Glasspaper the surfaces and polish with a good wax polish. Cover the base with a piece of baize by gluing the wood and pressing the baize on to the base. Allow to set and trim off the baize to the exact size.

MATCH HOLDER

MATERIALS

Hardwood, $4\frac{3}{4}$ ins. by 2 ins. by $1\frac{1}{4}$ ins. Small piece of medium glasspaper.

Method.—Plane up the wood on all four sides, mark the centres of the two holes, bore them 1 in. deep, and set out the shape as shown in the Diagram. A bevel of $\frac{1}{4}$ in. is taken off all round the block. Saw the ends and finish off with a finely set smoothing plane. Plane off the bevel on the sides.

Set out the position of the glasspaper with gauge and try-square and carefully take out a recess not more than $\frac{1}{32}$ in. deep.

Finish.—Glasspaper the block thoroughly and polish with wax polish. Scrape out any wax that has got into the recess and glue a piece of glasspaper of the exact size into it for the striker.

SHAVING MIRROR

And Dressing Table Mirror

SHAVING MIRROR

MATERIALS

The Mirror.—Mirror 7 ins. by 5 ins.
3-ply 6 ins. by 8 ins.
14 ins. of 1 in. by $\frac{1}{4}$ in. beading.
1 bar $6\frac{1}{2}$ ins. by $\frac{1}{4}$ in. by $\frac{1}{4}$ in.

The Stand.—Base $7\frac{1}{2}$ ins. by 5 ins. by $\frac{1}{2}$ in.
2 uprights $4\frac{3}{8}$ ins. by $\frac{3}{4}$ in. by $\frac{3}{4}$ in.
1 crossbar $7\frac{1}{2}$ ins. by $\frac{1}{2}$ in. by $\frac{1}{4}$ in.
2 stands 5 ins. by $\frac{1}{2}$ in. by $\frac{1}{4}$ in.

Method: The Mirror Frame.—To make the beading which fastens the mirror to its plywood back, first cut the 14-in. piece into two lengths of 6 ins. and 8 ins. A groove is then cut down the centre of each length, and finally the lengths are sawn down the middle, see Diagram 1. Clean the sawn edges with glasspaper. Next cut the beading (mitre the corners), so that it makes a frame round the mirror. When the frame has been made, glue and pin with $\frac{1}{2}$ in. pins three sides to the plywood. Then place the mirror

with a packing of cardboard at the back, if needed, and finally glue and pin the fourth side. When dry, the frame may be squared up with a finely set smoothing plane. Whilst the frame is drying the stand may be made.

The Stand.—The uprights are fixed to the base with $\frac{3}{8}$ in. dowels. Mark out the position of an upright, Diagram 2, on the top of, and underneath, the base. Pin the upright to the base with two 1 in. veneer pins, one in opposite corners, Diagram 2. Now mark the position of the dowel hole, grip the upright firmly in the vice and with the base resting on the top of the vice, bore a $\frac{3}{8}$ in. hole through the base right into the upright. Repeat for the other upright.

Each upright has a slot for the bar on the back of the mirror to slide into and a groove to take the crossbar joining the two uprights. Gauge the slot to size, Diagram 3 (page 125), and remove waste with $\frac{1}{4}$ in. chisel. Outline the slot deeply with a marking gauge on the face of the wood, marking the $\frac{1}{4}$ in.

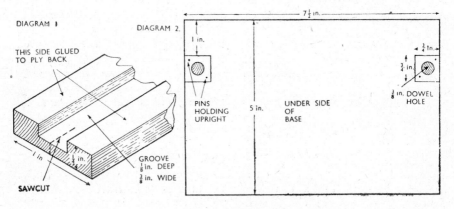

DIAGRAM 1

THIS SIDE GLUED
TO PLY BACK

1 in. $\frac{1}{4}$ in.

SAWCUT

GROOVE
$\frac{1}{8}$ in. DEEP
$\frac{3}{8}$ in. WIDE

DIAGRAM 2.

1 in.

PINS
HOLDING
UPRIGHT

$7\frac{1}{2}$ in.

5 in.   UNDER SIDE
OF
BASE

$\frac{1}{4}$ in.

$\frac{3}{4}$ in.

$\frac{3}{8}$ in. DOWEL
HOLE

FOR THE MAN OF THE HOUSE. *This compact little white painted shaving mirror will prove a very useful gift. The mirror fits into the slotted sides of the two uprights, or a hanger can be fixed on the back so that it may be hung up if desired.*

line with a sharp chisel. Mark the position of the slot on the end of the piece with light cuts with a ¼ in. chisel. Cut out the waste wood, working partly from the end and partly from the face of the wood. Keep the chisel sharp. Remove waste wood from the groove at the back with saw and chisel.

Before putting in the uprights, glue and pin on the two long stands to the base, Diagram 4. Then fix in the crossbar with glue and ½ in. pins and follow by gluing in the uprights and dowels,

getting them square with the base.
The Swivel Bar.—This is screwed on the ply back 2½ ins. from the top of the mirror and its ends are rounded, Diagram 5, so that the mirror slides easily up and down the slots, thus being adjustable, the base resting on the stand.
Finish.—Clean up with fine glasspaper, give a coating of glue size, followed by two coats of white enamel.

A hanger is fixed on the back of the mirror so that it may be hung up if desired.

FOR BIG BROTHER. *Just the right size for a man's dressing table, this neat looking hinged mirror is sure to please. The mirror is backed with plywood and can be conveniently tilted to any angle with an adjuster which is attached to the back.*

HINGED MIRROR

8 in. by 12 in.

MATERIALS

Wood base 9 ins. by $9\frac{5}{8}$ ins. by $\frac{1}{2}$ in.
2 uprights 9 ins. by $1\frac{1}{4}$ ins. by $\frac{3}{4}$ in.
2 sides 8 ins. by $\frac{3}{4}$ in. by $\frac{3}{4}$ in.
1 back $8\frac{1}{8}$ ins. by $\frac{3}{4}$ in. by $\frac{3}{4}$ in.
1 crossbar $8\frac{1}{8}$ ins. by $\frac{3}{4}$ in. by $\frac{3}{4}$ in.
Mirror 8 ins. by 12 ins.
Ply 8 ins. by 12 ins.
4 feet each $1\frac{1}{2}$ ins. by $1\frac{1}{2}$ ins. by $\frac{1}{2}$ in.
Wood for adjuster 3 ins. by 1 in. by $\frac{1}{2}$ in.
4 clips for mirror and ply.
1 pair $1\frac{1}{4}$ in. hinges.
1 1 in. hinge.
2 ins. of $\frac{3}{8}$ in. dowel stick.
(Finished sizes).

Method.—The crossbar to which the mirror is hinged, is joined to the uprights by dowels. Alternatively, long, thin, roundhead brass screws could be used.

Set a marking gauge to $\frac{3}{8}$ in. and mark two lines at right angles on an end of the crossbar and on one side of an upright, Diagram 1.

Carefully bore $\frac{3}{8}$ in. hole in each piece of wood about $\frac{1}{2}$ in. deep. Cut a piece of $\frac{3}{8}$ in. dowel stick to join the two. Unless the brace is kept upright, the hole may turn out too loose for the dowel. In any case it is wise to bore a test hole in a piece of waste wood, and try in the dowel rod.

Repeat for other end of crossbar. Round the top front corner of each upright, Diagram 2. Before gluing, the uprights are screwed to the base $2\frac{1}{2}$ ins. from the back as in Diagram 2. This will make the assembling easier. Now remove screws and glue in the crossbar, using the other $8\frac{1}{8}$ ins. piece of wood to keep the uprights square. Leave in a cramp or bind together (tourniquet fashion). Whilst this is drying the sides and legs may be prepared.

The Sides.—Cut each of the 8-in. pieces

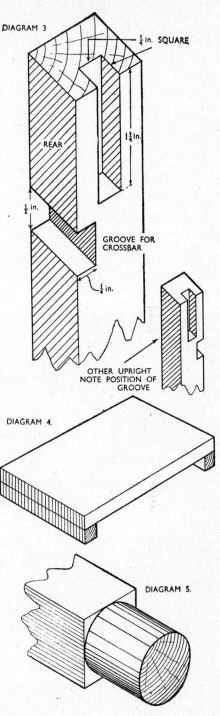

DIAGRAM 3

$\frac{1}{4}$ in. SQUARE

REAR

$1\frac{1}{4}$ in.

$\frac{1}{2}$ in.

GROOVE FOR CROSSBAR

$\frac{1}{4}$ in.

OTHER UPRIGHT
NOTE POSITION OF GROOVE

DIAGRAM 4.

DIAGRAM 5.

into two so that, after shooting all ends, they are $2\frac{1}{2}$ ins. and $5\frac{1}{4}$ ins. long. One $\frac{3}{4}$ in. edge of each of the $5\frac{1}{4}$ in. pieces is rounded—this edge will go to the front.

The four legs are prepared by simply rounding all 8 edges of a $1\frac{1}{2}$ in. by $1\frac{1}{2}$ in. by $\frac{1}{2}$ in. and then drilling a screwhole in the middle.

The rounding is done with a fine-set block plane (if available) or by chisel and rasp. Finish off with a medium then fine glasspaper. The feet may be fixed into place, each one projecting $\frac{1}{4}$ in. from under the base, Diagram 3. Remove prior to polishing.

The Mirror.—This is backed with plywood equal in size to the glass. The two are held together with 4 clips made of any suitable material, such as thin zinc or brass sheet, Diagram 4. A small screw fixes each clip about $\frac{3}{4}$ in. from the corner.

The Adjuster.—Is cut from a 3in. by 1 in. by $\frac{1}{2}$ in. piece of wood shaped as in Diagram 5, and fixed to the bottom of 3-ply as in Diagram 5, with a 1 in. hinge. Small depressions into which the point rests are cut later on.

Finish.—Assemble all pieces to ensure correct fitting, then carefully clean up the crossbar and uprights before finally gluing and screwing them on base. Next glue on the $2\frac{1}{2}$ ins. pieces, then the $5\frac{1}{4}$ ins. pieces, finally the back 8 in. piece, pinning all from underneath the base with 1 in. veneer pins.

When the glue has set, hinge the mirror to the crossbar, the base of the former being level with the tops of the sides (i.e., there is a $\frac{3}{4}$ in. gap between the mirror and the base). Before fixing the mirror, cut a line of 5 depressions $\frac{1}{2}$ in. apart with a gouge in the base so that the point of the adjuster can rest comfortably in each, so tilting the mirror.

Now remove the mirror, polish or wax all pieces and when this has been done, screw on legs and mirror.

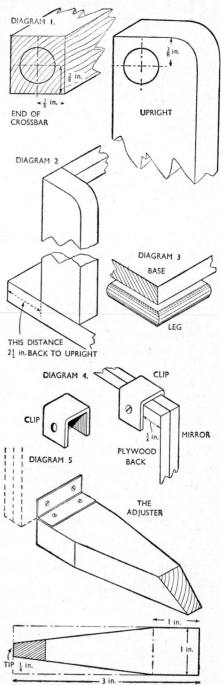

DIAGRAM 1.

END OF CROSSBAR

UPRIGHT

DIAGRAM 2

DIAGRAM 3

BASE

LEG

THIS DISTANCE $2\frac{1}{2}$ in. BACK TO UPRIGHT

DIAGRAM 4.

CLIP

CLIP

DIAGRAM 5

PLYWOOD BACK

MIRROR

THE ADJUSTER

1 in.

1 in.

TIP $\frac{1}{4}$ in.

3 in.

BEDSIDE LAMP

With a Light Switch

MATERIALS

1 top $4\frac{1}{2}$ ins. by $3\frac{1}{2}$ ins. by $\frac{1}{4}$ in.

1 upright 7 ins. by $2\frac{1}{4}$ ins. by $\frac{3}{8}$ in.

4 sides—2 pieces $2\frac{1}{2}$ ins. by $\frac{7}{8}$ in. by $\frac{1}{2}$ in.

        2 pieces $4\frac{1}{2}$ ins. by $\frac{7}{8}$ in. by $\frac{1}{2}$ in.

1 strip 6 ins. by $\frac{5}{8}$ in. by $\frac{1}{4}$ in.

1 arm $2\frac{1}{4}$ ins. by 1 in. by $\frac{1}{4}$ in.

Ply base $4\frac{1}{4}$ ins. by $2\frac{1}{2}$ ins.

Bulb holder and small shade.

2 terminals on panel $1\frac{1}{2}$ ins. by $\frac{3}{4}$ in.

1 small switch.

Method.—Glue and pin the top to the 4 sides, using $\frac{1}{2}$ in. veneer pins, as in Diagram 1. Punch in the pins. Next mark out the upright as in Diagram 2. Saw out the waste wood, clean the edges with a sharp chisel, then round off the 4 corners as indicated. Use a chisel and medium glasspaper for this.

The front corners of the box may then be rounded as in Diagram 3, using a chisel and spokeshave or chisel and medium glasspaper. Cut out a groove at the back of the box to take the width of the upright, which should eventually be flush with the back of the box. Make a good fit as the upright will not be glued in, only fixed with two screws. This is to facilitate removing the back for wiring and possible repairs.

The Arm.—The shape of the arm depends somewhat on the type of bulb holder used. The holder used in the model was of a circular type, 1 in. in diameter. An arm, as in Diagram 4, was made to fit the holder. This arm fits into a hole cut in the upright, Diagram 2. Make this hole by first boring a $\frac{1}{4}$ in. hole, then enlarging this to

FOR GRANDPA. *An extremely useful little bedside lamp which is operated by a push-button type switch and a small flat torch battery.*

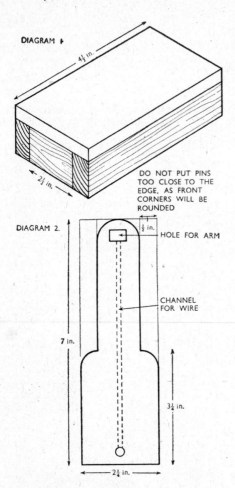

DIAGRAM 1

4½ in.

2¼ in.

DO NOT PUT PINS TOO CLOSE TO THE EDGE, AS FRONT CORNERS WILL BE ROUNDED

DIAGRAM 2.

½ in. HOLE FOR ARM

CHANNEL FOR WIRE

7 in.

3¼ in.

2¼ in.

the correct shape by means of a chisel, or rasping it with a square-taper coarse file. Do not glue in the arm yet.

Fitting in the battery.—The space in the box takes a flat type battery. Procure two terminals (if unobtainable, two ¾ in. gauge 2 B.A. screws with nuts will do). Mount these terminals on a panel of insulating material, such as a plastic material, thick rubber, ebonite and so on, as in Diagram 5 ; so that, when the panel is screwed to one end of the box, the brass tabs of the battery will press against them. It may be necessary to glue a piece of wood at the other end of the box in order to keep the battery against the terminals.

The Switch.—A small (1 in. by ½ in.) push-button type switch was used. Other type switches may be used, of course, or one devised. The switch is fixed at the base of the upright, either outside or let into the wood, the latter being a neater finish.

The Wiring.—Cotton covered or enamelled wire, about the thickness of strong thread, gauge 18 to 20, is used. Cut out a channel in the arm, Diagram 4, wide and deep enough to take two strands of wire. Use a small chisel, or a V-shaped carving chisel. Cut a similar channel down the back of the upright shown as dotted in Diagram 2.

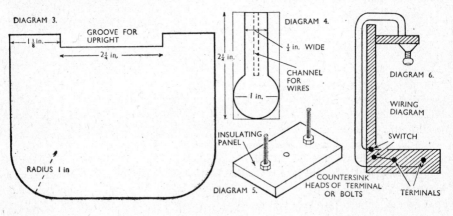

DIAGRAM 3.

GROOVE FOR UPRIGHT

1⅛ in.

2¼ in.

RADIUS 1 in

2¼ in.

DIAGRAM 4.

½ in. WIDE

CHANNEL FOR WIRES

1 in.

INSULATING PANEL

DIAGRAM 5.

COUNTERSINK HEADS OF TERMINAL OR BOLTS

DIAGRAM 6.

WIRING DIAGRAM

SWITCH

TERMINALS

A marking gauge will be found useful here to mark and cut out the width of the channel. A $\frac{1}{8}$ in. hole must be bored just above the switch to allow the wires to enter the box.

First connect wires to the lamp holder, fix in the arm and lead the wires down the groove into the box. Connect to the switch and terminals as in Diagram 6. Wire loosely at first to ensure correct working. When this has been done, pull the wires tight and thus get the correct amount of wire needed.

Finish.—Remove wires. Glue in the arm but keep the channel clear of glue. When the arm is firm, re-wire, then pin on the back strip to cover over the channel. Shape the ply base so that it can be screwed on to the bottom of the box, thus holding in the battery. Glasspaper well with a fine paper, then stain, polish or wax. A reflector from an old torch soldered to the holder may be used as a shade, or if desired, a small shade of paper or material could be made.

Take out a spent battery as soon as it fails; if left in, it will corrode the terminals and soil the inside of box.

LEATHER WALLET

MATERIALS

Morocco or fine grained sheepskin.

1 piece, $13\frac{3}{4}$ ins. deep by $6\frac{3}{8}$ ins. wide for wallet.

1 piece, $6\frac{1}{2}$ ins. deep by $6\frac{3}{8}$ ins. wide for flap pocket.

1 piece, $3\frac{1}{4}$ ins. deep by $6\frac{3}{8}$ ins. wide for pocket.

1 piece, 3 ins. deep by $\frac{3}{8}$ ins. wide for band.

1 piece, $2\frac{1}{2}$ ins. deep by $\frac{3}{8}$ ins. wide for tab.

Skiver lining to suit above.

1 piece, $11\frac{1}{4}$ ins. deep by $6\frac{3}{8}$ ins. wide.

1 piece, $6\frac{1}{2}$ ins. deep by $6\frac{3}{8}$ ins. wide.

Thread for stitching.

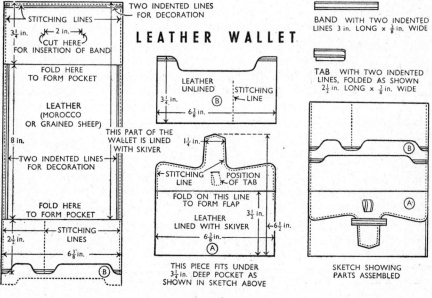

FOR THE BUSINESS MAN. *A pocket-size gift that will prove useful as well as pleasing—a handy-size wallet in blue morocco, lined with beige skiver.*

N.B.—All of these measurements are net and $\frac{1}{8}$ to $\frac{1}{4}$ in. extra all round should be allowed for margins on all pieces which are lined.

Method.—Cut a paper pattern, as shown in the Diagrams on page 129, for all the parts except the band and the tab. Place the patterns on the leather, mark round the edge with a pencil and cut out with scissors leaving a small margin all round the pieces which are lined. The unlined pocket can be cut to the exact size with knife and ruler and the lines indented. Use a smooth penny as a guide when cutting the curves. Cut out the two pieces of lining, but before sticking them to the leather make the little band and tab. These, of course, should be in

leather. Cut the necessary slots as shown in the Diagram, insert the ends of the band and tab through the cuts and glue the ends in position. Cut the curved edge of the $2\frac{1}{2}$ ins. deep pocket and indent the lines. Mark the position of the stitching line on this pocket, glue the $3\frac{1}{4}$ ins. deep pocket in position, make holes with stitch spacer and stitch the two pockets together.

Paste the skiver to the wallet and line the other pocket.

When dry cut to exact size, stitch round the upper edge of the flap pocket, fold the wallet to form pockets and insert the flap pocket as shown in the sketch.

Stitch along edges of wallet, lightly hammer stitching and folds.

BATH MITTS

And Shampoo Cape

MITTS

MATERIALS

½ yd. 24 in. wide terry towelling.
¾ yd. narrow blue ribbon.
3 ins. narrow elastic.
6 ins. white tape, slightly wider than the elastic. Embroidery thread.

Method.—The mitts have, inside each palm, a concealed pocket that can be filled with toilet oatmeal.

To make a pattern for the mitts, take a glove of a suitable size and lay it, palm upwards, on a piece of paper. Draw round the outline only and cut out the shape along the pencilled line. An average-size mitt will measure about 9 ins. in depth and 7 ins. in width across centre of palm and thumb.

Fold the terry towelling double and cut out the shape, reverse the pattern and cut it again. Before stitching the halves together, make the concealed pocket in the following way:

Cut two circles, one 5 ins. in diameter and one 3 ins. In the larger one, cut a round hole in the centre, 2 ins. across. Using the embroidery thread, work blanket stitching round the inner cut edge of this hole and also round the outer edge of the 3 in. wide circle, as shown in Diagrams 1 and 2. Turn both circles on to the wrong side, place the smaller one

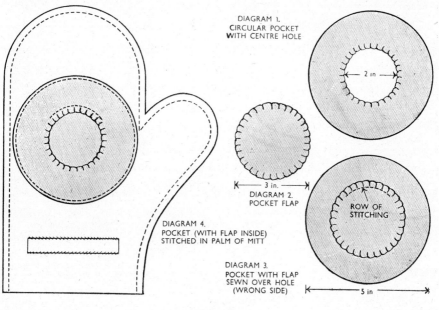

DIAGRAM 1.
CIRCULAR POCKET
WITH CENTRE HOLE

2 in

3 in.

DIAGRAM 2.
POCKET FLAP

ROW OF
STITCHING

DIAGRAM 4.
POCKET (WITH FLAP INSIDE)
STITCHED IN PALM OF MITT

DIAGRAM 3.
POCKET WITH FLAP
SEWN OVER HOLE
(WRONG SIDE)

5 in

over the hole in the larger one so that it overlaps about ½ in. all round. Stitch the two together for about 1 in. at the top as shown in Diagram 3. Take a very narrow turning, on to the wrong side, all round the outer edges of the large circle, using small running stitches and drawing the thread up slightly. Turn the work on to the right side and pin it in the centre of the palm of one of the mitt shapes. Sew it securely all round as shown in Diagram 4.

Cut a piece of tape about 3 ins. long, pin it across the mitt shape, approximately 1½ ins. up from the bottom edge and hem it down on the long sides to make a casing for the elastic. Thread 1½ ins. of elastic through this casing and stitch it firmly at both ends.

The front half of one mitt is now finished. Pin it to a back half with the pocket uppermost and machine both layers together, whipping the raw edges over afterwards to prevent fraying. Insert a piece of ribbon in the seam at each side of the wrist, then make a narrow turning along the bottom edge and work blanket stitch over it.

To fill the pocket, pull the circular flap through the centre hole, put in as much toilet oatmeal as the pocket will conveniently hold, then tuck the flap back in again. Turn the mitt right side out and tie the ribbon ends in a bow at the back across the wrist.

Make another mitt in exactly the same way, but this time attach the pocket to the reverse palm for the opposite hand.

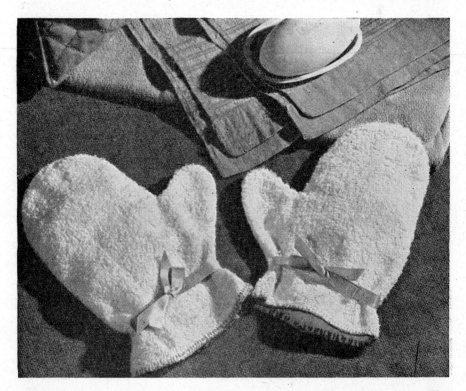

FOR ANY GIRL FRIEND. *Feminine yet practical are these bath mitts. They have, inside each palm, a concealed pocket which can be filled with toilet oatmeal.*

FOR THE GIRL WHO WASHES HER HAIR AT HOME. *This charming little shampoo cape is made of blue spotted plastic. The outer edges are cut into scallops, and it fastens at the front with a narrow band that fits tightly round the neck.*

SHAMPOO CAPE

MATERIALS

1 yd. plastic material, 36 ins. wide.

1 press fastener.

Method.—Cut the plastic material into a large circle, 36 ins. in diameter. Fold this circle in half and mark the centre of the fold. From this centre point cut out a semicircle in the double material, 2½ ins. in radius, for the neck opening. On the right-hand side of the semicircle mark a point at the edge of the material approximately 9 ins. down from the fold and from this point cut diagonally up to the fold at the right of the neck opening. This will be the opening at the centre front of the cape.

From the remaining pieces of plastic cut a strip 2 ins. wide and 17 ins. long and bind the neckline with this. Sew on a press fastener to fasten the band at the front of the neck.

Cut the outer edges of the cape in small scallops all round.

FOR THE 'TEEN-AGE GIRL. *A felt jerkin to slip over light dresses when summer breezes blow. The original was in a delicate shade of lime green with blue and cerise flowers appliquéd to the side fronts. The edges were outlined with blue ric-rac braid.*

'TEEN-AGE JERKIN

Trimmed with Braid

MATERIALS

⅞ yd. of 36-in. wide felt.
3½ yds. contrasting ric-rac braid.
Scraps of felt in contrasting colours.
4 small hooks and eyes.

MEASUREMENTS

Bust 32-34 ins.
Centre back, neck to lower edge, 18 ins.

Method.—Cut the pattern for the waistcoat as shown in Diagram 1, pin it on to the folded felt as in Diagram 2 and cut out. Mark in the darts and stitch them, then trim away surplus material to leave only a narrow turning, open and press. Join the shoulder and side seams and press these well.

Take a narrow turning on to the wrong side along the outer edges and the armholes, tack and press well. Slip-stitch the raw edges down so that the stitches do not show on the right side, remove the tackings and press again. Sew the ric-rac braid along these edges on the right side of the garment.

From the scraps of contrasting felt cut four small flowers as the shape given in Diagram 3, in each of two colours, and from dark coloured felt, cut eight narrow stems, each slightly curved. Arrange the flowers and stems in pairs of different colours, as shown in the illustration on the facing page, tack them in place and appliqué them.

Arrange four hook and eye fastenings under the front edges of the waistcoat.

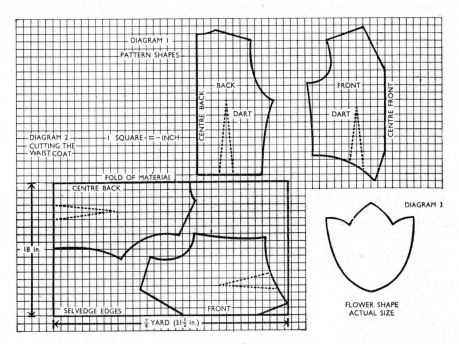

DIAGRAM 1
PATTERN SHAPES

BACK

CENTRE BACK

DART

FRONT

DART

CENTRE FRONT

DIAGRAM 2
CUTTING THE
WAIST COAT

I SQUARE = INCH

FOLD OF MATERIAL

CENTRE BACK

18 in.

SELVEDGE EDGES

FRONT

⅞ YARD (31½ in.)

DIAGRAM 3

FLOWER SHAPE
ACTUAL SIZE

FOR BIG SISTER. *A most attractive "threesome," this smart matching hat, bag and belt set is in braid, high-lighted with gilt studs. Two bags are made, and then joined together with a wide strip of braid, so that it can be carried over the arm or worn tucked under the belt as shown above.*

HAT, BAG & BELT SET

In Braid, with Stud Trimming

MATERIALS

12 yds. braid 3¼ ins. wide.
6 yds. braid 1 in. wide.
Studs for trimming.
Thick cord for piping.

THE BELT

Method.—Cut a piece of wide braid 30 ins. long (or waist measurement).

Lay a length of thick piping cord along 14 ins. of centre and stitch braid round it, to form a pleat at back. Mitre both ends to form a point. Trim with studs in triangular pattern.

Make a button by rolling up a length of 1-in. braid to size required and sew to one end.

Make a loop using 1-in. braid folded double and sew to the other end.

THE HAT

Method.—Cut two strips of wide braid 19 ins. long, and join lengthwise.

Cut two strips of wide braid 7 ins. long for back. Join lengthwise, overlapping so that back measures 5½ ins. at top and 4½ ins. at neck edge, see Diagram at foot of page.

Join the 19-in. piece along the three sides of back, leaving the neck edge free. Pipe along the join folding the braid with cord and stitching.

Make a ½ in. pleat at each side of front, as Diagram, then bind round neck edge with the narrow braid, securing the pleats with this bind and turning the piped tuck towards the back. Trim with studs along join of front strip, as shown in Diagram.

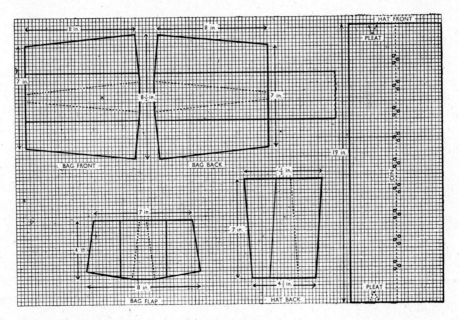

THE BAG

Cut the braid as follows :—

  1 piece 27 ins. long.
  2 pieces 8 ins. long.
  2 pieces 7½ ins. long.
  3 pieces 4 ins. long.

Method.—For the back, join the 8-in. pieces one each side of the 27-in. piece, overlapping so that the work measures 8½ ins. wide at the edge and 7 ins. wide at top, see Diagram, page 137.

For the front, join 3 pieces 7½ ins. long to match the back.

Join 3 pieces 4 ins. long for the flap to measure 7 ins. at top and 8 ins. at bottom, as Diagram on page 137.

For all these the centre panel of braid is sewn on top of the other pieces.

Bind sides and edge of flap with the narrow braid.

Bind top of front with narrow braid.

Stitch flap to back, neatening inside with narrow braid.

Cut two pieces of narrow braid 29 ins. long and join together lengthwise.

This makes the gusset which goes round the three sides of the bag.

Stitch this gusset in place, with the join to the inside, neatening both ends.

Make a button as given for belt and sew a loop to the flap.

Make a similar bag on the other end of the 27-in. strip, to match.

DAINTY HEAD SCARF

With Embroidered Names

GIRL'S HEAD SCARF

MATERIALS

Square of silk suitable for scarf, approximately 36 ins. by 36 ins.
Embroidery thread in three or four contrasting colours.

Method.—On a piece of thin white paper, write the recipient's name in your own handwriting in four different sizes, the largest approximately 9 ins. in length, the smallest about 2 ins. in length.

Transfer the handwriting to the fabric by placing a piece of well-worn typing

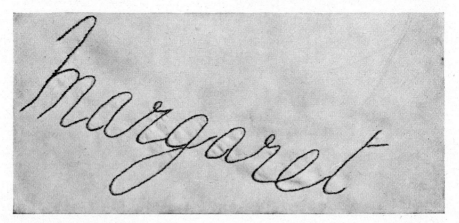

Close-up of embroidered name showing style of lettering and actual size.

FOR A GIRL COUSIN. *This delightful head scarf would make a most personal and original gift. The recipient's name is hand-written in four different sizes and transferred to the material. They are then embroidered in contrasting shades.*

carbon paper under the white paper and going over the lines with a sharp pencil. Try to avoid pressing your hands on the carbon around the writing, so that the material will not be soiled. Space the names out all over the square, putting them at angles to one another.

Work over the lines of the names with any narrow line embroidery stitch, such as outline stitch, chain stitch, back stitch and so on, varying the colours and mixing them, so that no adjacent ones are worked in the same shade.

Finish the scarf with a rolled hem.

SOFT TOYS

Adorable Gifts for the Nursery

TOYMAKING HINTS

Materials to Use.—Any firm, closely-woven fabrics can be used, such as cotton print, blanket-cloth, felt, velvet, oil-baize. Avoid real fur (except for tails, and so on) or loosely-woven fabrics. The former needs special skill in seaming, and the latter will not stand the strain of too much stuffing.

Colourful scraps of leather, ribbon, plastics, embroidery thread and wool can also be put to good advantage in giving gay finishing touches. If you haven't the materials mentioned for the models, substitute what you can obtain. A great part of the charm of home-made toys is the clever use of unlikely materials.

Stuffing.—Use lightweight filling such as kapok, cushion-filling, flock, millpuff, or wadding. If you *must* use snipped-up rags, shred them finely, and pack in loosely, or the toy will be heavy, but they cannot be moulded as easily as other fillings. Use *very* little stuffing at a time, filling first the parts furthest from the opening, and getting the extremities very firm before adding more. The blunt end of a pen-holder or pencil will help. If the position for the opening is not stated, choose a place which will not show very much, or one that can easily be covered by a coat, saddle, and so on.

Using the Patterns.—Instead of cutting out the patterns (to be found on the loose inset at the back of the book), and thus spoiling the sheets, trace off the shapes on to tracing or greaseproof paper. The patterns will last longer and be easier to cut if you mount them on waste cardboard.

To cut out, place the patterns to the best advantage on your material, hold in place with any small weights (such as cotton-reels), mark round *very exactly* with a sharp pencil, then remove the pattern and cut out with extreme care. Where the pattern sheet mentions *fold*, the material should be doubled and placed against the fold.

Pile fabrics must be cut on the wrong side, with short snips to avoid damaging the surface. Do not attempt to cut thick fabrics double. Pencil out the half-shape, then turn over the pattern and mark out the other half.

Where pairs of pieces are to be cut, as for the two sides of a head, make sure they will face each other correctly when made up.

Seams and Turnings.—Large, simply-shaped toys are seamed on the wrong side, taking ¼-in. turnings and using firm backstitching with very strong double cotton. Smaller toys, or those with many curves, are seamed on the right side with close oversewing, using strong double cotton. On non-fraying edges, such as felt, sew over the raw edge. On printed cotton and similar fabrics, turn in the edges to face, and sew over the folded edges.

The method of seaming used in each model is given in the directions, and sufficient turnings are left on the patterns for that particular method.

Where hats and other garments are made from felt in the models, no turnings are left on raw edges. If using other fabrics, allow for neatening the edges; if using soft fabrics, cut them double or add an interlining of stiff muslin.

Sew eyes very firmly.

FOR BABY. *Noah's family at the fair—six quaint and appealing toy animals for nursery Christmas trees. Above is shown from left to right, Lucky Cat, Flying Fish, Denis the Dachshund, Pet Lamb, Feeding Horse, and Freddie Frog.*

FREDDIE FROG
(Illustrated above)

(No. 1 on pattern sheet).—The model uses oil-baize, green, black and white striped on top, plain yellow underneath. Orange and black felt makes the eyes (or real glass eyes could be used), and the edges are stitched with black cotton over the raw edges on the right side.

Coloured print or velvet is also suitable. This should be stitched on the wrong side and turned out through the

opening, but take care not to narrow the limbs where they join the body.

Cut out parts as directed on pattern, seam up, stuff lightly and sew up the opening. Sew black centres to each eye, sew the eyes down to the body, adding a little cotton-wool beneath each.

FLYING FISH
(Illustrated above)

(No. 2 on pattern sheet).—Oil-baize striped in deep yellow and white was used for the model, with the eyes and mouth marked in Indian ink. Felt would also look well, especially if you use a contrasting shade for the base and the inside of the fins. The eyes can be made like the frog's, if preferred. The seams are made on the right side with yellow cotton, and the fins stitched with black.

Cut out parts as directed on pattern sheet and seam the sides together, inserting the base where shown and matching letters A and B. An opening may be left one side of the base, near the tail, but with oil-baize it is often better to stuff as you go, to save strain on the seams. Stuff the tail as soon as it is sewn up, then work round to the head and stuff that, leaving the centre of the body till last. Sew up the opening, join the fins together in pairs and stitch them in place. Mark eyes and mouth as shown on the loose pattern sheet.

FOR THE VERY YOUNG. *Modelled for the nursery, these two intriguing little animals will delight the heart of a small boy or girl. The Floppy Dog is a " character " animal : he does not stand up but falls into all sorts of amusing attitudes. Bobby Bunny is a soft cuddly toy made from gaily patterned print.*

FOR THE TODDLER. *This Dusky Darkie is particularly lovable with his cheeky face, jaunty beret, and gaily striped trousers. The winsome Teddy Bear strikes a new note with " girl " clothes. She wears a gay gingham skirt with knickers to match, and a charming little bonnet trimmed with felt flowers and ribbon.*

LUCKY CAT
(Illustrated on page 141)

(No. 3 on pattern sheet).—The model uses shiny black patent leatherette, with black and white circles for eyes, green cotton whiskers and a tartan braid bow. Felt or cloth could also be used, but be sure to add a very gay touch with the bow, or to use real eyes in blue or green glass to add a bright spot of colour. It must be stitched on the right side.

Cut out parts as directed on pattern sheet. Note that you have a pair of *whole* body pieces, and a pair of under-body pieces, which are the same shape as the lower part of the body. This method of obtaining four separate legs is used for most animal toys.

Seam the under-body sections together along the upper curved edge, keeping both right sides touching. Place them between the two sides of the body, with body right sides outwards, and seam the under-body in place on each side. Join the tail to the body, each side separately, then stitch up remainder of body, stuffing as you go. Leave the ears free, stitching along their base.

For each eye, place a black circle over a white circle, and secure with two or three stitches on the centre of the black circles, taking the cotton through the head from one eye to the other and pulling tightly. Mark whiskers with coloured cotton, and add neck-bow.

DENIS THE DACHSHUND
(*Illustrated on page* 141)

(No. 4 on pattern sheet).—Denis was made from light brown felt, and he wears a jade-green felt coat. Felt is ideal for these small animals, for it is colourful and very easy to use. Edges of ears and coat need no neatening. With a little extra trouble, he could be made in velvet. His eyes and mouth are made with tiny snippets of black felt.

Cut out the parts as directed on pattern sheet. In this case the under-body is cut in one piece, with the front end extended to make a gusset which goes right round the nose and gives the distinctive shape to the head.

Place the under-body between sides of body, with the long narrow piece coming round the nose and over the head as far as the back of the neck (match letters A and B on patterns). Stitch parts together on the right side, leaving a stuffing-space across the middle of the back. Stuff, then sew up space.

Add nose, mouth and ears. Stitch coat together across top and along short front edge, put on back of dog and stitch securely together underneath.

FEEDING HORSE
(*Illustrated on page* 141)

(No. 5 on pattern sheet).—This model uses a piece of fur plush in an oyster shade, with scraps of real fur for mane and tail. The raw edges were turned in before stitching. Blanket-cloth or velvet could also be used. If the main colour is dull, make the under-body in a bright contrasting shade.

Cut out the parts as directed on pattern sheet. Seam the under-body along the upper edge, place it between sides of body and stitch all round, turning in raw edges as you go and inserting mane and tail as they are reached. Stuff from centre of back. Fold ears in half and sew to head. Add tiny black circles for nostrils and eyes.

BOBBY BUNNY
(*Illustrated on page* 142)

(No. 6 on pattern sheet).—This is an example of many soft cuddly toys which can be made from strong cotton print. This one has a design of gaily-coloured nursery toys on a white background. Floral or spot designs are also good. The ears are lined with pieces cut from a yellow duster; the under-body could be made from the same fabric if desired. Hunt for a bit of white fluffy cloth or lamb's wool for the tail.

Cut out parts as directed on pattern sheet. Stitch the under-body together along the upper edge, then place between sides of body and stitch in position. Insert the gusset between the sides of body along the head and back, matching letters A and B.

In the model, the edges were turned in to face, and the folded edges oversewn on the right side, but this toy could also be stitched up on the wrong side, and turned out through a stuffing-space in the centre of the under-body. In any case, it is best to tack all the parts together first, to make both sides well-balanced.

Stuff bunny very softly and sew up opening. Mark the eyes with dark circles, a few stitches, or real glass eyes, in every case taking the needle through

FOR A TINY TOT. *Curved and cuddlesome, this amusing Elf Doll is a specially good toy for a small child, as the arms and legs are easy to take hold of. The original was made in magenta plush, with trousers and soles, gloves and collar in emerald green.*

the head and pulling cotton, to shape head slightly. Seam up the darts in all ear sections, join ears in pairs, sew to head with linings facing outwards. Add tail.

PET LAMB
(*Illustrated on page* 141)

(No. 7 on pattern sheet).—This is an ideal pram toy if made in soft pastel-toned fabric and filled with very light stuffing. The model uses rose-pink felt, with ear-linings and oversewing in pale lime green. A buttercup-chain of felt

and a scrap of braid make a dainty finishing touch.

Cut out parts as directed on pattern sheet. Seam the under-body along upper edges, place between sides of body, and stitch all parts together on the right side, stuffing as you go. Sew the ears together in pairs and attach to head. Add eyes of black circles, stitches or real glass, and finish with one buttercup sewn to the mouth and a few others draped round the neck on a scrap of narrow green cord or braid.

SIX-YEAR-OLDS *will love this intriguing two-in-one doll. Two dolls are made complete, as far down as the hips, and joined end to end. A double skirt is sewn over the join so that it can be turned either way up—the skirt hides the doll not required. A sloe-eyed black mammy is at one end, and a " white " doll is at the other.*

FLOPPY DOG

(Illustrated on page 142)

(No. 8 on pattern sheet).—This is an example of a " character " animal. It is not meant to stand up (though it will do with care), but to fall into all sorts of amusing attitudes. The model uses a novelty " House that Jack Built " cotton print in strong clear colours. Other novel effects could be obtained with plain cloth, velvet or felt in contrasting shades.

Cut out parts as directed on pattern sheet. Cut also two straight strips, both 1½ ins. wide, one 21 ins. long to go round the upper part of body and one 7 ins. long to go along the lower edge of body.

Seams are best made on the right side, turning in the edges and tacking parts together before oversewing, but they could be made on the wrong side by hand or machined if preferred. Stitch the short gusset between sides of body along the base, A to B, then stitch the long gusset right round the rest of the body, meeting the short gusset A and B. Leave ends of gussets open, stuff the body through them, but still leave open.

Seam up the four legs, add soles, and stuff, taking the stuffing fairly near the top and packing it firmly. Fold each leg flat across the top from side to side, then stitch the two front legs into the front gusset opening, and the two back legs into the back gusset opening. They may need rather more length than the length of the gusset-ends, as the legs must be sewn side by side. If so, take up a small tuck to extend the gusset opening and fit the legs into it. When finished the legs should flop loosely, but be very securely attached.

Make up and stuff the tail and sew to body, rounding the base of the tail. Stitch the ears together in pairs, preferably using a contrast for linings, and attach to head. For each eye, place a small dark circle over a larger white one, and stitch to head, placing a fringed strip of black oil-baize or felt behind it to form eye-lashes. Sew a black nose in place, and a few stitches in black wool or a strip of braid to indicate the mouth. Finish with a collar at neck.

GIRL TEDDY BEAR

(Illustrated on page 143)

(No. 9 on pattern sheet).—Every child loves a teddy bear, and this one strikes a new note with " girl " clothes. You can of course dress the same model in shorts for a boy, or leave it without clothes. The original was made with thick rough blanket-cloth, brushed up afterwards to form a fluffy pile. Real glass eyes or shoe buttons are needed, as they help to mould the correct contour of the head. Pink and white checked gingham makes skirt and knickers. Bonnet and trimmings are emerald-green felt, with red ribbon to tie bonnet and red felt soles to feet.

Cut out parts as directed on pattern sheet. All seams for this toy must be *very firmly* stitched on wrong side. First stitch head gusset between sides of head, matching A and B, and fitting in the short straight nose end of the gusset evenly. Stitch down the front of the body from A to C, then from B to C down the back, but leave the space marked on the pattern for the opening. Sew up the darts each side of neck. Attach each felt sole from D to D on each leg.

Now pull the sides of body apart and make separate legs by sewing from F, round foot and up to C, each leg the same. Turn body right side out through stuffing-space and stuff very firmly. Turn up feet and hold with a few strong stitches across front ankles. Fold each arm in half, make up and stuff, sew very securely to body with strong double thread.

Stitch ears together in pairs, stitch to head, curving towards front. Twist the wires on eyes into small shanks (as on shoe-buttons) make a hole with scissor-points in head for eye-shank to sink into (you *must* have a good-sized hole), attach each eye on separate double thread, taking it through the head and bringing all the ends out together at the back of neck. Pull all threads *very* tightly, to pull head into shape, knot together, cut off ends. Mark nose and mouth as in photograph. Brush up body with wire brush.

Join knickers at narrow ends, turn in or bind the straight edges. Turn in and gather up curved waistline, place on body, catching points between legs with a few stitches. Bind, hem or otherwise trim the wide circular edge of skirt, turn in waist and sew to body. Add a waistband with a bow at the back.

The bonnet is left quite flat, but is held in place by the ribbons and two cords which slip over the ears. Place bonnet on back of head and mark position for ends of cords, then add these, either by sewing on short lengths of cord, or taking long stitches across several times and buttonholing the strands together. Sew on ribbon tie-ups ; add a few felt flowers for trimming and place bonnet on head so that the ears show.

NIGGER BOY
(*Illustrated on page* 143)

(No. 10 on pattern sheet).—Every child loves a " black doll," though actually it is better to use brown, rather than black fabric. The original was made up in brown velvet, but a very good alternative is an old brown cashmere stocking, as worn by schoolgirls.

The model has trousers of bright striped silk, with a flame-coloured felt beret and belt, and braces of multicoloured cord. Any similar gaily-coloured pieces can be used. The hair is dark brown bouclé wool, and the face is stitched with white, black and scarlet embroidery thread. A ready-made mask can be used if preferred.

All doll toys depend largely for their success upon the face, and the secret of this is to work—or at any rate, prepare—the face before making up the doll. Faces may be painted with poster-colour, stitched as in the " nigger " model, or appliquéd, that is, shapes for eyes and mouth cut out in felt or leather and caught down with tiny stitches.

For the nigger boy's face, cut a piece of firm fabric as shown on the pattern sheet, and trace the features as shown. (If this is difficult on dark material, the best way is to trace the features on to very thin paper, tack over the face for working, then tear the paper away.) Cut a similar piece of stiff fabric such as book muslin or canvas, tack behind the case, then stitch or paint the features. Satin-stitch is used for eyes and mouth, outlined with tiny back-stitches to give a tidy edge. To make sure of getting the mouth well balanced, begin in the middle, do a stitch first one side, then one the other side, till the corners are reached. A very little stuffing may be inserted between face and backing, on chin, cheeks and forehead, to give added shape.

When the face is complete, cut out all parts as directed on pattern sheet. All seams in the model were made on the right side, turning in the edges and over-sewing with matching cotton, but they could be stitched on the wrong side with care. Remember that the stiffened face will not turn inside out easily.

Seam the head together down centre-back, leaving space where shown. Stitch head centrally round face, leaving about an inch of the face free beneath the chin.

Add felt ears if desired, and sew wool (or dolls' hair) all over the head, or on the parts left free of the hat. Stuff head, sew up opening, but leave neck open.

Make and stuff upper body, leaving neck and waist open. Make and stuff trousers ; stitch up lower ends, but leave waist open and push up into waist of upper body, stitching firmly. Push neck into a well-rounded shape on both head and body, press well together and stitch *very securely*. For extra strength, insert inside neck, head and body a strip of wood or strong cardboard, bound round with stuffing strongly tied on with cotton.

Make and stuff feet, mark toes (and fingers also) with black cotton, sew to lower edges of trousers. Add braces and a belt. Make up beret and stitch to head.

ELF DOLL
(Illustrated on page 145)

(No. 11 on pattern sheet.) This is a specially good cuddly doll for a small child, as the arms and legs are easy to take hold of. Use your very gayest materials. The model uses magenta plush, with emerald green cotton brocade for the trousers and soles, gloves and collar of felt in the same shade. A ready-made mask was used on the original, with the kiss-curl added in black crayon, but you can make the face yourself as described for " nigger boy " ; details of the " elf " face are given on the pattern.

Cut out parts as directed on pattern sheet. Cut also a straight strip for trousers, 18 ins. long and 4½ ins. wide. Seams on this doll are all made on the *wrong* side. First stitch cap from A round the point and down to B at back of neck. Sew gloves to ends of sleeves, then stitch all round gloves and down sleeves. Stuff arms firmly, pushing stuffing into thumbs and hand, mark fingers with stitches, then sew top of arms into slit C-D on each side of tunic. Sew down front of tunic, from E to F, and stitch face into front of cap.

Fold each leg in half, sew from G to H and add felt soles. Stuff legs very firmly and sew across top to hold stuffing. Join the long trouser section down the back, gather up one long side to fit the tunic, sew the two together, taking care to get gathers even on both sides. Turn in and gather the other edge evenly and

sew legs in *flat*. Stuff body and sew up opening. Sew on the felt collar, catching it up at centre-back and down in front, add pompons on tunic and shoes.

TWO-WAY DOLL
(Illustrated on page 146)

(No. 12 on pattern sheet.) No toy-making series is complete without a doll, and this design is specially useful as it gives two patterns in one. Two dolls are made, complete as far down as the hips, and joined end to end. A double skirt is gathered and sewn over the join so that it can be turned either way up—the skirt hides the doll not required.

The original had flesh-coloured and brown felt respectively for the two bodies; pieces from old stockings or undies would do equally well. Clothes are in felt too, light blue for the white doll, scarlet for the black one. Cotton print in suitable designs makes skirts (candy stripes for the black doll, and tiny floral print for the other doll), and bonnet-backs. Yellow wool and black fur respectively make the hair, and the faces are stitched in natural colours.

Cut out parts as directed on pattern sheet. Work faces as explained for nigger doll. Make up bodies, stitching on right side, sew together at hips, adding stuffing down centre so that bodies are very firm. Make each bodice and place on dolls, adding basques at waist and a frill and gathered sleeves for the " white " doll. Add ribbon or braid for belt.

For each bonnet, bring A to B at back and stitch up two short seams, then join up back seam C-B. Bind edges with braid, add bow or other trimming. Sew hair on in loops, sew bonnet to head. Make a double skirt about 30 ins. wide and 8 ins. long (when finished). Face in lower edge, and add a narrow band of trimming at the hem. Turn in and gather upper edge, draw up to fit, and sew firmly over hip join of dolls.

TINY HAT SHOP

With Mirror, Hat-Box and Stands

MATERIALS

3 empty cotton reels.
3 wooden meat skewers.
6 domed button moulds.
Small mirror.
Round box, Cellophane or cardboard approximately 4 ins. wide by $2\frac{1}{2}$ ins. deep.
Small tin pink enamel.
Scraps of felt, with feathers, ribbon, net, flowers, and so on, for trimming.
Glue, tacks, and cardboard.

Method

The Hat Stands.—Saw each cotton reel in half to make six bases and glue a small circle of cardboard under each one. Cut the wooden skewers up to make six stems, three 3 ins. long, and three $3\frac{1}{2}$ ins. long. Glue a stem into the centre hole of each base then secure a button

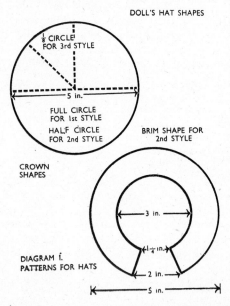

DOLL'S HAT SHAPES

$\frac{1}{8}$ CIRCLE FOR 3rd STYLE

5 in.

FULL CIRCLE FOR 1st STYLE

HALF CIRCLE FOR 2nd STYLE

BRIM SHAPE FOR 2nd STYLE

CROWN SHAPES

3 in.

$1\frac{1}{4}$ in.

2 in.

5 in.

DIAGRAM I. PATTERNS FOR HATS

mould to the top of each stem by driving a tack through the hole in the mould and into the stem. Paint the stands with pink enamel.

The Mirror.—Cut a strip of cardboard, bend it near the top and glue it to the back of the mirror to form a strut. Make a frame round the mirror with gummed paper and paint the frame and the back of the mirror with pink enamel.

The Hat-box.—A discarded bath powder or face powder box is ideal for the hat-box. Paint pink enamel stripes across the top and down the sides, then add a decorative label with a name lettered on it. Fill the hat-box with tissue paper.

The Hats.—The shapes for the hats are given in Diagram I. Felt is the most suitable material for making them, but fabric could be used.

First Style.—Cut a 5-in. wide circle of felt. Leave 6 ins. of its outer edge plain for the back of the hat and gather the remainder up to about 4 ins. for the front. Sew a narrow band of felt about 9 ins. long, round the edge of the circle, easing the plain back section into it. Join the ends of the band at the back, then twist a scrap of net and tack it over the band. A similar shaped hat could have its edge bound with ribbon and a bow of the ribbon at the front.

Second Style.—For the crown cut a 5-in. wide semicircle of felt, fold in half and join the two straight edges, then turn right side out. Push the point down to shape the top of the hat. Cut the brim as shown in Diagram I. Beginning at the seam at the back of the crown, sew the crown down over the

FOR A LITTLE GIRL. *Proud owners of dolls always love to get new acquisitions for their dollies' wardrobe, and this miniature French hat shop will delight the heart of a small girl. Five perfect felt models in miniature are shown above standing on their tiny hat stands, and one model is already packed in its gaily striped hat-box.*

inner edge of the brim, stretching the brim and easing in the crown. Join the open ends of the brim at the back. This style can have a feather through the crown and its brim turned down at the front and up at the back, or the brim stitched up at one side with a flower, or up at the front with a decorative bow of felt or ribbon.

Third Style.—Cut a semicircle into four quarters and join them together on their straight sides. Turn right side out and with the fingers work the felt until the crown is rounded out at the top, as much as possible. Tuck the top point in. Stretch the outer edge of the crown then stitch a straight strip of felt round it for a brim. Turn the brim down at the back and up at the front and trim with a tiny veil and feathers.

FELT PRAM COVER

And Toy Rattle made with Ribbon

PRAM COVER

MATERIALS

Felt, 36 ins. deep by 24 ins. wide in any suitable colour.

4 yds. contrasting corded ribbon, 1½ ins. wide.

Beige felt approximately 11 ins. square.

Scraps of white felt and green wool.

Method.—Cut the edges of the oblong piece of felt in scallops, each approximately 2½ ins. wide and ½ in. deep, letting the two end scallops at the corners merge into one large scallop. Fold the corded ribbon in half lengthways and press well. Tack this folded ribbon under the scalloped edges of felt, with

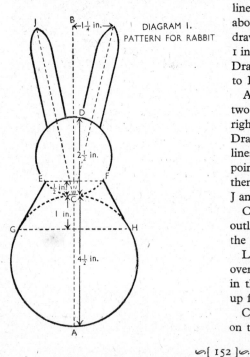

DIAGRAM 1.
PATTERN FOR RABBIT

the fold projecting about ⅛ in. beyond the outer curves of the scallops. Mitre the ribbon at each corner so that it forms a neat border round the scallops. Hem the double edges of ribbon to the felt on the wrong side of the cover, then slip-stitch the felt scallops to the ribbon on the right side, taking care not to let the stitches show on the other side of the ribbon border.

To cut the pattern for the rabbits, follow Diagram 1. Draw a vertical line A to B, 10 ins. long. Mark a point C, 4½ ins. above A and using A—C as diameter, draw in a 4½ ins. wide circle. Mark another point D, 2½ ins. above C and using C—D as diameter describe another circle, 2½ ins. wide. Draw a line across this smaller circle ½ in. above C, marking its ends E and F, then draw another line across the larger circle 1 in. below C, marking the ends G and H. Draw lines to connect E to G and F to H.

At the top of the original line mark two points J and K, 1¼ ins. to left and right of B. Join J to C and K to C. Draw parallel lines ⅜ in. each side of the lines J—C and K—C from the top to the point where they cross the small circle, then taper these lines off to a point at J and K, for the tops of the rabbit's ears.

Cut the pattern out round the thick outline shown in the diagram and cut the shape in beige felt.

Line the right ear with ribbon, fold it over to one side and appliqué the rabbit in the centre of the cover, about 5 ins. up from the lower edge.

Cut a pattern for the smaller rabbits on the same principle as the larger one,

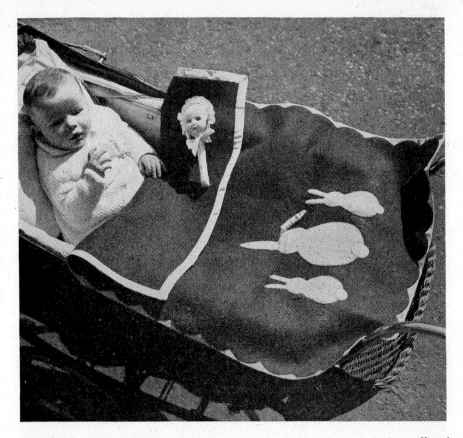

FOR BABY. *A warm and cosy pram cover in felt, with attractively scalloped edges backed with contrast corded ribbon. The original was in maroon with peach-coloured ribbon. The delightful little rabbits are cut out in beige felt and appliquéd to one end of the cover. The turn-back ear of the centre rabbit is lined with ribbon. A close-up of the rattle is shown on the next page.*

but with the following measurements :—
A—B, 6 ins. ; A—C, 2¾ ins. ; C—D, 1½ ins. ; E—F, ¼ in. above C ; G—H, ½ in. below C ; B—K and B—J, each ¾ in. ; and the ears ⅜ in. wide. Cut two of these shapes in beige felt and appliqué one each side of the larger rabbit. For the tails cut one circle of white felt 1¼ ins. wide (for the centre rabbit) and two ¾ in. wide and appliqué in place. Work groups of stitches in varying lengths, in green wool, between the rabbits and at both sides to represent blades of grass.

BABY'S RATTLE

MATERIALS

2 doll masks, about 3 ins. wide.
3 yds. blue or pink ribbon, ¾ in. to 1 in. wide.
1 small tin containing few buttons.
1 wooden clothes peg.
Small piece of wadding.

Method.—Cover the peg with several layers of wadding. Cut a piece of ribbon about 3 ins. long, gather it at one edge and stitch it over the wadding at the split end of the peg, to make a small cap.

Bind over the edge of this cap and up the stem of the peg with ribbon, and put a stitch or two to keep the binding secure at the knob end of the peg. This completes the handle.

Cut two thick circles of wadding, the same width as the masks, put the tin containing the buttons between them and whip the edges together except for about 1 in. Insert the top of the handle in this open space and stitch the wadding on to the handle back and front. This foundation is shown in Diagram 1.

Now take one of the masks and bind all round its edge with the ribbon, folded in half. Gather another length of ribbon to make a frill and sew it to the ribbon binding from the bottom of one cheek round the top of the head to the bottom of the other. Now make up the other mask in exactly the same way.

Put the two masks, one each side of the foundation and stuff in a little more wadding between foundation and masks to prevent denting. Whip the bound edges together as far as the handle on each side, then stitch the masks to the top of the handle back and front.

Draw the masks together round the remainder of the faces with stitches through the gathered frills, as near to the ribbon binding as possible.

TIN ENCLOSED IN WADDING

DIAGRAM 1.
PEG HANDLE BOUND AND STITCHED INSIDE RATTLE FOUNDATION

FOR BABY AGAIN. *This delightful little rattle is made of two masks joined back to back, with a gathered ribbon frill round the join. The handle is bound with ribbon, and the rattle is finished with a ribbon bow under the chin.*

BERET AND MITTS

Trimmed with Heart-shapes

MATERIALS

3 oz. 3-ply wool in red.
2 oz. 3-ply wool in white.
2 No. 12 knitting needles.
A small ball of wool in a bright contrasting colour.

MEASUREMENTS

Beret : Width across top, 9 ins.
Mitts : Length of hand, 6½ ins.
Width all round, 7 ins.

TENSION

8½ sts. to 1 in.

ABBREVIATIONS

K. knit, p. purl, st. stitch, tog. together, r. red, w. white, sl. slip, p.s.s.o. pass slipped st. over, g.st. garter stitch. *N.B.*—Do not weave wool when working heart patt., but where there are more than 5 sts. in one colour catch up the contrasting wool once or twice on the wrong side. Where wool is changed at the same place in 2 or more consecutive rows twist the 2 colours on the wrong side to prevent a hole.

THE BERET

Using w. wool cast on 112 sts. and work in k. 1, p. 1 rib for ¾ in.

Next row.—K. twice in every st. to the end.   (224 sts.)

Next row.—P. to the end.

Now work in patt. thus :—

1st row.—K. 2 r., * (1 w., 1 r.) 17 times, 1 w., 2 r., rep. from * to the end.

2nd row.—P. 2 r., * (1 r., 1 w.) 17 times, 3 r., rep. from * to the end. Rep. these 2 rows 5 times more.

13th row.—K. 2 r., * (1 w., 1 r.) 8 times, 3 w. (1 r., 1 w.) 8 times, 2 r. rep. from * to the end.

14th row.—P. 2 r., * (1 r. 1, w.) 7 times, 1 r. 5 w., 1 r. (1 w., 1 r.) 7 times, 2 r., rep. from * to the end.

15th row.—K. 2 r., * (1 w., 1 r.) 7 times, 7 w. (1 r., 1 w.) 7 times, 2 r., rep. from * to the end.

16th row.—P. 2 r. * (1 r., 1 w.) 6 times, 1 r., 9 w., 1 r. (1 w., 1 r.) 6 times, 2 r., rep. from * to the end.

Continue thus sloping white panels by working an extra w. st. at both ends of each panel in every row and keeping the continuity of spot patt. and r. bands in between until there are 21 w. sts. in each panel, thus ending with a p. row.

Now work heart patt. thus :—

1st row.—K. 2 r., * (1 w., 1 r.) 3 times, 6 w., 4 r., 3 w., 4 r., 6 w. (1 r., 1 w.) 3 times, 2 r., rep. from * to the end.

2nd row.—P. 2 r., * (1 r., 1 w.) twice, 1 r., 6 w., 6 r., 1 w., 6 r., 6 w., 1 r. (1 w., 1 r.) twice, 2 r., rep. from * to the end.

3rd row.—K. 2 r., * (1.w., 1 r.) twice, 6 w., 15 r., 6 w. (1 r., 1 w.) twice, 2 r., rep. from * to the end.

4th row.—P. 2 r., * 1 r., 1 w., 1 r., 7 w., 4 r., 1 w., 5 r., 1 w., 4 r., 7 w., 1 r., 1 w., 3 r., rep. from * to the end.

5th row.—K. 2 r., * 1 w., 1 r., 8 w. (3 r., 3 w.) twice, 3 r., 8 w., 1 r., 1 w., 2 r., rep. from * to the end.

6th row.—P. 2 r., * 1 r., 9 w., 4 r., 3 w., 1 r., 3 w., 4 r., 9 w., 3 r., rep. from * to the end.

7th row.—K. 2 r., * 10 w., 5 r., 5 w., 5 r., 10 w., 2 r., rep. from * to the end.

8th row.—P. 2 r., * 11 w., 5 r., 3 w., 5 r., 11 w., 2 r., rep. from * to the end.

9th row.—K. 1 r., * sl. 1, k. 1 r., p.s.s.o., 11 w., 5 r., 1 w., 5 r., 11 w., k. 2 tog. r., rep. from * to the last st., 1 r.

THE 'TEEN-AGE GIRL *will love this jaunty knitted set of beret and mitts for frosty days. The heart-shaped motif is cleverly worked into the sections of the beret and the deep gauntlet of the mitts. The set was originally knitted in beige and maroon.*

10th row.—P. 2 r., * 12 w., 9 r., 12 w., 2 r., rep. from * to the end.

11th row.—K. 1 r., * sl. 1, k. 1 r., p.s.s.o., 12 w., 7 r., 12 w., k. 2 tog. r., rep. from * to the last st., 1 r.

12th row.—P. 2 r., * 14 w., 3 r., 14 w., 2 r., rep. from * to the end.

13th row.—K. 1 r., * sl. 1, k. 1 r., p.s.s.o., 14 w., 1 r., 14 w., k. 2 tog. r., rep. from * to the last st., 1 r.

14th row.—P. 2 r., * 29 w., 2 r., rep. from * to the end.

15th row.—K. 1 r., * sl. 1, k.1 r., p.s.s.o., 27 w., k. 2 tog. r., rep. from * to the last st., 1 r.

16th row.—P. 2 r., * 27 w., 2 r., rep. from * to the end.

17th row.—K. 1 r., * sl. 1, k. 1 r., p.s.s.o., 8 w., 3 r., 3 w., 3 r., 8 w., k. 2 tog. r., rep. from * to the last st., 1 r.

18th row.—P. 2 r., * 7 w., 5 r., 1 w., 5 r., 7 w., 2 r., rep. from * to the end.

19th row.—K. 1 r., * sl. 1, k. 1 r., p.s.s.o., 6 w., 3 r., 1 w., 3 r., 1 w., 3 r., 6 w., k. 2 tog. r., rep. from * to the last st., 1 r.

20th row.—P. 2 r., * 6 w., 4 r., 1 w., 1 r., 1 w., 4 r., 6 w., 2 r., rep. from * to the end.

21st row.—K. 1 r., * sl. 1, k. 1 r., p.s.s.o., 5 w., 5 r., 1 w., 5 r., 5 w., k. 2 tog. r., rep. from * to the last st., k. 1 r.

22nd row.—P. 2 r., * 6 w., 4 r., 1 w., 4 r., 6 w., 2 r., rep. from * to the end.

23rd row.—K. 1 r., * sl. 1, k. 1 r., p.s.s.o., 6 w., 7 r., 6 w., k. 2 tog. r., rep. from * to the last st., 1 r.

24th row.—P. 2 r., * 8 w., 3 r., 8 w., 2 r., rep. from * to the end.

25th row.—K. 1 r., * sl. 1, k. 1 r., p.s.s.o., 8 w., 1 r., 8 w., k. 2 tog. r., rep. from * to the last st., 1 r.

26th row.—P. 2 r., * 17 w., 2 r., rep. from * to the end.

27th row.—K. 1 r., * sl. 1, k. 1 r., p.s.s.o., 15 r., k. 2 tog. r., rep. from * to the last st., 1 r.

28th row.—P. 2 r., * 15 w., 2 r., rep. from * to the end.

29th row.—K. 1 r., * sl. 1, k. 1 r., p.s.s.o., 4 w., 2 r., 1 w., 2 r., 4 w., k. 2 tog. r., rep. from * to the last st., 1 r.

30th row.—P. 2 r., * 3 w., 7 r., 3 w., 2 r., rep. from * to the end.

31st row.—K. 1 r., * sl. 1, k. 1 r., p.s.s.o., 2 w., 2 r., 1 w., 1 r., 1 w., 2 r., 2 w., k. 2 tog. r., rep. from * to the last st., 1 r.

32nd row.—P. 2 r., * 2 w., 3 r., 1 w., 3 r., 2 w., 2 r., rep. from * to the end.

33rd row.—K. 1 r., * sl. 1, k. 1 r., p.s.s.o., 2 w., 5 r., 2 w., k. 2 tog. r., rep. from * to the last st., 1 r.

34th row.—P. 2 r., * 3 w., 3 r., 3 w., 2 r., rep. from * to the end.

35th row.—K. 1 r., * sl. 1, k. 1 r., p.s.s.o., 3 w., 1 r., 3 w., k. 2 tog. r., rep. from * to the last st., 1 r.

36th row.—P. 2 r., * 7 w., 2 r., rep. from * to the end.

37th row.—K. 1 r., * sl. 1, k. 1 r., p.s.s.o., 5 w., k. 2 tog. r., rep. from * to the last st., 1 r.

38th row.—P. 2 r., * 5 w., 2 r., rep. from * to the end.

39th row.—K. 1 r., * sl. 1, k. 1 r., p.s.s.o., 3 w., k. 2 tog. r., rep. from * to the last st., 1 r.

40th row.—P. 2 r., * 3 w., 2 r., rep. from * to the end.

41st row.—K. 1 r., * sl. 1, k. 1 r., p.s.s.o., 1 w., k. 2 tog. r., rep. from * to the end.

42nd row.—P. 1 r., * p. 3 tog. r., rep. from * to the last st. p. 1 r.

Break off w. wool and fasten off.

Break off a long length of r. wool and thread through remaining sts.

Draw up tightly and fasten securely then sew up seam on the wrong side.

Press. Cut a piece of stiffish muslin the size of the crown and tack in position.

THE MITTS

Using w. wool cast on 86 sts. and work in g. st. (every row k.) for ½ in.

Now work in patt. thus :—

1st row.—K. 2 r., * 4 w., 4 r., 3 w., 4 r., 4 w., 2 r., rep. from * to the end.

2nd row.—P. 2 r., * 3 w., 6 r., 1 w., 6 r., 3 w., 2 r., rep. from * to the end.

3rd row.—K. 2 r., * 2 w., 15 r., 2 w., 2 r., rep. from * to the end.

4th row.—P. 2 r., * 2 w., 4 r., 1 w., 5 r., 1 w., 4 r., 2 w., 2 r., rep. from * to the end.

5th row.—K. 2 r., * 2 w. (3 r., 3 w.) twice, 3 r., 2 w., 2 r., rep. from * to the end.

6th row.—P. 2 r., * 2 w., 4 r., 3 w., 1 r., 3 w., 4 r., 2 w., 2 r., rep. from * to the end.

7th row.—K. 2 r., * 2 w., 5 r., 5 w., 5 r., 2 w., 2 r., rep. from * to the end.

8th row.—P. 2 r., * 3 w., 5 r., 3 w., 5 r., 3 w., 2 r., rep. from * to the end.

9th row.—K. 1 r., * sl. 1, k. 1 r., p.s.s.o., 3 w., 5 r., 1 w., 5 r., 3 w., k. 2 tog. r., rep. from * to the last st., 1 r.

10th row.—P. 2 r., * 4 w., 9 r., 4 w., 2 r., rep. from * to the end.

11th row.—K. 2 r., * 5 w., 7 r., 5 w., 2 r., rep. from * to the end.

12th row.—P. 2 r., * 7 w., 3 r., 7 w., 2 r., rep. from * to the end.

13th row.—K. 2 r., * 8 w., 1 r., 8 w., 2 r. rep. from * to the end.

14th row.—P. 2 r., * 17 w., 2 r., rep. from * to the end.

15th row.—K. 2 r., * 17 w., 2 r., rep. from * to the end.

16th row.—P. 2 r., * 17 w., 2 r., rep. from * to the end.

17th row.—K. 2 r., * 4 w., 3 r., 3 w., 3 r., 4 w., 2 r., rep. from * to the end.

18th row.—P. 2 r., * 3 w., 5 r., 1 w., 5 r., 3 w., 2 r., rep. from * to the end.

19th row.—K. 1 r., * sl. 1, k. 1 r., p.s.s.o., 2 w. (3 r., 1 w.) twice, 3 r., 2 w., k. 2 tog. r., rep. from * to the end.

20th row.—P. 2 r., * 2 w., 4 r., 1 w., 1 r., 1 w., 4 r., 2 w., 2 r., rep. from * to the end.

21st row.—K. 2 r., * 2 w., 5 r., 1 w., 5 r., 2 w., 2 r., rep. from * to the end.

22nd row.—P. 2 r., * 3 w., 4 r., 1 w., 4 r., 3 w., 2 r., rep. from * to the end.

23rd row.—K. 2 r., * 4 w., 7 r., 4 w., 2 r., rep. from * to the end.

24th row.—P. 2 r., * 6 w., 3 r., 6 w., 2 r., rep. from * to the end.

25th.—K. 2 r., * 7 w., 1 r., 7 w., 2 r., rep. from * to the end.

26th row.—P. 2 r., * 15 w., 2 r., rep. from * to the end.

27th row.—K. 2 r., * 15 w., 2 r., rep. from * to the end.

28th row.—P. 2 r., * 15 w., 2 r., rep. from * to the end.

29th row.—K. 1 r., sl. 1, k. 1 r., p.s.s.o., 4 w., 2 r., 1 w., 2 r., 4 w., k. 2 tog. r., rep. from * to the last st. 1 r.

30th row.—P. 2 r., * 3 w., 7 r., 3 w., 2 r., rep. from * to the end.

31st row.—K. 2 r., * 3 w., 2 r., 1 w., 1 r., 1 w., 2 r., 3 w., 2 r., rep. from * to the end.

32nd row.—P. 2 r., * 3 w., 3 r., 1 w., 3 r., 3 w., 2 r., rep. from * to the end.

33rd row.—K. 2 r., * 4 w., 5 r., 4 w., 2 r., rep. from * to the end.

34th row.—P. 2 r., * 5 w., 3 r., 5 w., 2 r., rep. from * to the end.

35th row.—K. 2 r., * 6 w., 1 r., 6 w., 2 r., rep. from * to the end.

36th row.—P. 2 r., * 13 w., 2 r., rep. from * to the end.

Break off r. wool and continue with w.

37th row.—* k. 2 tog., k. 6, rep. from * to the last 6 sts., k. 2 tog., k. 4. (54 sts.)

Now work in k. 1, p. 1 rib. for 1 in. ending with a row on the wrong side.

Next row.—* k. twice in the first st , k. 8, rep. from * to the end. (60 sts.)

Next row.—P. to the end.

Now work in spot patt. thus :—

1st row.—* k. 1 w., k. 1 r., rep. from * to the end.

2nd row.—* p. 1 w., p. 1 r., rep. from * to the end.

Rep. these 2 rows until work measures

Contrast coloured wool is used to outline the top and bottom rows of hearts on the gauntlets and the beret is embroidered to match. The beret is lined with stiff muslin.

2 ins. from end of ribbing, ending with a row on the wrong side.

Thumb row for Left Hand.—Patt. 20 sts., **, k. the next 10 sts. with an odd length of different coloured wool, slip the 10 sts. back on left-hand needle, then k. with r. and w. wools tog., **, patt. 30 sts.

Thumb row for Right Hand.—Patt. 30 sts., rep. from ** to * *.

Next row.—Patt. all sts. including those knitted with odd wool.

Now continue in patt. until work measures 5 ins. from ribbing at wrist, ending with a row on the wrong side.

Break off r. wool and continue with w.

Shape Top thus.—

Next row.—K. 1, sl. 1, k. 1, p.s.s.o.,

k. 24, k. 2 tog., k. 2, sl. 1, k. 1, p.s.s.o., k. 24, k. 2 tog., k. 1.

Next row.—P. to the end.

Next row.—K. 1, sl. 1, k. 1, p.s.s.o., k. 22, k. 2 tog., k. 2, sl. 1, k. 1, p.s.s.o., k. 22, k. 2 tog., k. 1.

Next row.—P. to the end.

Next row.—K. 1, sl. 1, k. 1, p.s.s.o., k. 20, k. 2 tog., k. 2, sl. 1, k. 1, p.s.s.o. k. 20, k. 2 tog., k. 1.

Next row.—P. to the end.

Continue thus dec. after the first st., at both sides of the 2 centre sts. and before the last st. in every right-side row until 24 sts. remain.

Next row.—P. 12.

Now graft the 2 sets of 12 sts. together.

The Thumb.—Unpick the piece of odd

wool for thumb and pick up the 2 sets of 10 sts. thus formed on to 2 needles.

Keeping the continuity of the spot patt. work on one of these sets of 10 sts. in patt. for 2 ins. ending with a row on the wrong side.

Break off r. wool and continue with w.

Next row.—K. 1 (k. 2 tog., k. 1) 3 times.

Next row.—P. to the end.

Next row.—K. 1 (k. 2 tog.) 3 times.

Break off the wool and thread through the remaining sts.

Draw up tightly and fasten off.

Work on the second set of sts. in the same way.

Make-up.—Press work with a hot iron and damp cloth.

Join side and thumb seams.

Press seams.

Embroidery

Using the contrasting colour outline the top and bottom rows of hearts on the gauntlets with chain-stitch. Embroider the heart-shapes on the top of the beret to match.

SLEEVELESS PULLOVER

Trimmed with Fair-Isle

MATERIALS
3 oz. 4-ply wool in medium colour.
2 oz. 4-ply wool in dark colour.
1 oz. 4-ply wool in light colour.
2 No. 12 and 2 No. 9 knitting needles.

MEASUREMENTS
Length : 19 ins.
Chest : 32 ins.

TENSION
6½ sts. to 1 in. on No. 9 needles.

ABBREVIATIONS
K. knit, p. purl, st. stitch, inc. increase, dec. decrease, tog. together, m. medium colour, lt. light colour, dk. dark colour, st.st. stocking st.

N.B.—When working fair-isle patt. wool not in use should be stranded on wrong side, not woven in.

The Front.—Using No. 12 needles and dk. coloured wool cast on 96 sts. and work in k. 1, p. 1 rib for 3½ ins., inc. 1 st. at the end of the last row (97 sts.).

Change to No. 9 needles and work 4 rows in st.st. (1 row k., 1 row p.).

Now work in fair-isle patt. thus :—

1st row.—K. dk. to the end.

2nd row.—P. 3 dk. ; * 1 lt., 5 dk., rep. from * to the last 4 sts., 1 lt., 3 dk.

3rd row.—K. 2 dk., * 3 lt., 3 dk., rep. from * to the last 5 sts., 3 lt., 2 dk.

4th row.—P. * 1 dk., 5 lt., rep. from * to the last st., 1 dk.

5th row.—K. lt. to the end.

6th row.—P. 1 lt., * 1 lt., 3 m., 1 lt., 1 m., 1 lt., 3 m., 2 lt., rep. from * to the end.

7th row.—K. * 1 lt., 3 m., rep. from * to the last st., 1 lt.

8th row.—P. 3 m., * 1 lt., 5 m., rep. from * to the last 4 sts., 1 lt., 3 m.

9th row.—K. * 2 m., 1 lt., 7 m., 1 lt., 1 m., rep. from * to the last st., 1 m.

10th row.—P. 1 dk., * (1 lt., 4 dk.) twice, 1 lt., 1 dk., rep from * to the end.

11th row.—K. * 1 lt., 4 dk., 3 lt., 4 dk., rep. from * to the last st., 1 lt.

12th row.—As 10th row.

13th row.—As 9th row.

14th row.—As 8th row.

FOR A SCHOOLBOY. *Every schoolboy hankers after a pullover with his school colours knitted into it. Here is a good design that he will be proud to wear, a sleeveless pullover with colour introduced at the high round neck, armholes and waist.*

15th row.—As 7th row.

16th row.—As 6th row.

17th row.—As 5th row.

18th row.—As 4th row.

19th row.—As 3rd row.

20th row.—As 2nd row.

21st row.—As 1st row.

This completes patt.

Continue with m. coloured wool in st.st., inc. 1 st. at both ends of every 6th row until there are 109.

Then continue without shaping if necessary until work measures 11 ins. from lower edge.

Shape Armholes thus.—Cast off 5 sts. at the beginning of the next 2 rows, then dec. 1 st. at both ends of every row until 72 sts. remain.

Now continue without shaping until work measures 16½ ins. from lower edge, ending with a row on the wrong side.

Shape Neck thus.—

Next row.—K. 27, turn, and leave remaining sts. on a spare needle.

Now work on these 27 sts., dec. 1 st. at neck edge in every row until 13 sts. remain. Then continue in st.st. with-

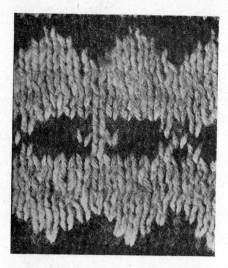

Close-up of fair-isle design showing exact size of stitch.

out shaping if necessary until work measures 19 ins. from lower edge, ending at armhole edge.

Shape Shoulder thus.—

Next row.—Cast off 6, work to the end.

Next row.—Work to the end.

Cast off remaining sts.

Return to sts. on spare needle and beginning at neck edge slip the first 19 sts. on to a spare needle, rejoin wool and k. to the end.

Now work on these 27 sts. to match first side.

The Back.—Work exactly as given for front until armhole shaping is completed and there are 72 sts., then continue in st.st. without shaping until work measures 18½ ins. from lower edge, ending with a row on the wrong side.

Shape Neck thus.—

Next row.—K. 17, turn, and leave remaining sts. on a spare needle. Now work in st.st. on these 17 sts., dec. 1 st. at neck edge in every row until 13 sts. remain.

Continue without shaping if necessary until work measures 19 ins. from lower edge, ending at armhole edge.

Shape Shoulder thus.—

Next row.—Cast off 6, work to the end.

Next row.—Work to the end.

Cast off remaining sts.

Return to sts. on spare needle and beginning at neck edge slip the first 39 sts. on to spare needle, rejoin wool and k. to the end.

Now work on these 17 sts. to match first side.

The Armhole bands.—With right side of work facing and using No. 9 needles and m. wool pick up and k. 61 sts. evenly along armhole edge.

Next row.—P. Now work the first five rows of the fair-isle patt. as given for the front.

Change to m. wool and p. 1 row.

Now change to No. 12 needles **and**

The pullover is in stocking stitch with a fair-isle band in three colours at the waist; a welt in plain coloured rib, and a narrow fair-isle band at the neck and armholes.

work in k. 1, p. 1 rib for 1 in.

Cast off loosely in rib.

Work remaining 3 armhole bands in the same way.

The Front Neck band.—With right side of work facing and using No. 9 needles and m. wool pick up and k. 27 sts. along neck edge beginning at shoulder, k. the 19 sts. from spare needle, then pick up and k. 27 sts. from other side of neck. (73 sts.)

Next row.—P. to the end.

Now work the first 5 rows of fair-isle patt. as given for the front.

Change to dk. wool and p. 1 row.

Change to No. 12 needles and work in k. 1, p. 1 rib for 1 in.

Cast off loosely in rib.

The Back Neck band.—With right side of work facing and using No. 9 needles and m. wool, begin at shoulder and pick up and k. 5 sts. along neck edge, then k. the 39 sts. from spare needle, then pick and k. 5 sts. along other side of neck. (49 sts.)

Next row.—P. to the end.

Now work the first 5 rows of fair-isle patt. as given for the front.

Change to dk. wool and p. 1 row.

Change to No. 12 needles and work in k. 1, p. 1 rib for 1 in.

Cast off loosely in rib.

Make-up.—Press pieces carefully with a hot iron and damp cloth.

Join side and shoulder seams.

Press seams.

TODDLER'S CARDIGAN

In Bands of Fair-Isle

MATERIALS

2 oz. 3-ply wool in white.
About ½ oz. each 3-ply wool in green, pink, blue and yellow.
2 No. 12 and 2 No. 10 knitting needles.
6 buttons.

MEASUREMENTS

Length, 11 ins.
Chest, 21 ins.
Sleeve, 8 ins.

TENSION

8 sts. to 1 in.

ABBREVIATIONS

K. knit, p. purl, st. stitch, tog. together, dec. decrease, inc. increase, rep. repeat, wh. white, pk. pink, bl. blue, gr. green, yl. yellow.

Begin at lower edge and with No. 12 needles and bl. wool cast on 168 sts. and work ½ in. in k. 1, p. 1 rib.

Now work a buttonhole thus :—

Next row.—Rib to the last 4 sts., cast-off 2, rib 2.

Next row.—Rib 2, cast on 2, rib to the end.

Continue in rib until work measures 1 in. from lower edge, ending at buttonhole edge if garment is for a girl or opposite end to buttonhole if for a boy.

Next row.—Slip the first 6 sts. on to a safety pin, k. with wh. wool to the last 6 sts., slip the last 6 sts., on to a safety pin and turn.

Next row.—Using wh. wool p. 77, p. twice in the next st., p. to the end.

Change to No. 10 needles and work in patt. on these 157 sts. thus :—

1st row.—K. * 1 gr., 3 wh., 1 gr., 1 wh., 1 gr., 2 wh., 1 gr., 3 wh., 1 gr., 3 wh., 1 gr., 2 wh., 1 gr., 1 wh., 1 gr., 3 wh., rep. from * to the last st., 1 gr.

2nd row.—P. 1 wh., * 2 wh., 1 gr., 1 wh., 1 gr., 6 wh., 1 gr., 1 wh., 1 gr., 6 wh., 1 gr., 1 wh., 1 gr., 3 wh., rep. from * to the end.

3rd row.—K. * (1 gr., 1 wh.) 4 times, (1 wh., 1 gr.) twice, 3 wh., (1 gr. 1 wh.) twice, 1 wh., (1 gr., 1 wh.) 3 times, rep. from * to the last st., * 1 gr.

4th row.—P. 1 wh., * 2 wh., 1 gr., 1 wh., 1 gr., 2 wh., 1 gr., 1 wh., 1 gr., 5 wh., 1 gr., 1 wh., 1 gr., 2 wh., 1 gr., 1 wh., 1 gr., 3 wh., rep. from * to the end.

5th row.—K. * 2 wh., 1 gr., 1 wh., 1 gr., 2 wh., (1 gr., 1 wh.) 7 times, 1 wh., (1 gr., 1 wh.) twice, rep. from * to the last st., 1 wh.

6th row.—P. 1 wh., * 1 gr., 6 wh., 1 gr., 1 wh., 1 gr., 5 wh., 1 gr., 1 wh., 1 gr., 6 wh., 1 gr., 1 wh., rep. from * to the end.

7th row.—K. * 1 gr., 3 wh., 1 gr., 2 wh., 1 gr., 1 wh., 1 gr., 3 wh., 1 gr., 3 wh., 1 gr., 1 wh., 1 gr., 2 wh., 1 gr., 3 wh., rep. from * to the last st., 1 gr.

8th row.—Break off gr. wool and p. wh. to the end.

9th row to 13th row.—K. bl.

14th row.—Break off bl. wool and p. wh. to the end.

15th row.—K. * 1 yl., 3 wh., 1 yl., 2 wh., 1 yl., 1 wh., 1 yl., 3 wh., 1 yl., 3 wh., 1 yl., 1 wh., 1 yl., 2 wh., 1 yl., 3 wh., rep. from * to the last st., 1 yl.

16th row.—P. * 1 wh., 1 yl., 6 wh., 1 yl., 1 wh., 1 yl., 5 wh., 1 yl., 1 wh., 1 yl., 6 wh., 1 yl., rep. from * to the last st., 1 wh.

17th row.—K. * 2 wh., 1 yl., 1 wh., 1 yl., 2 wh., (1 yl., 1 wh.) 7 times, 1 wh., (1 yl., 1 wh.) twice, rep. from * to the last st., 1 wh.

FOR THE TODDLER. *A lightweight cardigan will make a lovely gift for any small boy or girl. This charming little garment is knitted in bands of pastel shaded fair-isle on a white ground, separated with narrow bands of darker coloured wool.*

18th row.—P. 1 wh., * 2 wh., 1 yl., 1 wh., 1 yl., 2 wh., 1 yl., 1 wh., 1 yl., 5 wh., 1 yl., 1 wh., 1 yl., 2 wh., 1 yl., 1 wh., 1 yl., 3 wh., rep. from * to the end.

19th row.—K. * (1 yl., 1 wh.) 4 times, (1 wh., 1 yl.) twice, 3 wh., 1 yl., 1 wh., 1 yl., 2 wh., (1 yl., 1 wh.) 3 times, rep. from * to the last st., 1 yl.

20th row.—P. 1 wh., * 2 wh., 1 yl., 1 wh., 1 yl., 6 wh., 1 yl., 1 wh., 1 yl., 6 wh., 1 yl., 1 wh., 1 yl., 3 wh., rep. from * to the end.

21st row.—K. * 1 yl., 3 wh., 1 yl., 1 wh., 1 yl., 2 wh., 1 yl., 3 wh., 1 yl., 3 wh., 1 yl., 2 wh., 1 yl., 1 wh., 1 yl., 3 wh., rep. from * to the last st., 1 yl.

22nd row.—Break off yl. wool and p. wh. to the end.

23rd row to 27th row.—K. bl.

28th row.—Break off bl. wool and p.

wh. to the end.

Rep. rows 1 to 27 once more but working with pk. wool instead of gr. in rows 1 to 7, and working with gr. wool instead of yl. in rows 15 to 21.

Work should now measure about 7 ins.

Shape Armholes thus.—

Next row.—Using wh. wool, p. 36, cast off next 5 sts., p. 75 (including st. already on right hand needle after casting off), cast off next 5 sts., p. to the end.

The Right Front.—Work on this last set of 36 sts., keeping the continuity of the patt. beginning with the 1st patt. row but working with yl. wool instead of gr. and dec. 1 st. at armhole edge in every row until 31 sts. remain. Then continue without shaping working through the patt. and keeping the colour sequence with bl. bands in between until work measures 9½ ins. from lower edge, ending at front edge.

Shape Neck thus.—Keeping the continuity of the patt. cast off 4 sts. at beginning of next row, then dec. 1 st. at neck edge in every row until 18 sts. remain.

This summer-weight woollie has a round neck in ribbing, and it buttons right up the front. Oddments of pastel shaded wool can be used for the attractive fair-isle design.

Continue in patt. without shaping until work measures 11 ins. from lower edge, ending at armhole edge.

Shape Shoulder thus.—

Next row.—Cast off 6, work to the end.

Next row.—Work in patt. to the end.

Repeat these 2 rows once more.

Cast off remaining sts.

The Back.—Keeping the continuity of the patt., beginning with a row on the right side work on the centre set of sts. dec. 1 st. at both ends of every row until 65 sts. remain, then continue in patt. without shaping until work measures 11 ins. from lower edge.

Shape Shoulders thus.—Cast off 6 sts. at the beginning of the next 6 rows.

Cast off remaining sts.

The Left Front.—Work on the remaining 36 sts. to match first side.

The Sleeves.—Using No. 12 needles and bl. wool cast on 53 sts. and work 2 ins. in k. 1, p. 1 rib.

Next row.—K. wh. to the end.

Next row.—P. wh. to the end.

Change to No. 10 needles and work in patt. as given for main part of garment, inc. 1 st. at both ends of the 15th and every following 4th row until there are 61 sts., then continue without shaping until 2 complete patts. have been worked from lower edge, thus ending with bl. band following fair-isle patt. in gr.

Work should now measure about 8 ins.

Shape Top thus.—Keeping the continuity of the patt. dec. 1 st. at both ends of every row until 28 sts. remain.

Cast off 4 sts. at the beginning of the next 4 rows.

Cast off remaining sts.

The Front Borders.—Slip the 6 sts. of buttonhole border on to a No. 12 needle and, with bl. wool, continue in k. 1, p. 1 rib until work measures 1¾ ins. from cast off edge of first buttonhole, then work another buttonhole thus :—

Next row.—Rib 2, cast off next 2 sts., rib to the end.

Next row.—Rib 2, cast on 2 sts., rib to the end.

Continue in k. 1, p. 1 rib working further buttonholes at intervals of 1¾ ins. in the same way until there are 5 buttonholes altogether then work in rib until border measures same length as front when slightly stretched (about 9½ ins.), ending with a row on the wrong side.

Leave these 6 sts. on a safety pin.

Slip the 6 sts. of button border on to a No. 12 needle and with bl. wool work in k. 1, p. 1 rib until work measures same length as buttonhole border ending with a row on the wrong side.

Leave these sts. on a safety pin.

The Neck Border.—Join shoulder seams. With right side of work facing and using No. 12 needles and bl. wool rib the 6 sts. of right front border, pick up and k. 70 sts. evenly all round neck edge, then rib the 6 sts. of left front border.

Next row.—Rib to the end.

If the garment is for a girl work buttonhole thus :—

Next row.—Rib 2, cast off next 2 sts., rib to the end.

Next row.—Rib to the last 2 sts., cast on 2, rib 2.

If the garment is for a boy work buttonhole thus :—

Next row.—Rib to the last 4 sts., cast off next 2 sts., rib to the end.

Next row.—Rib 2, cast on 2, rib to the end.

Now continue in k. 1, p. 1 rib until work measures ¾ in.

Cast off loosely in rib.

Make-Up.—Press work lightly with a hot iron and damp cloth.

Join the side and sleeve seams and sew in the sleeves matching the seams to side seams.

Sew front borders to front edges.

Sew on the six buttons to match the buttonholes. Press seams.

OUTFIT FOR OUTINGS

Pram Coat with Hood Attached

MATERIALS

3 oz. 3-ply wool in main colour.
1 oz. 3-ply wool in 1st contrast.
1 oz. 3-ply wool in 2nd contrast.
1 oz. 3-ply wool in 3rd contrast.
2 No. 10 and 2 No. 12 knitting needles.
4 buttons.

MEASUREMENTS

The Coat.—Length 12 ins.
Chest 24 ins.
Sleeve 7½ ins.
The Hood.—Depth 6½ ins.
Width all round 13 ins.

TENSION

7½ sts. to 1 in.

ABBREVIATIONS

k. knit, p. purl, st. stitch, inc. increase, dec. decrease, tog. together, st.st. stocking st., g.st. garter st., wl. fwd. wool forward, wl. bk. wool back, c. contrast, mn. main, patt. pattern, sl. slip, beg. beginning, ins. inches, rep. repeat.

N.B.—These instructions give button-holes in right front for a girl. If garment is for a boy, buttonholes are worked in the same way but in left front.

THE COAT

The Back.—Using No. 10 needles and mn. wool cast on 90 sts. and work 2 rows in g.st. (every row k.).

Now work in patt. thus :—
With 1st c. work 2 rows in g.st.
With mn. work 2 rows in g.st.
With 2nd c. work 2 rows in g.st.
With mn. work 2 rows in g.st.
With 3rd c. work 2 rows in g.st.
With mn. work 12 rows in st.st. (1 row k., 1 row p.).

These 22 rows form the patt.

Continue in patt. until work measures about 8 ins., ending with 2 rows in g.st. with 3rd c.

Shape Armholes thus.—Keeping continuity of patt. cast off 3 sts. at beg. of next 2 rows, then dec. 1 st. both ends of every row until 74 sts. remain.

Continue in patt. without shaping until work measures 12 ins. from cast on edge.

Shape Shoulders thus.—Cast off 8 sts. at beg. of next 6 rows.

Cast off remaining sts.

The Right Front.—Using No. 10 needles and mn. wool cast on 48 sts. and work 2 rows in g.st.

Next row.—Sl. first 6 sts., with 1st c. k. to end.

Next row.—With 1st c. k. to last 6 sts., sl. 6.

With mn. work 2 rows in g.st.

Next row.—Sl. first 6 sts., with 2nd c. k. to end.

Next row.—With 2nd c. k. to last 6 sts., sl. 6.

With mn. work 2 rows in g.st.

Next row.—Sl. first 6 sts., with 3rd c. k. to end.

Next row.—With 3rd c. k. to last 6 sts., sl. 6.

Now work in patt. thus :—

1st row.—With mn. k. to end.

2nd row.—With mn. p. to last 6 sts., k. 6.

Rep. these 2 rows 5 times more.

13th row.—Sl. 6, with 1st c. k. 5, sl. 8, k. to end.

14th row.—With 1st c. k. 29, wl. fwd., sl. 8, wl. bk., k. 5, wl. fwd., sl. 6.

15th row.—With mn. k. to end.

FOR BABY AGAIN. *In palest blue, this delightful little pram set will make a perfect gift for a baby girl or boy. The edge of the hood and coat borders are in garter stitch, and the narrow plain panels on the coat and round the bonnet are attractively decorated with " lazy daisy " embroidery.*

16th row.—With mn. k. 29, p. 8, k. to end.

17th row.—Sl. 6, with 2nd c. k. 5, sl. 8, k. to end.

18th row.—With 2nd c. k. 29, wl. fwd., sl. 8, wl. bk., k. 5, wl. fwd., sl. 6.

19th and 20th rows.—As 15th and 16th rows.

21st row.—Sl. 6, with 3rd c. k. 5, sl. 8, k. to end.

22nd row.—With 3rd c. k. 29, wl. fwd., sl. 8, wl. bk., k. 5, wl. fwd., sl. 6.

These 22 rows form patt.

Continue patt. until work measures about 4½ ins. from cast-on edge, ending at front edge (g.st. border in mn. colour) and so that the next row will be worked in mn. colour and not a c. Now work a buttonhole thus :—

Next row.—K. 2, cast off nest 2 sts., patt. to end.

Next row.—Work to last 2 sts., cast on 2, k. 2.

Work 3 more buttonholes in the same

way at intervals of 2 ins. from cast-off edge of previous buttonhole.

Continue in patt. with buttonholes in front border until work measures about 8 ins., ending at side edge with 1st patt. row.

Shape Armhole thus.—Cast off 3 sts. at beg. of next row, then dec. 1 st. at armhole edge in every row until 40 sts. remain.

Continue in patt. without shaping until work measures 10½ ins. from cast-on edge, ending at front edge. (4th buttonhole should now be completed.)

Shape Neck.—Keeping continuity of patt. cast off 8 sts. at beg. of next row, then dec. 1 st. at neck edge in every row until 24 sts. remain.

Continue without shaping until work measures 12 ins. from cast-on edge, ending at armhole edge.

Shape Shoulder thus.—

Next row.—Cast off 8, work to end.
Next row.—Work to end.
Rep. these 2 rows once more.
Cast off remaining sts.

The Left Front.—Using No. 10 needles and mn. wool cast on 48 sts. and work 2 rows in g.st.

Next row.—With 1st c. k. to last 6 sts., turn.
Next row.—With 1st c. k. to end.
With mn. work 2 rows in g.st.
Next row.—With 2nd c. k. to last 6 sts., turn.
Next row.—With 2nd c. k. to end.
With mn. work 2 rows in g.st.
Next row.—With 3rd c. k. to last 6 sts., turn.
Next row.—With 3rd c. k. to end.
Now work in patt. thus :—
1st row.—With mn. k. to end.
2nd row.—With mn. k. 6, p. to end.
Rep. these 2 rows 5 times more.
13th row.—With 1st c. k. 29, sl. 8, k. 5, turn.
14th row.—With 1st c. k. 5, wl. fwd., sl. 8, wl. bk., k. to end.

15th row.—With mn. k. to end.
16th row.—With mn. k. 11, p. 8, k. to end.
17th row.—With 2nd c. k. 29, sl. 8, k. 5, turn.
18th row.—With 2nd c. k. 5, wl. fwd, sl. 8, wl. bk., k. to end.
19th and 20th rows.—As 15th and 16th rows.
21st row.—With 3rd c. k. 29, sl. 8, k. 5, turn.
22nd row.—With 3rd c. k. 5, wl. fwd., sl. 8, wl. bk., k. to end.

These 22 rows form the patt.

Continue in patt. (with buttonholes in front border if garment is for a boy) until work measures about 8 ins. from cast-on edge, ending at side edge with a 22nd patt. row.

Shape armhole and complete as given for right front.

The Sleeves.—Using No. 12 needles and mn. wool cast on 40 sts. and work 2 rows in g.st.

With 1st c. work 2 rows in g.st.
With mn. work 2 rows in g.st.
With 2nd c. work 2 rows in g.st.
With mn. work 2 rows in g.st.
With 3rd. c. work 2 rows in g.st.
Change to mn.

Next row.—* k. 3, k. twice in next st., rep. from * to end. (50 sts.)
Next row.—P. to end.
Now work 10 rows in st.st.

Change to No. 10 needles and work in patt. as given for back, inc. 1 st. both ends of the next and every following 4th row until there are 62 sts.

Then continue without shaping until work measures about 7½ ins. from cast-on edge, ending with 2 rows in g.st. with 3rd c.

Shape Top thus.—Keeping the continuity of the patt. dec. 1 st. both ends of every row until 54 sts. remain.

Now dec. 1 st. both ends of every 4th row until 42 sts. remain. Continue with mn. wool and cast off 4 sts. at the beg.

The hood of this pram set is attached to the coat with a narrow band of ribbing which helps it to fit snugly. The coat buttons right up to the neck.

of next 4 rows.   Cast off remaining sts.

THE HOOD

Join shoulder seams.

Using No. 12 needles and mn. wool and with right side of work facing pick up and k. 61 sts. evenly round neck edge, omitting front border sts. at each end.

Next row.—K. 6, * p. 1, k. 1., rep. from * to last 7 sts., p. 1, k. 6.

Next row.—K. 6, * k. 1, p. 1., rep. from * to last 7 sts., k. 7.

Rep. these 2 rows until work measures 1 in., ending with a row on wrong side.

Next row.—K. 6 (k. twice in next st., k. 1) 6 times, (k. twice in next st.) 25 times, (k. 1, k. twice in next st.) 6 times, k. 6.   (98 sts.)

Next row.—K. 6, p. to last 6 sts., k. 6.

Change to No. 10 needles and work in patt. thus :—

1st row.—Sl. 6, with 1st c. k. 5, sl. 8, k. to last 19 sts., sl. 8, k. 5, turn.

2nd row.—With 1st c. k. 5, wl. fwd., sl. 8, wl. bk., k. to last 19 sts., wl. fwd., sl. 8, wl. bk., k. 5, wl. fwd., sl. 6.

3rd row.—With mn. k. to end.

4th row.—With mn. k. 11, p. 8, k. to last 19 sts., p. 8, k. 11.

5th row.—As 1st row but with 2nd c.

6th row.—As 2nd row but using 2nd c.

7th and 8th rows.—As 3rd and 4th rows.

9th row.—As 1st row but with 3rd c.

10th row.—As 2nd row but with 3rd c.

11th row.—With mn. k. to end.

12th row.—With mn. k. 6, p. to last 6 sts., k. 6.

Rep. last 2 rows 5 times more.

These 22 rows form patt.

Continue in patt. until hood measures about $7\frac{1}{2}$ ins. from commencement, ending with a 10th patt. row.

Cast off.

Make-up.—Press pieces lightly with a hot iron and damp cloth.

Join the side and the sleeve seams and sew in the sleeves with the seams to the side seams.

Join hood seam at top.

Sew on the buttons to match the buttonholes.

Press seams.

Work a little simple " lazy daisy " embroidery with the contrast coloured wools, in the plain panels, at each side front of the coat and round the hood as shown in the illustration at top left of this page.

GIFTS TO MATCH

Cycle Bag, School Satchel, Tennis Hold-all

CYCLE BAG
MATERIALS

1 piece strong canvas, 29 ins. by 12 ins.
1 piece strong canvas, 15½ ins. by
6½ ins. (or both can be cut from
1 piece, 36 ins. by 15½ ins.).
4 yds. 1-in. strong binding.
Two 9-in. straps.
Three 6-in. straps.
10 ins. of ¾-in. iron strap.
2 buckles.

Method.—Cut the 3 pieces of canvas
as in Diagram 1 below. The corners are
radius 2 ins. Cut each 9-in. strap into
2 pieces, the buckle end being 3 ins. long.
Stitch on the buckles, using the same

stitch as for the Tennis Racquet Hold-all
on the next page, and in position as in
Diagram 1. Stitch on a piece of leather
cut as in Diagram 2, 13 ins. from the
flap, and centrally (see also Diagram 1),
This leather has slits cut in it to take a
6-in. strap which is needed to fasten the
bag to the seat pinion.

Machine on the two sides starting
from the flap. Don't forget to nick the
rounded corners to facilitate the work.
The Binding.—Commence as follows :—
With the edge marked A in Diagram 3.
Then from point B go along the side,
then the flap.

A join is made somewhere on the way

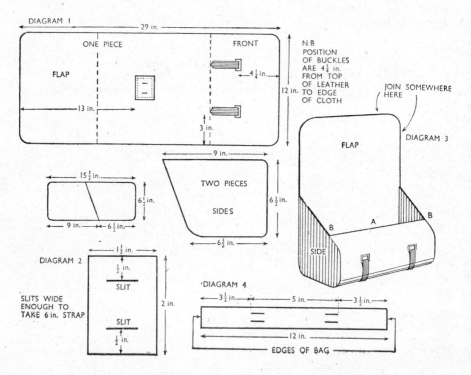

FOR THE SCHOOLGIRL. *A gift that cannot fail to please is this practical school set consisting of a tennis racquet hold-all, cycle tool bag, and satchel. They are made in strong material, bound with leather, and finished with leather straps.*

as two starts are made, both at points B.

Stitch on the straps to the flap.

Machine or hand-stitch a piece of very strong material, 11 ins. by 1½ ins. (such as leather) 7 ins. from the flap and on top. This is to form the pocket for the 10-in. iron bar which keeps the bag rigid. The bar may be put into the pocket and closed up with stitching.

Four slits are made in the leather as shown in Diagram 4 to take 2 straps which are used to suspend the bag. The straps should go under the iron bar.

TENNIS HOLD-ALL

MATERIALS

1 piece strong canvas, 27 ins. by 36 ins.

Gusset, 46 ins. long by 3½ ins. wide (2 pieces may be joined).

1 attaché case handle (with ⅝-in. rivets).

Three 9-in. straps and buckles.

26 ins. of ¾-in. strap iron.

5 yds. 1-in. strong binding.

Method.—Cut out the pieces of canvas as shown in Diagram 1. The rounded

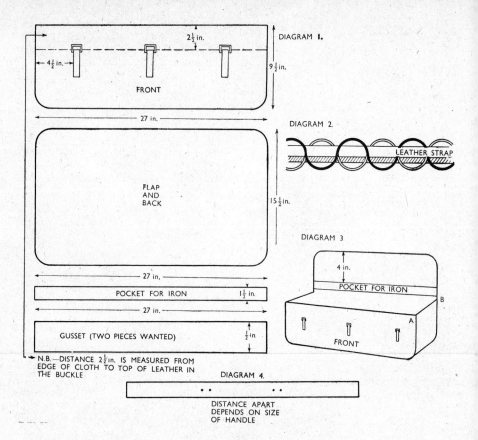

DIAGRAM I.

2½ in.

4½ in.

FRONT

9½ in.

27 in.

DIAGRAM 2.

LEATHER STRAP

FLAP
AND
BACK

15½ in.

DIAGRAM 3

4 in.

27 in.

POCKET FOR IRON

1½ in.

POCKET FOR IRON

B

27 in.

A

GUSSET (TWO PIECES WANTED)

½ in.

FRONT

N.B.—DISTANCE 2½ in. IS MEASURED FROM
EDGE OF CLOTH TO TOP OF LEATHER IN
THE BUCKLE

DIAGRAM 4.

DISTANCE APART
DEPENDS ON SIZE
OF HANDLE

corners are all radius 2 ins. Cut each 9-in. strap into 2 pieces, the buckle end 3 ins.

Fix the buckles on the front first (positions are indicated in Diagram 1 shown above). The method of stitching is shown in Diagram 2 and is the usual way of stitching except the stitches must be worked back through the same holes. Make the holes for the stitches first. A stitch-marker is useful but, if one is not obtainable, an old clock wheel would do, or failing that, use a ruler and sharp point. A brown waxed thread should be used for the stitching.

Having attached the buckles, machine on the gusset, which should be about 45 ins. long ; two pieces joined together will do if only one yard of material is bought. Machining round corners is simplified by cutting 4 or 5 little nicks in the rounded edge.

Having joined all pieces, machine inside the flap the 1½-in. wide strip to form the pocket containing the iron bar which keeps the hold-all rigid. Leave one end open, as in Diagram 3. Also machine on the outside of the flap a piece of leather (3 ins. by 1½ ins.) at each end of the pocket to strengthen it, and to prevent the iron bar wearing through the hold-all.

The Binding.—Starting from point A, do the side, bottom and side of the front, then from point B, do the gusset, top of front and the other gusset, and the edges of the back and flap, leaving one end of the pocket for the iron, open.

Now stitch on to the flap the other parts of the straps.

The Handle.—4 holes, wide enough to take the $\frac{5}{8}$-in. rivets, are drilled in the bar of strap iron, Diagram 4. The holes are in the centre of the bar and the distance apart is determined by the size of the handle bought.

Push the bar into the pocket and then, with a sharp pointed instrument (such as an awl) make holes in the cloth to correspond with the holes in the bar. Now attach the handle.

Finally finish binding the open end of the pocket as neatly as possible.

SCHOOL SATCHEL
MATERIALS

30 ins. by 14¼ ins. strong canvas.
10 ft. of 1-in. binding.
One 42-in. strap.
Two 9-in. straps.

Method.—Cut out pieces according to the pattern. Cut each of the 9-in. straps into 2 pieces, the buckle ends being 3 ins. Sew these latter pieces on the pocket, Diagram 1 shown below. The edges of the pocket can now be bound and then machined or sewn on to the front as in Diagram 1.

Now join the front and gusset, follow by putting on the back. It will be found easier, when machining or binding the

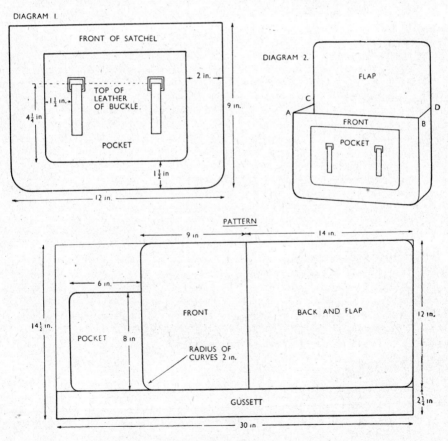

DIAGRAM 1.

FRONT OF SATCHEL

TOP OF LEATHER OF BUCKLE.

POCKET

2 in.

1½ in.

9 in.

4¼ in.

1½ in.

12 in.

DIAGRAM 2.

FLAP

FRONT

POCKET

C

A

D

B

PATTERN

9 in

14 in.

6 in.

FRONT

BACK AND FLAP

12 in.

14½ in.

POCKET

8 in

RADIUS OF CURVES 2 in.

GUSSETT

2¼ in

30 in

edges of the gusset, to have the gusset uppermost, and cut 4 or 5 nicks in the rounded corners when machining the gusset. This makes the machining of the corners easier.

Binding.—See Diagram 2, commence by binding A to B, then join C to D via the side of gusset, side and bottom of front, then to B and D. Finish by binding the back.

Now sew the straps on to the flap and, when this has been done, cut the 42-in. strap into 12 ins. and 30-in. lengths, the smaller piece being used for the buckle end. Sew these pieces carefully on to the sides of the gusset.

LEATHER CASE

To Hold Small Mirror and Comb

MATERIALS

9½ ins. by 5½ ins. leather or two similar size pieces of skiver.

2½ ins. by 2 ins. leather or two similar size pieces of skiver.

1 yd. thonging (see note 2 below).

Mirror 5 ins. by 3 ins. (if backed, another piece of skiver or leather 6 ins. by 4 ins.).

Comb, 5 ins.

Gum.

Punch to make slits for thongs.

N.B.—(1) If the case is to be made of skiver, it is necessary to use the material double, by gumming two pieces together.

(2) The case may be machine-stitched instead of thonged.

(3) The punch makes three slits at once.

(4) Plastic thonging is quite suitable and can be obtained in all colours.

Method.—Turn over 2½ ins. of leather one end and 1½ ins. the other end of the larger piece of leather to form the pockets, Diagram 1. Gum down the two side edges of the pockets and leave under pressure for a few hours.

The Thonging.—The punch has three prongs which make the slits, and these

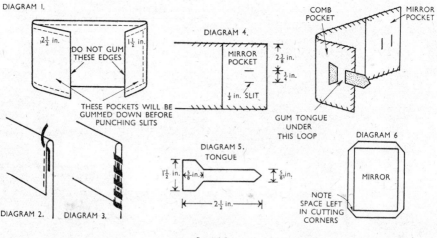

DIAGRAM 1.

2½ in. | DO NOT GUM THESE EDGES | 1½ in.

THESE POCKETS WILL BE GUMMED DOWN BEFORE PUNCHING SLITS

DIAGRAM 2. | DIAGRAM 3.

DIAGRAM 4.

MIRROR POCKET

2⅜ in.

¾ in.

½ in. SLIT

DIAGRAM 5.

TONGUE

1½ in. | ⅝ in.

⅝ in.

2½ in.

COMB POCKET | MIRROR POCKET

GUM TONGUE UNDER THIS LOOP

DIAGRAM 6

MIRROR

NOTE SPACE LEFT IN CUTTING CORNERS

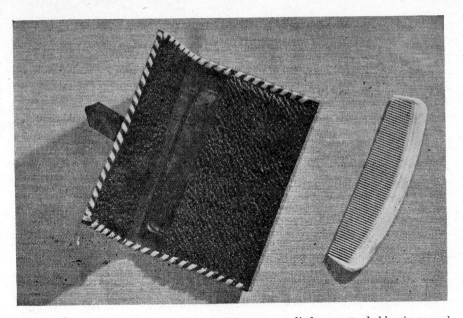

FOR THE SCHOOLGIRL AGAIN. *This compact little case to hold mirror and comb will delight the heart of a small girl. It is in dark brown leather and the seams are thonged with light tan leather which adds a neat finishing touch.*

are punched all round the edges of the case, as Diagram 1. Punch the first three holes then, in punching the next three, place one prong of the punch in a slit already cut, this ensures correct spacing and helps to keep the line of slits straight. The slits should be a thong's width from the edge. If leather thongs are used, it is helpful to slightly wax them before starting to thong.

Now carefully prise open the leather for about three slits' length, then thread the thong through, leaving about $\frac{3}{4}$ in. *between* the two layers of leather, as shown in Diagram 2. When work is commenced, the loose end is bound tightly down by the loops, Diagram 3. **Finish.**—This is starting in reverse. Prise the leather open for the last three holes, then thread the thong under the last three loops and gradually tighten so that the thong is pressed down.

Snip off the thong as closely as possible

to the loop with a pair of scissors. **To Fasten the Case.**—Cut two $\frac{1}{2}$ in. slits in the mirror pocket, Diagram 4, but before cutting, slip a piece of tin in the pocket to prevent the knife going through to the other side of the case. Now cut a strip of leather $\frac{1}{2}$ in. wide and about 2 ins. long. Thread this strip through the slits and gum down the ends inside the pocket.

A tongue of leather is fastened to the other pocket, Diagram 5. Two slots are cut on the outside of the comb pocket. Thread the tongue through and gum into place, Diagram 5.

The mirror may be backed with a piece of leather cut $\frac{1}{2}$ in. bigger all round. Gum the leather, place on mirror and cut the corners as in Diagram 6. Turn over the edges and press flat. Leave for a few hours to dry.

When ready trim the edges down to $\frac{1}{4}$ in. wide. Polish the leather.

PENCIL BOX

With Two Compartments

MATERIALS

Hardwood, all planed to given sizes, and $\frac{1}{4}$ in. thick.

2 pieces $10\frac{1}{4}$ ins. by $1\frac{1}{8}$ ins. for sides.

1 piece $9\frac{1}{2}$ ins. by $1\frac{1}{8}$ ins. for ends and division.

2 pieces $10\frac{1}{4}$ ins. by $3\frac{1}{8}$ ins. for top and bottom.

2 brass hinges $\frac{3}{4}$ in. long and $\frac{1}{4}$ in. wide.

Method.—Place the two side pieces together in the vice and mark out the position of the shoulder lines of the joints and also the position of the division to the measurements shown in the diagram on the opposite page.

Remove from the vice and square the

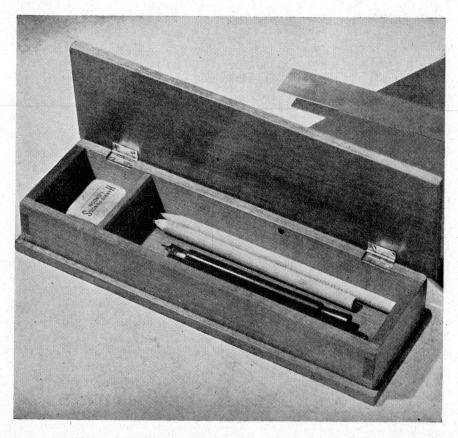

FOR THE 10-TO-12 YEAR-OLD. *An extremely practical and delightful little gift is this smart-looking polished wood pencil box. It is divided into two compartments, one for a rubber and the other for pens and pencils.*

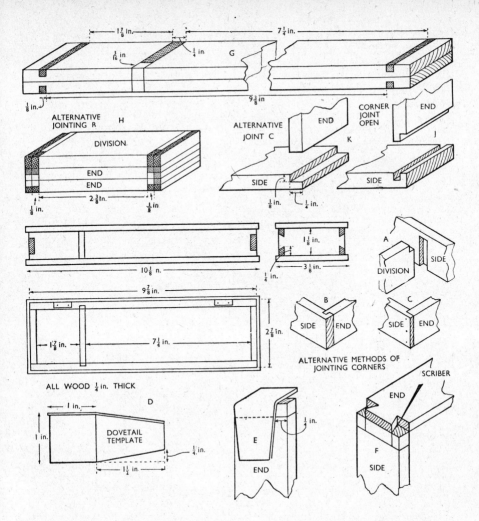

shoulder lines round on to both faces. Cut the other piece into three equal parts and place them in the vice together as before.

Square off the shoulder line across all three pieces, remove from the vice and square the lines round on to the faces of each piece. Make a dovetail template from a piece of metal $2\frac{1}{2}$ ins. by 1 in. and cut to the shape shown in the figure D, in diagram above, and bend it over at right angles at the dotted line. Place one end piece upright in the vice and using the template mark out the shape of the dovetail as in the figure E.

Saw down the lines and saw off square at the shoulders to complete the tails. Place the side upright in the vice and place the tail in position on top as shown in the figure F. Mark round the tail carefully with a sharp point. Continue these lines down to the shoulder line on the side and saw carefully to the line. Chop out the waste with a chisel and fit the joint.

Saw and chisel the stopped groove for the division and cut the division piece to fit. Glasspaper the inside of the box, glue the joints in place and allow to set, making certain that the box is square before leaving.

Finish.—When dry, clean up the outside of the box and pin- or screw the bottom in place leaving $\frac{1}{8}$ in. projecting all round the box. Fit the two hinges to the top. Glasspaper thoroughly and give it a coat of brush polish. When dry glasspaper lightly and finish with a good wax polish.

ALTERNATIVE JOINTS

Joint B.—Place the two side pieces in the vice together and mark out as shown in the figure G. Remove from vice and square the lines round on to the faces of the wood. Gauge the depth of the grooves $\frac{1}{8}$ in. and saw and chisel the grooves. Place the end pieces together in the vice and mark out as shown in the figure H. Remove and square the lines round as before. Gauge the tongues to fit the groove already cut in the sides and saw out the waste. Finish off as for the dovetailed box.

Joint C.—Mark out together as for the above joints as shown in figure K, sawing out the rebate at each end. The lengths of the end pieces in this case will be $2\frac{5}{8}$ ins. Finish as before and glue and pin the joints with fine panel pins.

CHILD'S DESK

With Sloping Hinged Lid

MATERIALS
Wood Required
3 pieces, 16 ins. by 6 ins. by $\frac{1}{2}$ in.

2 pieces, 17 ins. by 6 ins. by $\frac{1}{2}$ in.

2 pieces, 11 ins. by 6 ins. by $\frac{1}{2}$ in.

1 piece, 16 ins. by $3\frac{3}{4}$ ins. by $\frac{1}{2}$ in.

1 piece, 17 ins. by 4 ins. by $\frac{1}{2}$ in.

2 pieces, 8 ins. by 2 ins. by $\frac{1}{2}$ in.

4 legs, 20 ins. by 2 ins. by 1 in.

2 rails, $12\frac{1}{4}$ ins. by 2 ins. by 1 in.

Four 4-in. shelf brackets.

1 pair of 2-in. brass hinges.

$1\frac{1}{4}$-in. panel pins.

N.B.—Total amount of 6-in. wood required is 12 ft. 18 ft. of 4-in. wood could be used instead.

Method.—The two sides are prepared as in Diagram 1. The back, 16 ins. by 6 ins., the front, 16 ins. by $3\frac{3}{4}$ ins. ; and the base, 2 pieces, 16 ins. by 6 ins., are also prepared. Before assembling, it is advisable to clean up the faces of the wood which will form the inside of the desk, as they will be awkward to get at when the desk has been assembled.

First glue and nail the front and back to the sides using $1\frac{1}{4}$-in. panel pins, then add the two base boards. Note that the front needs to be chamfered to the same angle as the slope of the sides, Diagram 2. While the glue is setting, make the top and lid.

The Top measures 17 ins. by 4 ins. Prepare this top as in Diagram 3. The well for pens, pencils and so on, is a shallow groove that is hollowed out with a broad "outside ground" gouge. Glasspaper this groove thoroughly.

When finished, glue and nail this top to the frame of the desk, leaving a $\frac{1}{2}$-in. overlap.

The Lid.—The size of the lid should be found by laying the two boards on the desk, and marking to size, allowing for $\frac{1}{2}$-in. overlap all round. The two pieces are held together on under side of lid by two 8-in. battens as shown in Diagram 4. Round the overlapping edges of the lid, and also the two front corners, see

FOR THE SCHOOLGIRL OR BOY. *To have a desk at home, of one's very own, is the ambition of every small girl and boy. There is plenty of room in this neat little desk which is fitted with two ink wells, and a well for pens and pencils.*

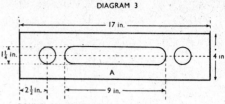

DIAGRAM I.

← 3 in →

6 in.

SIDE

3¾ in.

11 in.

DIAGRAM 3

← 17 in. →

1¼ in.

A

4 in

← 2½ in. →

← 9 in. →

ROUND ALL EDGES EXCEPT THE ONE MARKED "A"

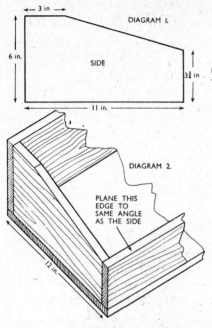

DIAGRAM 2.

PLANE THIS EDGE TO SAME ANGLE AS THE SIDE

12 in.

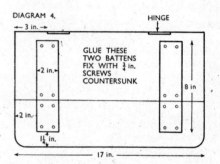

DIAGRAM 4.

← 3 in. →

HINGE

2 in.

GLUE THESE TWO BATTENS FIX WITH ¾ in. SCREWS COUNTERSUNK

8 in

2 in.

1¼ in.

← 17 in. →

Diagram 4.

Attach the lid to the top with a pair of 2-in. brass hinges.

The Legs.—Make two pairs of legs as in Diagram 5. When the rail has been joined to the legs (glue and nail), there is ⅛-in. overlap at each end. This overlap is planed off when the glue has set. The legs are attached to the desk by four 4 in. by 3 in. shelf brackets as shown in Diagram 6, thus being detachable when necessary. For a more permanent fixing, another rail should be added to join the two side rails in the centre. The joint is similar to that in Diagram 5.

Finish.—Punch in all nails, and fill cavities with plastic wood. Give the outside of the desk a coating of filler. Clean off, brush over a coat of glue size, and when hard, rub over with a fine sandpaper. Lastly, give the outside two coats of a good quality paint.

A length of chain may be fixed inside, from lid to front, to prevent the lid from falling backwards.

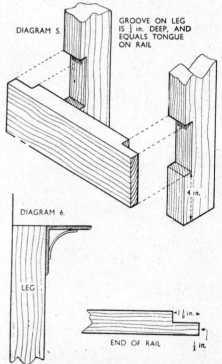

DIAGRAM 5.

GROOVE ON LEG IS ½ in. DEEP, AND EQUALS TONGUE ON RAIL

4 in.

DIAGRAM 6.

LEG

END OF RAIL

← 1⅛ in. →

½ in.

PUZZLES AND GAMES

Ring Board, Marble Board and Puzzle Cube

RING BOARD

MATERIALS

12-in. square of $\frac{1}{2}$ in. wood (or 3-ply).

4 pieces 12$\frac{1}{2}$ ins. by 1$\frac{1}{4}$ ins. by $\frac{3}{4}$ in.

9 dresser hooks (L type).

1 in. panel pins.

N.B.—If a 12-in. square of wood cannot be obtained, a frame is made, on which pieces of 12 in. wood, or a square of 3-ply is fixed.

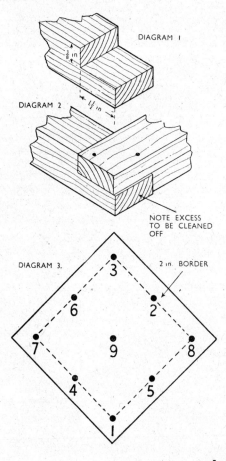

DIAGRAM I

DIAGRAM 2

NOTE EXCESS
TO BE CLEANED
OFF

DIAGRAM 3.

2 in. BORDER

Method.—The Frame.—Cut two 12$\frac{1}{2}$ in. pieces of wood as shown in Diagram 1 on the left. Try to remove the waste wood completely with a tenon saw. Fit these two ends as in Diagram 2. Remove any superfluous wood in the joint, and do the other three corners likewise.

Before gluing up, have the wood for the face (or the 3-ply) ready at hand.

Now glue and pin one corner, getting it square. Proceed with the other corners, keeping them square also. Finally glue and pin on the face and leave under a weight to dry.

Finish.—When ready, square and clean up corners with a finely set smoothing plane and mark holes for the hooks as in Diagram 3. If a 3-ply face be used, glue three strips of $\frac{3}{4}$ in. by $\frac{1}{2}$ in. wood at the back so that the hooks will hold. Fix in a screw eye for hanging the board. Remove hooks and rub over the wood with a medium, then fine, glasspaper. Coat the surface with glue size (to render the wood non-porous). When dry, rub over with fine glasspaper, then paint, using a light colour.

When dry, paint circles round the hooks, adding the numbers later (see Diagram 3). Replace hooks.

MARBLE BOARD

MATERIALS

Hardwood, 1 piece 15 ins. by 6$\frac{3}{4}$ ins. by $\frac{1}{4}$ in. for the base.

2 pieces 15 ins. by $\frac{3}{4}$ in. by $\frac{1}{4}$ in. for the sides.

1 piece 6$\frac{3}{4}$ ins. by $\frac{3}{4}$ in. by $\frac{1}{4}$ in. for the end.

1 piece 9 ins. by $\frac{5}{8}$ in. by $\frac{1}{4}$ in. for the divisions.

BOYS OR GIRLS *will get lots of enjoyment from these three jolly indoor games ; a gaily coloured ring board ; an intriguing and unusual puzzle cube played with small wooden blocks, and a marble board.*

1 piece 6¾ ins. by ¾ in. by ¾ in. for the foot.

27 panel pins 1 in. long.

Method.—Plane up the wood to the given sizes. Cut the mitre at 45 degrees at the ends of the sides and end and screw or pin them in position around the edge of baseboard from underneath.

Saw up the piece for the divisions into 2-in. lengths, shape one end of each with the chisel as shown in the diagram at the top of the next page, and pin or screw

them in position from underneath. It is easier if the pieces are glasspapered, given a coat of brush polish and then lightly glasspapered and waxed, finally fitting together (but the faces to be glued must be kept free from polish or wax.)

The panel pins are then driven into the baseboard in the positions indicated in the diagram and the divisions are numbered.

Plane up the foot so that it stands firmly and screw or pin it in position.

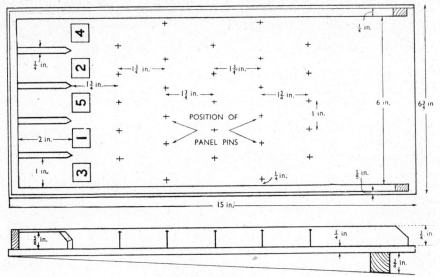

SECTION OF BOARD

Marbles are allowed to roll down from the back of the board.

PUZZLE CUBE

MATERIALS

Odd scraps of hardwood.

Method.—No dimensions have been shown on the diagram below as the cube may be made of any size although a cube 3 ins. each way will be found convenient so that all the pieces can be made from wood 1 in. thick.

Plane up the wood accurately to thickness and square off the edges. Set out each piece carefully with knife and try-square and saw and plane exactly to your marks. Make one each of the pieces marked A, C, E, F, H.

Make three pieces marked B, D, G.

Finish.—Glasspaper all the surfaces and give the pieces a coat of polish. When dry, glasspaper lightly and rub over with a little wax polish.

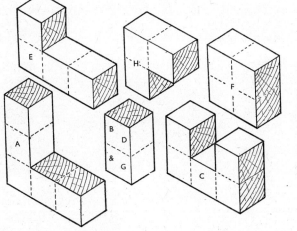

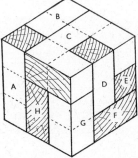

FOR THE SCHOOLBOY. *This realistic looking toy crane will delight any small boy. It has a roofed cabin which swivels easily on a square base. The boy is turning the winder which moves the crane up and down, and the lower winder is used for lifting.*

MINIATURE CRANE

With Cab and Wheeled Base

MATERIALS

Roof and floor : 12 ins. by 6 ins. by ½ in.

2 sides and back : 14 ins. by 6 ins. ply.

2 pieces : 4½ ins. by ⅜ in. by ⅜ in.

2 pieces : 3½ ins. by ⅜ in. by ⅜ in.

The Base

1 piece : 8 ins. by 5½ ins. by ½ in.

1 piece : 9 ins. by 2 ins. by ¾ in.

The Arm

3 ft. of ½ in. by ½ in.

1 pulley.

18 ins. of ⅛-in. rod (or 2 Meccano winders).

One 2½-in. bolt with 3 washers.

Method.—The crane is made in 3 parts—cab, base and arm.

The Cab.—From the ½-in. wood, prepare the roof, 5 ins. by 5 ins., and the floor, 6 ins. by 4 ins.

Cut the ply into 2 sides 6 ins. by 4½ ins. and 1 back 4 ins. by 4 ins. Round the top edges of the roof with a small plane and glasspaper.

Cut 2 windows out of each side with a fretsaw, Diagram 1. Smooth the edges with a rasp and paper. Glue and pin the cab together as in Diagram 2.

It is best to commence by fastening the roof to the 4½-in. pieces (note overlap for roof). Then pin and glue the other two 3½-in. pieces on the insides of the ply sides, so that the back may be fastened on to these.

Now join the roof and sides, then the base and the back. Set aside to dry.

The Base.—Cut the ¾-in. wood into three pieces ; two of them 6 ins. by 1 in., and the third, 3 ins. by 2 ins. Screw the 6-in. pieces under the baseboard as in Diagram 3. The wheels will be attached to the ends of these

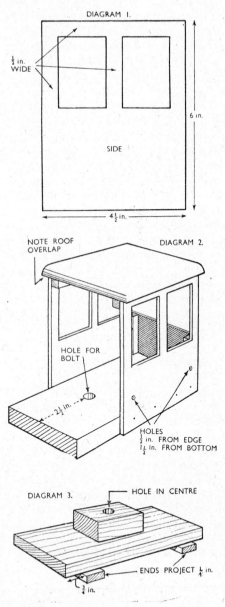

DIAGRAM 1.

¼ in. WIDE

SIDE

6 in.

4½ in.

NOTE ROOF OVERLAP

DIAGRAM 2.

HOLE FOR BOLT

2½ in.

HOLES ½ in. FROM EDGE 1½ in. FROM BOTTOM

DIAGRAM 3.

HOLE IN CENTRE

ENDS PROJECT ¼ in.

¾ in.

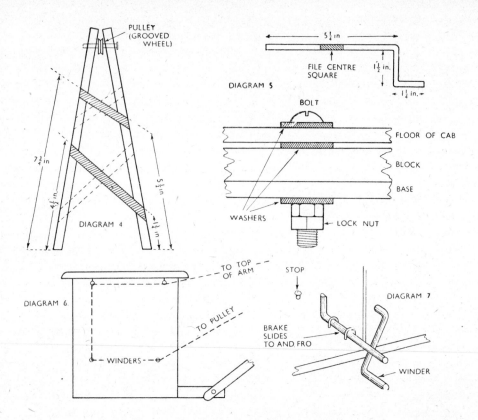

PULLEY (GROOVED WHEEL)

$7\frac{3}{4}$ in

$4\frac{1}{2}$ in.

$5\frac{1}{2}$ in.

$4\frac{1}{2}$ in.

DIAGRAM 4

$5\frac{1}{4}$ in

FILE CENTRE SQUARE

$1\frac{1}{2}$ in.

$1\frac{1}{4}$ in.

DIAGRAM 5

BOLT

FLOOR OF CAB

BLOCK

BASE

WASHERS

LOCK NUT

DIAGRAM 6

TO TOP OF ARM

TO PULLEY

WINDERS

STOP

BRAKE SLIDES TO AND FRO

DIAGRAM 7

WINDER

pieces. Then glue and nail from underneath the 3 in. by 2 in. in the centre of the baseboard, Diagram 3. The cab will swivel on this piece. Drive the nails in, leaving the centre free for a hole. **The Arm.**—Cut the 3-ft. length into two 12-in. pieces, and two pieces 6 ins. long. Cut these 6-in. pieces down the middle. The resulting slats are the girders for the arm.

Glue and pin ($\frac{1}{2}$-in. pins) as shown in Diagram 4. A nail cut to length, or a short Meccano spindle, will do as an axle for the pulley. Bore a hole to take this axle, the ends of which are burred over to prevent it from falling out. **Assembling.**—The front of the floor of the cab must be tapered so that the arm may be screwed on. The arm should move easily up and down.

The Winders are either made or bought (Meccano). Two 8-in. pieces of rod are cut and bent in the form shown in Diagram 5. One is used for moving the arm up and down and the other for lifting loads. File the centres of the winders square, so that the cord will grip when tied. Make holes in the sides as shown in Diagram 2 to take winders, which are prevented from coming out by a Meccano spring clip or a pin through a hole in the winder.

Mounting Cab on Base.—Bore a hole to take the $2\frac{1}{2}$-in. bolt in the centre of the block and base as shown in Diagram 3. Bore a similar hole in the floor of the cab as shown in Diagram 2. Now bolt the cab and base together as in Diagram 5.

The cab should move easily on the

block. Screw on the four wheels.

The arm is moved by the cord from the rear winder, passing directly up, to go through two screw eyes, as in Diagram 6, to be fixed to the top of the arm with a staple or screw. This avoids tangling of cords. Brakes may be fitted to the two winders as in Diagram 7. They consist of pieces of rod bent up at one end and moving to and fro through two staples and are prevented from coming out by a small screw in the floor of the cab.

Finishing.—Take to pieces, clean up, fill, and give a coat of glue size before painting. The cab of the original model had cream painted windows and roof, with a cream interior. A deep band of red paint decorated the lower part of the outside, and the base was black with silver painted wheels and arm.

Reassemble when dry.

A NOVEL TOY

Gaily Painted Peep-Show

MATERIALS

Box with lid about 9 ins. by 12 ins.
Coloured paper for covering the box.
A piece of transparent paper, such as greaseproof paper.

Method.—Pictures of trees, animals, people, and so on, are cut out and arranged inside to form a " show." One peeps through a hole in the side of the box, and the show inside is made visible by means of the light coming through the transparent paper.

Cover the outside of the box with gaily coloured paper cut to size and pasted on. Cut a large hole about half the area of the lid, at one end of the lid, and cover this hole from underneath with transparent paper.

Make a small hole at the end of the box as shown in the diagram on the right, large enough to see through.

Finish.—The arrangement of the scenery inside can be left to the individual, but it will add to the " show " if the inside of the box is covered with a suitable picture, such as trees, grass, and so on.

Against such a background, pictures of animals could be cut out and arranged on little cardboard stands.

The interior of the original peep-show can be clearly seen in the illustration at the bottom right of the next page.

A very realistic countryside scene is viewed through the peep-hole. The four sides of the box are decorated with painted trees and sky, and tiny animals such as rabbits, deer, squirrels, and so on, are fixed to little cardboard stands and arranged on a grass painted surface.

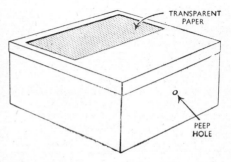

TRANSPARENT PAPER

PEEP HOLE

The interior of the peep-show is on the right showing painted scenery with cut-out animals. These are viewed through the hole at the side as shown above.

TOY XYLOPHONE

Played with Wooden Hammers

MATERIALS

Hardwood planed to given sizes.

2 pieces 19 ins. by $1\frac{1}{2}$ ins. by $\frac{3}{8}$ in. for sides.

1 piece $8\frac{1}{2}$ ins. by $\frac{3}{4}$ in. by $\frac{3}{4}$ in. for foot.

1 piece 5 ins. by $\frac{3}{4}$ in. by $\frac{3}{4}$ in. for foot.

8 pieces $1\frac{1}{8}$ in. wide and $\frac{1}{2}$ in. thick, and the following lengths for the notes —$3\frac{5}{8}$ ins., 4 ins., $4\frac{3}{8}$ ins., $4\frac{7}{8}$ ins., $5\frac{1}{2}$ ins., $5\frac{7}{8}$ ins, $6\frac{1}{2}$ ins, $7\frac{3}{8}$ ins.

4 ft. blind cord.

Method.—Place the two sides together and mark off the positions of the slots as shown in the diagram at S and detail A. Gauge the depth of the slots $\frac{3}{8}$ in.,

and saw down and chisel out the waste to the gauge line and shape the ends as shown in the diagram. Place the sides in their correct position on the feet and mark the slope of the notches on the feet by marking off from the sides. Gauge the depth $\frac{1}{8}$ in. and saw and chisel out the waste. Screw the feet up on to the sides so that they come immediately underneath the first and last notch on the sides.

Place the note pieces in their respective positions in the slots on the sides and draw a pencil line along the row of notes exactly over the centre of each side.

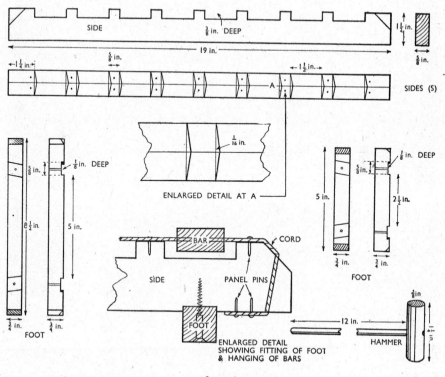

FOR BIG BROTHER. *An amusing toy that will delight the heart of a budding musician, is this jolly little xylophone. The notes are played with wooden hammers.*

This will indicate the direction in which a $\frac{1}{4}$-in. hole is to be bored through the edges of each note to take the suspending cord.

Bore a $\frac{1}{8}$-in. hole through each end of the sides in the centre of the sloping face. Thread the cord through this and fasten it underneath with panel pins. Thread each note in turn and fix the cord between each by means of a panel pin as shown in the enlarged detail. Thread the last of the cord through the sides and fix underneath. Keep the cord fairly taut all the while. Any polishing of the wood must be done before the notes are fixed.

Finish.—Make a hammer by boring a small hole in a short length of rod and gluing in a thin handle about 12 ins. long. A tap on the notes with a hammer should produce a fair scale.

DOLL'S BUNGALOW

With a Detachable Roof

MATERIALS

60 ft. of 4-in. matchboarding, 12 ft. of 2 ins. by 1 in., 3 ft. 6 ins. of 2 ins. by 2 ins., and just over 2 sq. ft. of plywood.

Stout cardboard for ceiling.

Ordinary 4-in. board is not so easy to work with as the matchboard, but can be used if joined by vertical struts, i.e., to convert into an 8-in. board.

If plywood is used, the areas required will be dealt with in the notes dealing with floor, and so on.

Cellophane for windows.

Method.—The Floor.—Join four pieces of 2 ins. by 1 in. to form a rectangle 20 ins. by 23 ins. Use the dowelling method described for the painted tray on page 67. On this frame, nail and glue 5 pieces of 4 ins. by 23 ins. matchboard, gluing the tongue and groove. Square up when dry.

Outside Walls.—Plywood is best here, but if unobtainable, use matchboard.

FOR A SMALL GIRL. *This delightful doll's bungalow is shown above with the roof off. It is divided into a bedroom ; kitchen and dining room with a hallway down the centre. The furniture was made from matchboxes and cardboard glued together.*

G

The bungalow complete with roof is shown above. The roof is red, and the outside walls are " roughcast." Inside the attic is a battery and switch that lights the interior.

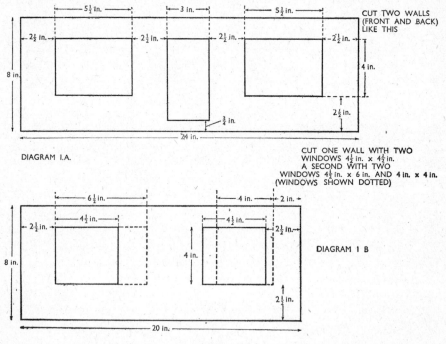

CUT TWO WALLS
(FRONT AND BACK)
LIKE THIS

DIAGRAM I.A.

CUT ONE WALL WITH TWO
WINDOWS 4½ in. x 4½ in.
A SECOND WITH TWO
WINDOWS 4½ in. x 6 in. AND 4 in. x 4 in.
(WINDOWS SHOWN DOTTED)

DIAGRAM 1 B

Cut out windows and doors as in Diagram 1, A, B, cutting each 4-in. piece separately and carefully. Use a fretsaw for plywood.

Now cut two pieces of 8 ins. by 2 ins. by 2 ins. into four triangular pieces (Diagram 2). Cut off the corners of the floor so that each triangular piece fits into place. Glue and nail (thin 1½-in. nails) each into its corner as in Diagram 2. Next glue and pin on the walls, and in attaching the first wall, drive pins in the frame first.

Partition Walls.—Cut and fit as in Diagram 3, fixing B last, so as to be able to fix in the partition C.

The Roof.—Make the two ends first as in Diagram 4 from two pieces of 12½ ins. by 2 ins. by 1 in. Cut as shown in the diagram, with two pieces of match-board nailed and glued. Cut off projecting shaded pieces. Make the two ends into a roof by nailing across 26-in. lengths of board. Attach so that the ends project 1 in. over the sides, and also over the front forming the eaves.

The Attic.—Make as in Diagram 5. This will house a battery and switch for the lights. Glue and pin from underneath the roof.

The Chimneys.—Cut two pieces of 6 ins. by 2 ins. by 2 ins. so that they can be glued and screwed from underneath the roof.

Cut a piece of stout cardboard to form a ceiling, size 21 ins. by 24 ins. and attach later.

The Doors.—Make these fit easily. Attach to walls by 1-in. strips of cloth glued on.

The Windows.—Make each frame ¼ in. bigger all round than the window opening. Those to open are attached by cloth hinges. Cut the inside of the frame with a fretsaw. See Diagram 6 for making up.

The Decoration.—Insides may be papered, distempered, or painted, but

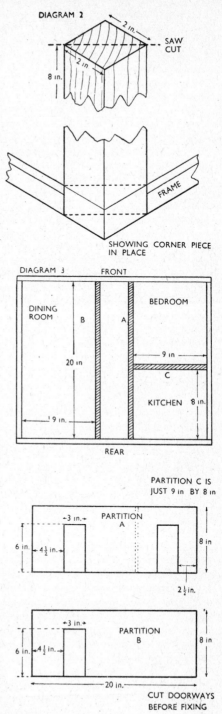

DIAGRAM 2

SAW CUT

8 in.

2 in.

2 in.

SHOWING CORNER PIECE IN PLACE

FRAME

DIAGRAM 3 FRONT

DINING ROOM

B A

BEDROOM

9 in

C

20 in

KITCHEN 8 in.

9 in.

REAR

PARTITION C IS JUST 9 in BY 8 in

PARTITION A

3 in.

6 in. 4½ in.

8 in

2½ in.

PARTITION B

3 in.

6 in. 4½ in.

8 in

20 in.

CUT DOORWAYS BEFORE FIXING

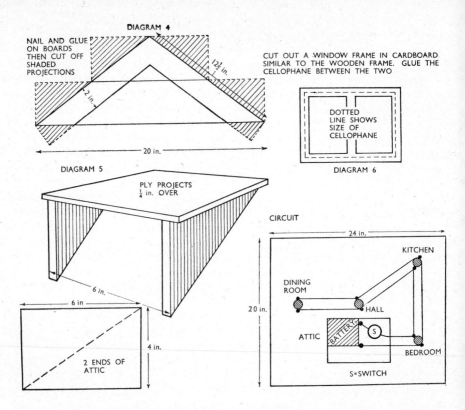

DIAGRAM 4

NAIL AND GLUE
ON BOARDS
THEN CUT OFF
SHADED
PROJECTIONS

12½ in.

2 in.

20 in.

CUT OUT A WINDOW FRAME IN CARDBOARD
SIMILAR TO THE WOODEN FRAME. GLUE THE
CELLOPHANE BETWEEN THE TWO

DOTTED
LINE SHOWS
SIZE OF
CELLOPHANE

DIAGRAM 5

PLY PROJECTS
¼ in. OVER

DIAGRAM 6

CIRCUIT

24 in.

KITCHEN

DINING
ROOM

20 in.

HALL

ATTIC

BATTERY

S

BEDROOM

S = SWITCH

6 in.

6 in

4 in.

2 ENDS OF
ATTIC

size the wood first if you are using paint. Outside walls are " roughcast " by stippling on a stiffish mixture of plaster-like filler which can be obtained from any hardware store. All faults and cracks are hidden when this coat is dry, and when painting size the walls first. The roof is painted red and if you wish can be marked out as tiles.

The Lighting.—You will require 4 screw-on bulb-holders, with bulbs, miniature switch, battery, and thin silk or cotton covered wire. The holders are screwed into position (use a backing of ply if the ceiling is cardboard) and wired as shown in the diagram ; before pinning on the ceiling, draw the two ends through a hole in the roof in the attic where the switch is located with the battery. Fasten the battery down with dresser hooks.

The roof is kept in position by two dowels projecting ½ in. in opposite corners of the bungalow. Two corresponding holes are made in the roof.

All the furniture in the bungalow was made from matchboxes, with the help of a few pieces of cardboard, scraps of cardboard wallpaper and some glue.

Where cupboards are required, the drawers of the boxes are removed, and cardboard doors are hinged on with narrow strips of cloth. Handles can be made with beads or paper-fasteners.

In making the armchairs, the matchboxes are arranged in position and padded with wadding before a printed covering is glued over them.

The saucepan is a measure from a tin of baby's food, and the flower bowl is the top of a bottle.

PORTER'S TRUCK

MATERIALS

2 pieces wood planed to 30 ins. by 2 ins. by $\frac{3}{4}$ in. for sides.

3 pieces wood, planed to 12 ins. by $1\frac{1}{2}$ ins. by $\frac{3}{4}$ in. for cross rails.

1 piece wood, planed to 13 ins. by $3\frac{1}{4}$ ins. by $\frac{1}{2}$ in. for end.

2 pieces wood, planed to 5 ins. by 2 ins. by $\frac{3}{4}$ ins. for feet.

2 pieces wood, planed to $4\frac{1}{2}$ ins. by $1\frac{3}{4}$ ins. by $\frac{3}{4}$ in. for axle pieces.

1 axle rod about $\frac{1}{2}$ in. to $\frac{3}{4}$ in. thick.

2 wheels about 4 ins. diameter.

Method.—Place the two sides together and square off the positions of the mortices. Similarly mark off the shoulders of the tenons on the three cross rails. Set the mortice gauge to a $\frac{1}{2}$ in., chisel and mark the tenons and mortices. Cut and fit the mortices and tenons, shape the handles, glue up the framework and wedge the tenons and allow to set, first seeing that the frame is square. Screw a 4-in. iron bracket to the end of each side and screw the end-piece on to the front of this bracket.

Bore a hole in each axle piece so that the axle rod will fit easily and shape them as indicated in the diagram. Screw these to the under side of the end of the truck. Bore holes in the wheels so that they will turn easily on the axle. Place a washer on the axle, add the wheel and another washer and fix in position with a cotter pin through a small hole bored across the axle outside the last washer.

Cut a step $1\frac{1}{2}$ ins. long and $\frac{1}{4}$ in. deep from each foot and screw these from the inside on to the side tight against the first cross rail. Glasspaper up the truck and paint a bright colour.

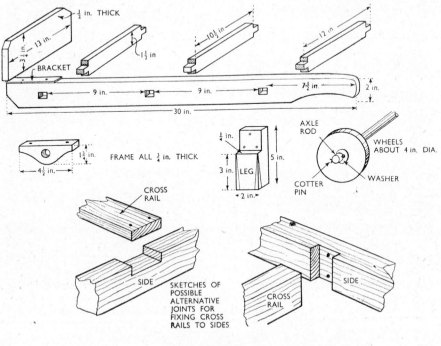

FOR A SMALL BOY. *A sturdy toy that will provide hours of enjoyment is this jolly looking porter's truck. The original was painted bright green with red wheels and yellow handles. It is very strong and will carry quite heavy loads.*

DOLL'S CRADLE

And Full Set of Bedclothes

CRADLE

MATERIALS
Wood required
End.—1 piece of ply, 14 ins. by 9 ins.
    2 pieces wood, 9 ins. by 1 in. by $\frac{1}{2}$ in.
    2 pieces wood, 12 ins. by $\frac{3}{4}$ in. by $\frac{1}{2}$ in.
    1 piece wood, $7\frac{1}{2}$ ins. by $\frac{3}{4}$ in. by $\frac{1}{2}$ in.
    Double above for 2 ends.
Bed.—1 piece ply, 16 ins. by 9 ins.
    2 rails 16 ins. by $\frac{3}{4}$ in. by $\frac{1}{2}$ in.
Side.—2 pieces wood, $15\frac{1}{2}$ ins. by $\frac{3}{4}$ in.
    by $\frac{1}{2}$ in.
    3 ft. $\frac{1}{2}$-in. dowel.
    Double above for 2 sides.
    Altogether 14 ft. of $\frac{3}{4}$ ins. by $\frac{1}{2}$ in.

Method.—The Ends.—Using $\frac{5}{8}$-in. veneer pins, pin and glue the 6 pieces of wood required for an end, as shown in Diagram 1a. Set aside to dry; when dry shape both ends as in Diagram 1b, using tenon saw and spokeshave.

The Bed.—Glue and pin stretchers to the ply as in Diagram 2, the end pins being at least $\frac{3}{4}$ ins. from the ends of the stretchers.
The Side.—One side will be fixed to the ends and will require 2 rails $15\frac{1}{2}$ ins. long and the other side will be hinged so that it may be let down. This side requires 2 15-in. rails. Cut 12 6-in. pieces of $\frac{1}{2}$-in. dowel. Mark out the two 15-in. rails as in Diagram 3a and the two $15\frac{1}{2}$-in. rails as in Diagram 3b. Bore $\frac{1}{2}$-in. holes and make up the sides —see that they are square. Now glue on the dowels, gluing one line of 6-in first, then gluing the holes of the opposite rails and inserting the other ends of the dowels. Place two $5\frac{1}{2}$-in. pieces of waste wood between the ends of the rails then tap down with a mallet. This ensures the rails being

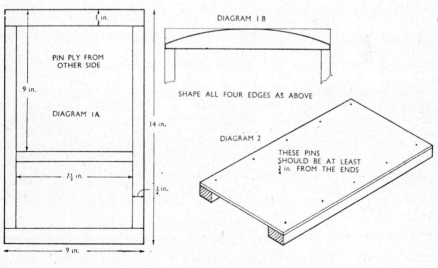

DIAGRAM 1 B

SHAPE ALL FOUR EDGES AS ABOVE

PIN PLY FROM
OTHER SIDE

9 in.

DIAGRAM 1A

$7\frac{1}{2}$ in.

9 in.

14 in.

$\frac{1}{2}$ in.

DIAGRAM 2

THESE PINS
SHOULD BE AT LEAST
$\frac{3}{4}$ in. FROM THE ENDS

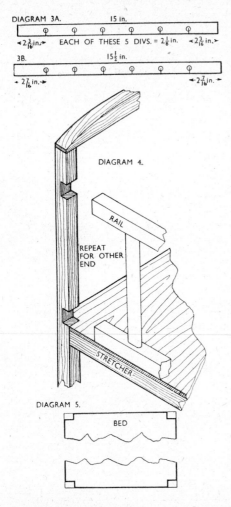

DIAGRAM 3A.

15 in.

2¾ in. — EACH OF THESE 5 DIVS. = 2⅛ in. — 2¾ in.

3B.

15½ in.

2⁷⁄₁₆ in. — 2⁷⁄₁₆ in.

DIAGRAM 4.

RAIL

REPEAT
FOR OTHER
END

STRETCHER

DIAGRAM 5.

BED

the nail and punch the rest in. A thin 1¼-in. screw may be screwed (from the outside of the cradle) into each end of the sides. Countersink the screw heads. The 15-in. side is hinged by two 1½-in. hinges so that it swings down. It is held up by two small hook catches, attached to the sides of the cradle.

Finish.—Clean up with glasspaper, fill with any proprietary brand of filler or plaster of paris, rub down with medium then fine paper, coat with thin glue or glue size then paint according to taste.

DOLL'S BEDCLOTHES

MATERIALS

The bedclothes can be made from oddments of material.

For the mattress use 2 pieces of strong material—preferably striped—measuring 16 ins. by 8 ins. and a strip about 2 ins. wide and 48 ins. long. A piece of wide braid could be substituted for the strip. Stuffing is also required and small pieces of leather cut into circles for the tufts, to make it look more realistic. Stitch the strip to one rectangle, and join the strip. Making sure that the corners match, stitch the other rectangle to the strip, leaving an opening in one long side. Stuff fairly firmly and over-sew the opening together neatly. Cut 10 circles of leather about ¾ in. across and sew these to the mattress at equal intervals, taking the thread through a piece of leather on each side and right through the mattress.

For the waterproof sheet use a piece of plastic, white or a light colour. Mark out the size about 16 ins. by 8 ins. with a pencil and cut out, preferably with pinking shears.

For the undersheet use a piece of white material, such as flannelette, measuring about 15 ins. by 22 ins. Hem all round.

The pillow is a piece of white calico

parallel. Set aside to dry; complete the other side.

Assembling.—Cut a piece out of each corner of the bed as shown in Diagram 5 so that it will rest on the rails glued on the ends of the cradle. Whilst resting on the rail, mark two grooves (as shown in Diagram 4), into which the ends of the 15½-in. side will fit. Cut the grooves, sawing inside the lines. Clean up before final assembly then glue and pin the bed on the rails and, driving one 1½-in. nail into each end of the stretchers, from the outside of the cradle, nip off the head of measuring 8 ins. by 12 ins. Fold it in half and machine round the three sides, leaving a 2-in. opening. Turn on to right side, stuff and oversew opening together.

Use two pieces of organdie or fine lawn measuring 7 ins. by 9 ins. for the pillowcase. Hem a short side of each piece, then join the other three sides together. Turn right side out and trim with lace or work a crochet edging into the material thus :—

1 dc. into the edge, 3 ch., 3 tr. all into same place as the dc. miss about ¼ in. and repeat.

For the top sheet use a piece of organdie or fine lawn measuring about 15 ins. by 20 ins. Hem all round and trim one end with lace or a crochet edging.

For the knitted blanket use about 2 ozs. 4-ply wool, No. 7 needles and work thus :—

Cast on 47 sts. and work in moss st.

FOR TINY FOLK. *Little girls will love to tuck up their dolls in this delightful little white-painted cradle. The bottoms of the two ends are curved so that dolly can be rocked gently to sleep. One side is hinged so that it may be let down.*

These enchanting little miniature bedclothes consist of a well-stuffed mattress finished with leather tufts; a pinked edge waterproof sheet; an undersheet of flannelette; a white calico pillow with an organdie pillowcase edged with crochet; a top sheet of organdie; a knitted blanket, and a quilted eiderdown with a frilled edge.

for 1 in. (k. 1, p. 1 alternately every row).

Next row.—Moss st. 7, * k. 6, moss st. 3. Rep. from * to last 4 sts., moss st. 4.

Next row.—Moss st. 7, * p. 6, moss st. 3. Rep. from * to last 4 sts., moss st. 4. Rep. last 2 rows twice more.

Work 4 rows in moss st.

Rep. the last 10 rows until work measures length required, ending with 1 in. in moss st. instead of 4 rows.

If a larger blanket is required add a number of sts. divisible by 9.

With the wool work a shell edging all round the blanket in the same way as given for the pillowcase on page 201.

For the eiderdown use two pieces of silk 8 ins. by 12 ins., and a strip about 60 ins. long and 1½ ins. wide. Join the strip into a ring and hem one long edge. Gather the other. Placing right sides together, stitch the frill all round one piece of silk, then pin the other piece of silk over this with the right sides facing and the frill in between. Stitch round 3 sides, then turn right side out. Stuff with wadding and turn in and hem the raw edge neatly. Quilt by working french knots through both thicknesses of silk and wadding in any desired pattern.

SWIMMING FISH

Simple to Make In Wood

MATERIALS

Wood 9 ins. by 2 ins. by 1 in.
Small piece of scrap lead.
2 wood screws.

Method.—The diagram shows the shape of the fish set out on a grid of 1-in. squares. Set out the shape on the wood and saw, chisel and spokeshave the fish to shape. Following the diagram exactly does not matter as any shape of fish will work just as well. Glasspaper to a fine finish.

Paint the fish with bright coloured enamel paints giving several coats and glasspapering lightly between each coat. **Finish.**—Tie a strip of lead about $\frac{1}{4}$ in. to $\frac{3}{8}$ in. wide to the middle of the fish and place it in water. Adjust the weight of the lead until the fish is just kept submerged. Make two holes to take the wood screws at each end of the lead

and screw the lead to the underside of the fish at its point of balance so that it will remain horizontal in the water.

Test the fish in water—it will probably sink—and remove small shavings of lead until the fish remains nicely balanced in the water. Use brass screws to avoid rusting.

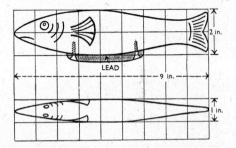

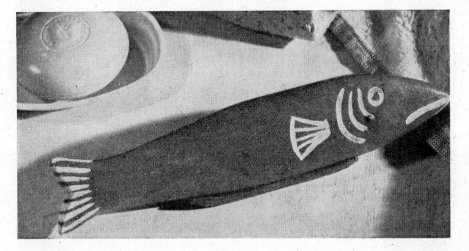

FOR TINY TOTS. *Designed for bath-time, this delightful little toy fish will cause endless amusement. A piece of lead is screwed to the underside of the fish so that it remains horizontal just under the surface of the water.*

DUCK ON WHEELS

With Flapping Wings

MATERIALS

The Duck.—3 pieces 3-ply 10 ins. by 6½ ins, or 1 piece 9-ply, 10 ins. by 6 ins.

2 Wings :—Each 6 ins. by 3 ins.

Base and Axle.— 1 piece, 11 ins. by 1½ ins. by ¾ in.

2 wooden wheels 3 ins. in diameter.

24 ins. of ½ in. dowel.

Two 1½ in. hinges and screws.

Screws.—Four, 1½ ins.

Two, 1 in.

Two, ½ in.

12 ins. of stout wire.

Method.—Cut the body of the duck according to Diagram 1. If 9-ply is used, cut with a coping saw or a padsaw. A fretsaw can be used for 3-ply, in which case 3 figures are needed, and are then glued together and left under a weight for the glue to dry.

If the duck is made from three pieces of 3-plywood, it is advisable to have an extra ½ in. so that tongues may be made and the duck fitted into slots cut in the baseboard (see Diagram 1 below).

When using this method glue the tongues into the slots and fix also with a ¾ in. No. 4 screw, driven in from underneath the base.

This way of attaching the duck to the

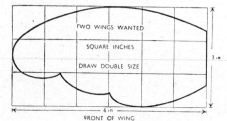

FRONT OF WING

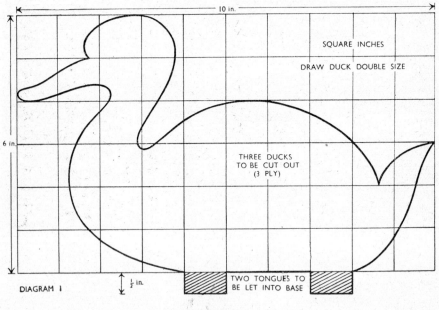

DIAGRAM 1

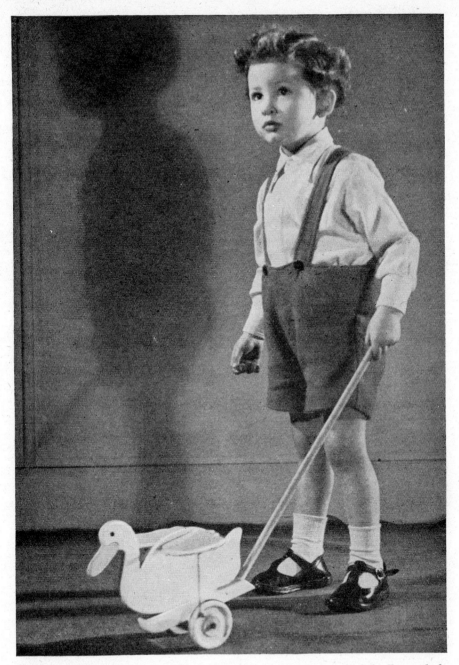

FOR A SMALL BOY. *This quaint little toy duck can be wheeled all round the nursery with his wings flapping as he moves. A long handle is attached to the back, and the front of the base is rounded to prevent the corners from catching in carpets.*

base is adopted to avoid the possibility of separating the pieces of 3-plywood, which might occur if thick screws are used from under the base as in the method employed in fixing the 9-plywood to the baseboard.

This latter way is quite safe for the 9-ply; in this case two $1\frac{1}{2}$ in. No. 8 screws are used, the screwholes being countersunk.

Whilst the duck is drying, cut out the wings as in Diagram 1, and then prepare the base and axle for the wheels shown in Diagram 2. The base is $7\frac{1}{2}$ ins. of the $1\frac{1}{2}$ in. wood, and the axle $3\frac{1}{2}$ ins. Note that the front of the base is rounded to prevent the corners from catching in carpets, and so on.

When the duck has dried, round off the edges of the ply with a chisel, rasp and glasspaper.

Finish.—Join the duck to base, either by slot or with two $1\frac{1}{2}$-in. screws as mentioned previously. Next fix the axle, counter-sinking the two 1-in. screws as in Diagram 3. Now screw on the wheels ($1\frac{1}{2}$ in. screws), then attach the wings by $1\frac{1}{2}$ in. hinges, as shown in Diagram 3.

Details of Movement.—A $\frac{1}{2}$-in. round-head screw is fixed into the wooden wheel, $\frac{3}{8}$ in. from the edge and a small screw-eye underneath the wing, not directly underneath the wheel. A piece of wire is looped at both ends, one loop going through the eye, and the other held by the screw in the wheel, Diagram 4. As the wheel rotates, the wire, acting as a piston rod, pushes the wing up and down. Repeat for the other wing, then attach the handle to the base, as shown in Diagram 5 at the foot of this page. After it has all been assembled and worked correctly, take to pieces, then clean up and glue in the handle and paint.

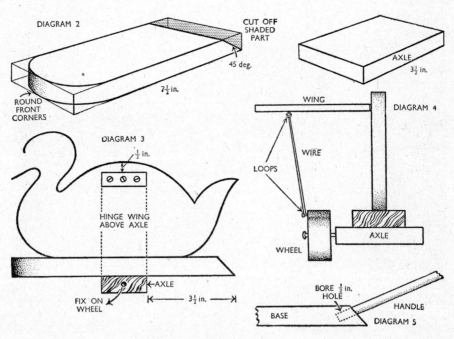

KALEIDOSCOPE

Amusing and Gay

MATERIALS

1 piece of glass 12 ins. by 9 ins.
Roll of black passe-partout.
Coloured paper for covering.
Piece of white card 2 ins. by 3½ ins.

Method.—Cut four pieces of glass, size and shape as indicated in Diagram 1. Draw the shapes on white paper, lay the glass on top and cut along the lines as seen through the glass. Join the two sides by the 9-in. edges with the passe-partout. Join the front piece of glass to the two 10½-in. edges of the sides.

Clean the inside of the kaleidoscope before joining.

Fix the white cardboard base next. It is advisable to reinforce all the edges with a second strip of passe-partout.

Before proceeding further, obtain a few scraps of brightly coloured tinsel, beads or other shining material and drop them into the kaleidoscope. A few experiments will soon determine how much

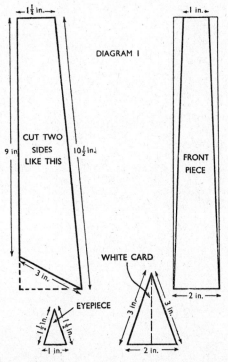

DIAGRAM 1

CUT TWO SIDES LIKE THIS

FRONT PIECE

WHITE CARD

EYEPIECE

Close-up of the kaleidoscope showing the decorative paper covering ; the 2-in. window on the face, and the passe-partout edging.

FOR A SMALL BOY OR GIRL. *An intriguing and unusual toy, this kaleidoscope will provide hours of fun and amusement for children of any age. The narrow end of the toy is placed against one eye and, as it is slowly turned, countless delightful patterns are formed at the other end by the scraps of brightly coloured tinsel beads or paper arranged in various sizes inside the kaleidoscope.*

coloured material will suit. Geometrical shapes of various sizes are the most successful.

Leave the pieces inside the box and fix on the glass top with binding.

Now black the outside glass, except the eye-piece, leaving a 2-in. window on the face. Use paint, paper or any other black material.

Finally cover the three sides and base with a brightly coloured paper, leaving about $\frac{1}{8}$ in. or $\frac{1}{4}$ in. edging of passe-partout showing.

The passe-partout edging round the window may be trimmed down to about $\frac{1}{8}$ in., thus letting in more light.

The glass should be ordinary window glass, not too thick, or it will prove difficult to cut cleanly. Lay it on a flat, level surface with stout packing paper beneath, while being cut. A " wheel " glass-cutter can be bought quite cheaply.

TOAST RACK

And Bread Board

TOAST RACK

MATERIALS

1 piece hardwood planed to 6 ins. by 3¼ ins. by ¼ in. for the base.

1 piece hardwood planed to 3½ ins. by 2½ ins. by ¼ in. for the handle.

1 piece hardwood planed to 7½ ins. by ¾ in. by ¼ in. for the feet.

Plastic (Perspex, Lactoid or Erinoid). 4 lengths of rod about ⅛ in. diameter and 5 ins. long.

Method.—Fit the handle to the base by two tenons ⅜ in. wide set ¼ in. from each side of the handle. Bore the hole in

the top to form a finger grip and shape the top as shown in the diagram. Drill holes in the base in the positions indicated exactly to fit the diameter of your plastic rod.

Clean up the base and handle and take off a small chamfer from all the edges. Saw the piece for the feet into two and shape the feet to fit the base. Glue the handle in position and glue and pin the feet with short panel pins. The whole can now be glasspapered and polished but it will be found very much more convenient to do this before the toast rack is glued up.

Plane a piece of scrap wood to 2½ ins. wide and round off one end to a perfect semicircle — this will give you a "former" for your plastic rod to form the 1¼ ins. radius required. Stand the former upright in the vice with the round end uppermost.

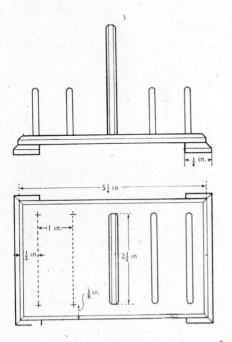

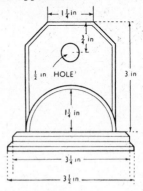

ALL WOOD ¼ in THICK

FOR THE HOUSEWIFE. *Two useful and easily made gifts which will be very pleasing additions to any household. A large size bread board with an addition at the side which is slotted (the blade of the knife slides into this when not in use) and a neat little wooden toast rack.*

Finish.—Place your plastic rods in boiling water for a few minutes to soften them and quickly take them out and bend them over the former and hold them there for a few minutes to set.

Cut the rods off to the length required and slip them into the holes bored in the base. See that all the semicircles of plastic are the same size or the job will look untidy.

Place a small drop of glue in each hole and press in the rod and allow it to set overnight and the rack is complete.

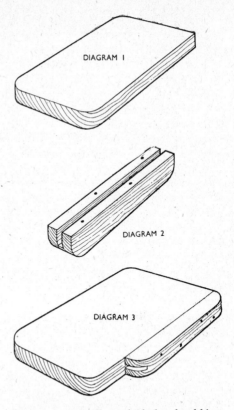

BREAD BOARD

MATERIALS

1 bread knife.

Piece of hardwood as long as the knife, and about 7 ins. wide and 1 in. thick.

Strip of hardwood as long as blade of knife and $\frac{1}{2}$ in. wider than knife.

Method.—Prepare the piece of hardwood, such as oak, walnut, birch, beech or sycamore, for the cutting board by planing both surfaces and edges. Then mark the three rounded corners shown in Diagram 1. Now saw off the waste wood close to the line and finish the rounding with a chisel or spokeshave.

Now prepare the strip which is to hold the knife, as shown in Diagram 2. Mark the groove, then with a tenon saw make a cut about $\frac{1}{4}$ in. deep along the groove, and also down the ends. Then with a hand saw widen the saw cut and cut deep enough to cover the knife. Now drill four $\frac{1}{16}$-in. holes right through the strip in the position shown in Diagram 2. Widen the holes on the outside to $\frac{3}{16}$ in. diameter and to a depth of $\frac{3}{4}$ in. Next glue and pin the strip to the board, see Diagram 3, using $1\frac{1}{2}$-in. panel pins punched right into the $\frac{3}{16}$-in. holes.

If desired $1\frac{1}{2}$ in. number 6 screws can be used to join the strip to the board. In this case, drill $\frac{3}{16}$ in. holes through the strip and enlarge them to $\frac{1}{4}$ in. on the outside. When the joint is completed and the screws are in place, the holes should be filled with wooden plugs instead of plaster of paris. Make these, by rounding with a rasp or chisel, a piece of wood off the same board as the strip. Whilst making the joint it is important to ensure that the groove which holds the knife is not obstructed with glue.

When set, clean the joint on both sides, then round all the outside edges, and finally scrape and glasspaper on both sides of the bread board.

Finger grips can be carved in the underside if required; use a carving tool or gouge and carve away a small boat-shape at each end of the board.

Finish.—The only finish required is a little wax polish well rubbed into the wood. The nail holes can be filled with a little wood filler or plaster of paris mixed with stain to tone with the wood.

IRON STAND

Copper Tongs and Teapot Stand

IRON STAND

MATERIALS

1 batten, 22 ins. by $1\frac{3}{4}$ ins. by $\frac{3}{4}$ in.
1 piece asbestos, 7 ins. by 7 ins.

Method.—Cut the batten into two equal parts and join with a half lap joint as shown in Diagram 1. The joint consists of a groove cut in the centre of each piece, $1\frac{3}{4}$ ins. wide and $\frac{3}{8}$ in. deep. Next cut the 7-in. square of asbestos. Drill two holes in opposite corners and countersink for screws, as shown in Diagram 2. Next mark the centre on each leg of stand, and place top in position as in Diagram 2. Mark the feet as shown in Diagram 2 and saw off the waste wood leaving $\frac{1}{4}$ in. of the top of the feet showing. Glasspaper the stand and paint; when dry screw on the top using two $\frac{5}{8}$-in. screws.

DIAGRAM 1.

2 in.

7 in.

DIAGRAM 1.

DIAGRAM 2.

X

C

B

$2\frac{1}{2}$ in.

$\frac{1}{2}$ in. E.

$\frac{3}{4}$ in.

DIAGRAM 3

SECTION X X

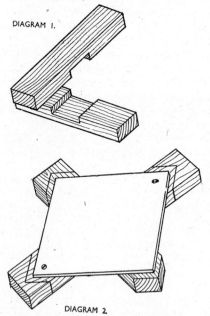

DIAGRAM 1.

DIAGRAM 2

COPPER TONGS

MATERIALS

1 deal batten, 17 ins. by $1\frac{7}{8}$ ins. by $\frac{7}{8}$ in.
1 deal batten, 4 ins. by 1 in. by $\frac{1}{4}$ in.
1 piece dowel $\frac{7}{8}$ in. long, $\frac{3}{4}$ in. diameter.
1 elastic band.

Method.—Mark out the batten as shown in Diagram 1 above, and at centres A and B bore $\frac{3}{4}$-in. diameter holes. Round the corners at both ends of batten and with a gouge make the grooves shown at C.

Cut out with a tenon saw the wedge-shape shown shaded in diagram which centres on B, and then drill two $\frac{1}{4}$ in. holes through the jaws of the tongs.

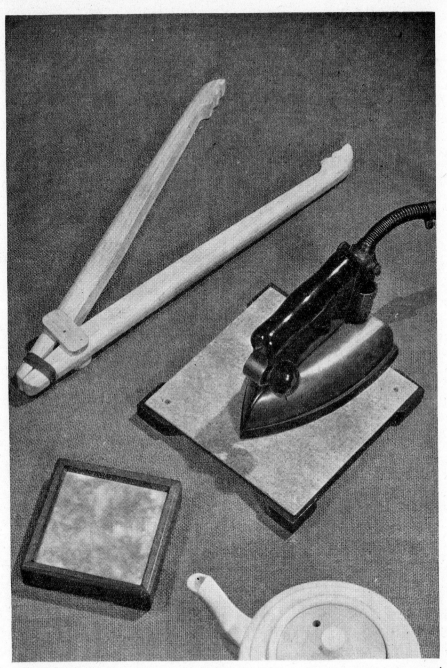

FOR MOTHER. *Three practical gifts for the kitchen that are sure to please. A square tile teapot stand with a wooden surround; an extremely useful iron stand of asbestos supported on a brightly coloured wooden base, and a pair of wood copper tongs.*

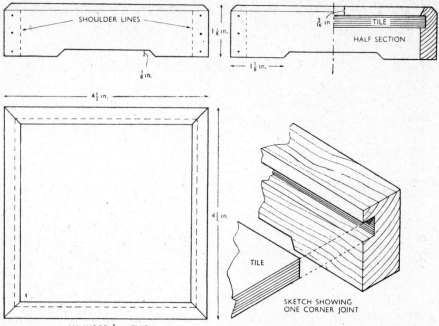

SHOULDER LINES

$1\frac{1}{8}$ in.

$\frac{1}{8}$ in.

$4\frac{1}{2}$ in.

$4\frac{1}{2}$ in.

$\frac{3}{16}$ in   TILE

HALF SECTION

$1\frac{1}{8}$ in.

TILE

SKETCH SHOWING
ONE CORNER JOINT

ALL WOOD $\frac{3}{8}$ in. THICK

With a plane round the outside edges (as shown in the Diagram) of the section cut through XX, and then saw apart down the centre line DE.

Clean the sawn edges with a plane or glasspaper, and then chisel the wood from the shaded part marked A. Cut a piece of $\frac{3}{4}$-in. round dowel $\frac{7}{8}$ in. long and nail to one arm with a fine panel pin to act as a hinge, Diagram 2. Next glasspaper the tongs well to smooth all the edges.

Make the two flanges 2 ins. long by 1 in. wide and nail over the hinge as shown in Diagram 3.

Finish.—The two arms of the tongs are held in place with a rubber band twisted round the groove as illustrated.

TILE TEAPOT STAND
MATERIALS
1 tile 4 ins. square.

Hardwood, 1 piece planed to 19 ins. by $1\frac{1}{8}$ ins. by $\frac{3}{8}$ in.

Method.—Plough a groove to a depth of $\frac{1}{8}$ in. and wide enough to fit the tile snugly (probably $\frac{1}{4}$ in.) and $\frac{3}{16}$ in. from the edge of the wood. Saw the wood into four equal pieces and place them together in the vice and mark off the distance between the shoulders of the joints across the four pieces at once with the try-square so that they are all the same length, $3\frac{3}{4}$ ins. in this case.

Remove the pieces from the vice and square the shoulder line round on to the inside of each piece. Set a sliding bevel to an angle of 45 degrees or use a mitre-square and set out the mitres for the corners carefully and saw each end accurately to the mitred line.

Fit the frame together, with tile in position, making any necessary adjustments.

Plane off a slight bevel on inside of top as indicated in the diagram above. Glasspaper and polish the inside and glue the job up, pinning the joints with fine nails or panel pins.

Finish.—Leave to set for 24 hours, and when dry clean, glasspaper and polish.

BATHROOM CABINET

And Tooth-brush Holder

CABINET

MATERIALS

2 sides, 12 ins. by 4 ins. by $\frac{1}{2}$ in. deal.
2 pieces for top and bottom, $10\frac{1}{2}$ ins. by 4 ins. by $\frac{1}{2}$ in.
1 shelf, $9\frac{1}{2}$ ins. by 4 ins. by $\frac{3}{8}$ ins.
1 door panel, $12\frac{1}{2}$ ins. by $10\frac{1}{2}$ ins. by $\frac{3}{16}$ in. ply.
2 door strips, $12\frac{1}{2}$ ins. by $1\frac{1}{4}$ ins. by $\frac{3}{4}$ in.
2 door strips, 8 ins. by $1\frac{1}{4}$ ins. by $\frac{3}{4}$ in.
1 door rack, 9 ins. by 1 in. by 1 in.
1 back, $12\frac{1}{2}$ ins. by $10\frac{1}{2}$ ins. by $\frac{3}{16}$ in. ply.
4 screw-eyes.

Method.—Construct the cabinet as shown in Diagram 1 using an open-housed joint, and glue and fix with inch panel pins. Mark the rebates with two marking gauges set to the width and the depth, doing all joints from same face of the wood. Then a vertical and a cross cut with a fine tenon saw should leave little work for the chisel in cleaning up.

Fit the back, glue and nail in place with $\frac{3}{4}$-in. nails, and then trim the edges and joints, finishing with glasspaper. Screw in screw-eyes $4\frac{1}{2}$ ins. down from the top of the cabinet to support the shelf. Now make the ply panel for the door to fit exactly over the front of the cabinet. Next glue the door strips in place in the order shown in Diagram 2; they must be flush with the edges, or the ply may be allowed to project a little, so that it can be rubbed down flush with glasspaper afterwards.

Secure the strips by nailing through the ply into the strips; sink the heads

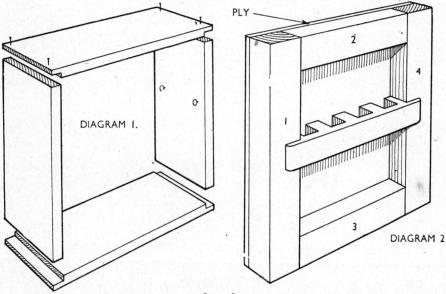

DIAGRAM 1.

PLY

DIAGRAM 2

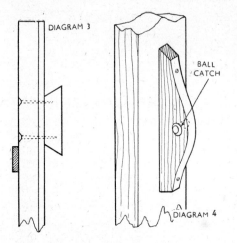

DIAGRAM 3

BALL CATCH

DIAGRAM 4

Next set out the shelf shown in Diagram 2 below, and then shape it by using a spokeshave, file, and glasspaper. Glue and pin the shelf to the backboard using 1-in. panel pins.

Now take the wire and bending round a piece of $\frac{1}{2}$-in. diameter rod, bend to form the two loops to hold tooth-brushes, as shown in Diagram 3. Set out the shape as in Diagram 4, on a piece of paper, and using this as a guide complete the shaping, bending the wire with pliers. Push the ends through the two holes in the backboard, bend the ends outwards, and hammer into two small grooves cut in the back with a chisel—Diagram 4a. Secure the ends by driving a

with a punch and fill the holes. Cut grooves in the rack (for the door) to take a tooth-brush, razor, and so on, then glue and nail the rack in place. The notches are outlined with two saw-cuts; then, working alternately from both faces of the rack, cut out the wood between saw-cuts with a sharp chisel.

A handle (Diagram 3) can be screwed on from the inside, and the door can then be hinged to the cabinet. Use 1$\frac{1}{2}$-in. hinges and sink them level with the surface of the cabinet and door.

A neat catch can be made by fitting a ball catch in a small piece of wood and then screwing this to the door so that it engages the plate let into the side of the cabinet, as shown in Diagram 4.

Finish.—Glasspaper the cabinet well, fill all nail holes, and then paint.

TOOTH-BRUSH HOLDER
MATERIALS

  Backboard, 8 ins. by 5 ins. by $\frac{1}{2}$ in.
  Shelf, 4 ins. by 3 ins. by $\frac{1}{2}$ in.
  Flexible wire, 16 ins.
  Round tin such as a cocoa tin.

Method.—First make the backboard and shape it as shown in Diagram 1. The positions of the shelf on which the tumbler stands, and of the tray to hold tooth-paste are also shown in Diagram 1.

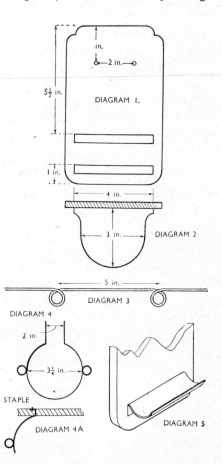

in.

2 in.

5$\frac{1}{2}$ in.

DIAGRAM 1.

1 in.

4 in.

3 in.

DIAGRAM 2

5 in.

DIAGRAM 3

DIAGRAM 4

2 in.

3$\frac{1}{4}$ in.

STAPLE

DIAGRAM 4A

DIAGRAM 5

THE HOUSEWIFE *will be sure to welcome these useful gifts for the bathroom. A white painted cabinet with two shelves and a rack inside the door, and a neat little tooth-brush holder with a shaped wire holding glass and brushes in place.*

small staple over each (a small staple can be made by shortening the prongs of an ordinary staple). Cut a 2-in. section from the side of a round tin, and fold in $\frac{1}{8}$ in. on the rough edges. To fold an edge, first bend with pliers and then hammer down on a piece of wood, using a round shape on which to hammer the curved ends. Bend the $\frac{1}{2}$-in. flap on the back and drill or punch two holes for screws, then screw into position as in Diagram 5 on page 216.

Finish by painting wood and metal parts with a good enamel.

SHOPPING REMINDER

With Book and Pencil

MATERIALS

Wood back 12 ins. by 8 ins. by $\frac{1}{2}$ in.
Box for book :—2 pieces $3\frac{1}{2}$ ins. by $\frac{1}{2}$ in. by $\frac{1}{4}$ in. 1 piece 5 ins. by $\frac{1}{2}$ in. by $\frac{1}{4}$ in. (in all 12 ins. by $\frac{1}{2}$ in. by $\frac{1}{4}$ in.). Plywood 5 ins. by $4\frac{1}{4}$ ins.

Method.—The shopping reminder consists of two parts, a wooden board with lists of commodities printed on each side of a central wooden pocket, and a loose-leaf notebook which is kept in the pocket.

Whilst directions are given for the making of this loose-leaf book, there is no reason why a similar kind of book may not be bought from any stationer. Also if need be, the central pocket used for storing the book could be altered in size to accommodate any other size notebook that the maker may wish to use.

The Back.—Mark out on the 12 in. by 8 in. piece of wood the shape shown in Diagram 1 on page 220. Remove waste wood from the corners first with a tenon saw, then by chisel and gouge.

A small sharp chisel is used on the top curves, which are finished off with a medium then fine glasspaper.

A small inside ground gouge is used for the lower curves, followed by a fine rasp, or glasspaper wound round a dowel stick.

The Box.—Round the top corners of the ply, then glue and pin on the 3 pieces as shown clearly in Diagram 2.

Now mark on the 12 ins. by 8 ins. back the place where box will be fixed, shown by dotted lines in Diagram 1. Make holes for the pins in the wood so that fixing will be made easier and more accurate. Glue on the box and drive in $\frac{5}{8}$-in. veneer pins from behind the back.

Finish.—Clean up with fine glasspaper, removing any glue with a sharp chisel. Give the whole a coat of thin glue, to render the surface non-porous before painting.

Prepare a shopping list on paper (see illustration on facing page) and glue to the wood after painting, with the most general household requirements set out in alphabetical order. Measure it out and

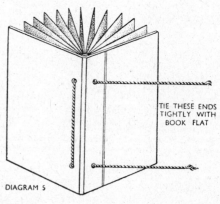

TIE THESE ENDS
TIGHTLY WITH
BOOK FLAT

DIAGRAM 5

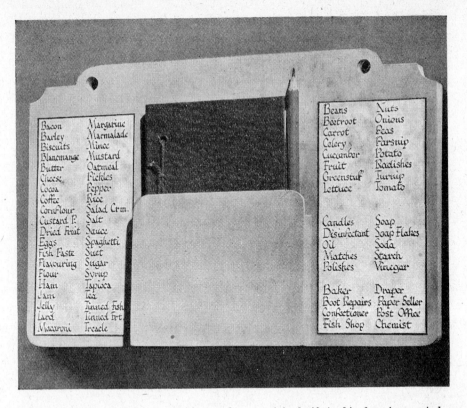

FOR MOTHER AGAIN. *A practical and most original gift is this shopping reminder to be hung near the larder. A list of household requirements is attached to each side to refresh your memory, and a box is fitted to the centre front in which is kept a loose-leaf notebook and a well-sharpened pencil.*

space it carefully in columns so that it looks neat and tidy. Box it in with a thick blackline as shown in the illustration above.

A square nib manuscript pen will be most suitable for the writing, but other methods of preparing the lists will occur to the maker. When fixed, give the paper a coat of paper varnish.

The book which fits into the pocket of the reminder is now made. It is simply a cover, with holes punched in it to take loose leaves, so that pages may be withdrawn or added as required. The book will wear better if covered with skiver or a smooth cloth, but stout paper could be used instead.

THE BOOK

MATERIALS

2 pieces thin cardboard, about 5 ins. by 4 ins.

1 piece of cloth, skiver, etc., $9\frac{1}{2}$ ins. by 6 ins., for covering.

Lining paper or thin cloth, $8\frac{1}{4}$ ins. by $4\frac{1}{2}$ ins.

Method.—Cut $\frac{3}{4}$ in. from a 5-in. side of one piece of card, then cut a further $\frac{1}{4}$ in. off. Save the $\frac{3}{4}$-in. piece and discard the $\frac{1}{4}$ in. Arrange the three pieces of card on the covering cloth as in Diagram 3; the positions should be marked out before gluing.

DIAGRAM 1.

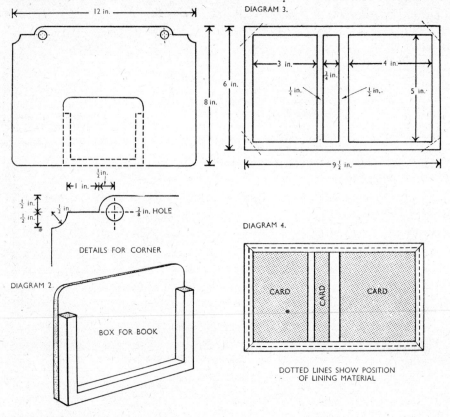

DETAILS FOR CORNER

DIAGRAM 2.

BOX FOR BOOK

DIAGRAM 3.

DIAGRAM 4.

CARD   CARD   CARD

DOTTED LINES SHOW POSITION
OF LINING MATERIAL

When all is ready glue the cloth, using thin, hot glue and quickly place on the cards. Cut off the 4 corners of cloth (not right up to the corner—see Diagram 3) and turn over the edges of the cloth. Press down edges with a ruler and place the book between the two boards in a press or under a weight. After a few minutes, take out the book, and try the lining material to see that it covers the inside of the book to leave a ¼ in. margin all round, Diagram 4. When satisfactory, glue on the lining, taking care to press down into the two gaps between the cards. Replace the book under weight.

When dry, two holes are punched in the ¾-in. card and two corresponding holes in the back of the book. Pages cut to 4½ ins. by 3¾ ins. have holes punched in them so that they can be attached inside the cover by a cord which is tied on the outside (Diagram 5 on page 218). **Finish.**—If eyelets can be obtained and fixed into the holes of the cover they will add to the appearance of the book. A small label stuck on the front of the book completes the work.

The book is kept in the box of the shopping reminder, as shown in the illustration on page 219.

A long pencil, sharpened and ready for use, should always be kept in the box next to the book.

BISCUIT BOX

Cheese Tray and Table Napkin Rings

BISCUIT BOX

MATERIALS

Wood required (finished sizes)

2 sides $6\frac{1}{2}$ ins. by 5 ins. by $\frac{3}{8}$ in.

2 sides $6\frac{1}{2}$ ins. by $4\frac{3}{8}$ ins. by $\frac{3}{8}$ in.

1 base $4\frac{1}{2}$ ins. by $4\frac{1}{2}$ ins. by $\frac{3}{8}$ in.

1 base ply 4 ins. by 4 ins.

1 lid 4 ins. by 4 ins. by $\frac{1}{2}$ in.

1 handle $2\frac{1}{4}$ ins. by 1 in. by $\frac{3}{4}$ in.

4 lid rests cut from 16 ins. of $\frac{1}{4}$ in. by $\frac{1}{2}$ in.

Approximate sizes :

4 pieces glass 4 ins. by $6\frac{1}{4}$ ins.

1 piece glass $3\frac{3}{4}$ ins. square.

N.B.—The glass should be cut when ready to fit into the box.

Method.—The four sides are joined as in Diagram 1. Note the slight projections of longer sides which, when planed off, will give clean joints.

A slat of wood, about 7 ins. by $\frac{1}{2}$ in. by $\frac{1}{4}$ in., lightly tacked on, is used as a guide when sawing the grooves, see Diagram 2 on page 222.

The saw cuts are $\frac{1}{4}$ in. and $\frac{5}{8}$ in. deep respectively in A and B. Saw down to the depth mark at the two ends first, then complete the cut by sawing across the width. Clean up grooves with a sharp chisel.

Before gluing the box, part drive two $\frac{1}{2}$-in. veneer pins into each joint, see Diagram 1, noting the position of the pins, being about $\frac{1}{4}$ in. from the finished corners of the box, so that, when the corners are rounded, the pins will not be in the way. Now glue up and drive home the pins, punching them in a little, finally putting the box into a cramp if one is available.

The Base.—This consists of two pieces, Diagram 3, the base proper and an added plywood top used as a stop for the glass lining. The four under edges of the base are lightly rounded off with a fine-set smoothing plane and a medium glasspaper, whilst the plywood stop is prepared so that it is $\frac{1}{8}$ in. smaller all round than the inside of the box. It is not yet fixed on.

The Lid.—This should be made to fit (not too loosely) into the top of the box and is prepared exactly as for the base (i.e., four edges are slightly rounded). The handle, Diagram 4, is then made, the corners being cut with a chisel and finished with a spokeshave or rasp, followed with a medium paper. Glue handle in the centre of the lid. Two veneer pins ($\frac{5}{8}$ in. long) can be drawn through lid from underneath as an additional fixing.

Cleaning the Box.—When the glued box is quite ready, clean off the projections and round off the corners of both the top and bottom of the box, as shown in Diagram 5. In rounding the corners, plane from the nearer corner always, as the wood of the further corner tends to split if planed otherwise. A rasp followed by a medium paper will finish the curves. After the top and bottom have been finished, round off the edges of the box.

Assembling.—Fix the base into position with a couple of $\frac{5}{8}$-in. pins partly driven in ; then reach inside the box and mark lines on the base where the sides touch it. Remove base and pin on the 3-ply stop, making sure that there is $\frac{1}{8}$ in. space between the pencilled lines and plywood, enough to take the thickness of the glass. Clean the inside of the box next then pin and glue on the base.

Fitting the Glass Linings.—Four pieces of $\frac{1}{8}$ in. by $\frac{1}{4}$ in. are prepared to act as catches for the glass and rests for the lid. Each piece must be the same length as the inside width of the box, which should be 4 ins. Cut two of these pieces $3\frac{1}{2}$ ins. long and pin and glue them as in Diagram 6, $\frac{1}{4}$ in. from the top of the box.

Now cut a rebate $\frac{1}{8}$ in. by $\frac{1}{8}$ in. in each of the other 2 pieces, see Diagram 7. This is done by marking the $\frac{1}{8}$ in. with a marking gauge, and cutting out waste wood with a $\frac{1}{8}$-in. or $\frac{1}{4}$-in. chisel, or by cutting a $\frac{3}{8}$-in. groove in a $1\frac{1}{4}$ in. wide piece of wood, splitting the wood down the groove, then planing to size. This rebate holds the glass upright. These 2 pieces are fixed each by one small screw, level with the other glued-on pieces. Bore holes for the screws with a fine fretwork drill. They are not glued, so that by removing them the glass may be easily taken out for cleaning.

Two pieces of glass are cut a shade less than 4 ins. wide (to ensure easy fitting) and long enough to fit between the base and top of the glued-on rest.

Remove the screwed-on rests and cut two pieces of glass $3\frac{3}{4}$ ins. wide and long enough to fit under the rebates of the screwed-on rests to the base. These two pieces of glass hold the other pieces in position when the screwed rests are put back into place.

Finish.—When assembling has been done, remove glass, fill holes with plastic wood, clean up and stain, replace glass.

N.B. — When cutting glass, rest it on an absolutely flat surface ; cut first a sufficiently long strip to the *width*, and then afterwards divide this into the required number of pieces for the *length* by cutting across.

It is wise to drill starting holes for all pins in thin wood.

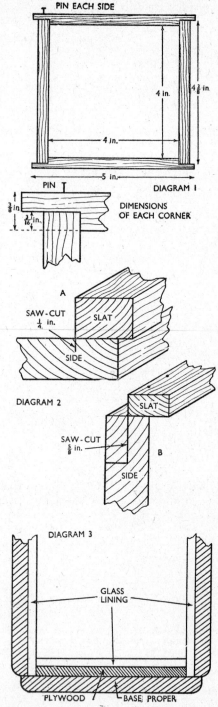

DIMENSIONS OF EACH CORNER

DIAGRAM 2

DIAGRAM 3

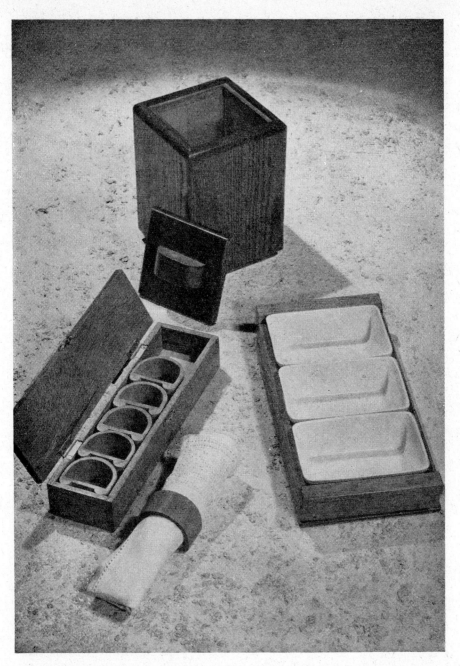

FOR THE HOUSEWIFE AGAIN. *A choice between three useful and very accept-*
able gifts, a wooden box with a hinged lid to hold six attractively shaped serviette rings ;
a butter, cheese and biscuit tray, and a polished wood biscuit barrel with a glass lining.

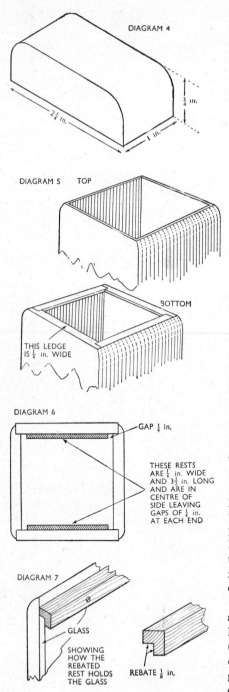

DIAGRAM 4

DIAGRAM 5   TOP

BOTTOM

THIS LEDGE
IS ¼ in. WIDE

DIAGRAM 6

GAP ¼ in.

THESE RESTS
ARE ¼ in. WIDE
AND 3½ in. LONG
AND ARE IN
CENTRE OF
SIDE LEAVING
GAPS OF ¼ in.
AT EACH END

DIAGRAM 7

GLASS

SHOWING
HOW THE
REBATED
REST HOLDS
THE GLASS

REBATE ⅛ in.

BUTTER, CHEESE AND BISCUIT TRAY

MATERIALS

3 rectangular dishes ; the ones shown are $4\frac{3}{4}$ ins. by $3\frac{1}{4}$ ins. by $1\frac{1}{2}$ ins. deep. Hardwood to suit dishes of above size.

1 piece 11 ins. by $1\frac{1}{2}$ ins. by $\frac{3}{4}$ in. for the ends.

1 piece $10\frac{3}{4}$ ins. by $1\frac{3}{16}$ in. by $\frac{3}{8}$ in. for the sides.

1 piece $11\frac{1}{4}$ ins. by $5\frac{1}{2}$ ins. by $\frac{3}{16}$ in. for the base.

N.B. Get your dishes before starting to make the tray, as adjustments may have to be made to these measurements in order to suit your own dishes.

Method.—Plane up the wood to the sizes given above and shown on diagram on the facing page. Place the two sides together in the vice and with a try-square and knife, mark out the shoulder line and joints so that they are both exactly the same size. Remove from the vice and square the line round on to the sides of the wood and complete the setting out of the joint. Saw out the joint accurately. Cut the piece for the ends into two equal parts and place in the vice and mark out lengths as before, remove and square the lines round. Complete the setting out of the joint and fit all the joints carefully.

Cut out the step forming the handle 1 in. wide and ¼ in. deep with a rebate plane. Clean up all the inside of the tray with glasspaper, give a coat of brush polish, and when dry, glasspaper again lightly and polish with wax. Glue up the sides and pin the joints with 2 panel pins and allow to set, making certain that the frame is square.

Plane up the base so that ⅛ in. projects all round tray ; glasspaper and polish.

Finish.—When the sides have set (about 24 hours), clean up the joints carefully with the smoothing plane and glasspaper and polish the outside. Pin or screw the base in position.

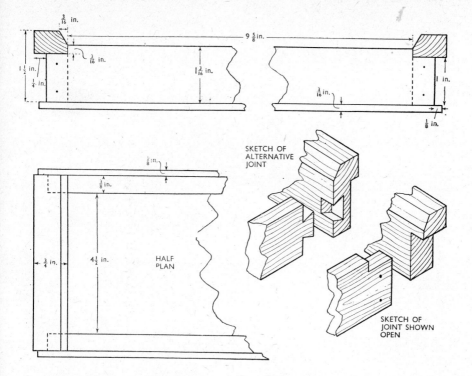

$\frac{3}{16}$ in.

$\frac{3}{16}$ in.

$9\frac{5}{8}$ in.

$1\frac{1}{2}$ in.

$\frac{1}{4}$ in.

$1\frac{3}{16}$ in.

1 in.

$\frac{3}{16}$ in.

$\frac{1}{8}$ in.

SKETCH OF
ALTERNATIVE
JOINT

$\frac{1}{8}$ in.

$\frac{3}{8}$ in.

$\frac{3}{4}$ in.

$4\frac{1}{2}$ in.

HALF
PLAN

SKETCH OF
JOINT SHOWN
OPEN

SERVIETTE HOLDERS

MATERIALS

1 piece hardwood 10 ins. by 2 ins. by $1\frac{3}{4}$ ins. (planed). This will make 6 holders.

Method.—Beechwood is most admirable for this work, although other hardwood will do. Shoot one end of the block then mark the ends of the wood as in Diagram 1 on page 226, and using a smoothing plane, take off the corner portion of the block. Now saw off a piece slightly larger than $1\frac{1}{4}$ ins. and by planing the rough end, reduce to $1\frac{1}{4}$ ins. Before proceeding further, smooth the curved part with a rasp and fine glasspaper. Mark each end as in Diagram 1, and commence taking out waste wood by boring a $\frac{3}{4}$-in. hole. Continue removing wood with an inside ground gouge and mallet. Don't attempt to chisel right through the wood ; cut a little from each

face, and work alternately thus, towards the middle. When nearing the line, the mallet should be dispensed with. A chisel is used for the flat part and the corners. Now smooth the inside curve with a half-round rasp followed with fine glasspaper wrapped round the rasp.

The small rests on the holder are made by cutting out a groove, see Diagram 2. Saw carefully down for $\frac{1}{4}$ in. then remove waste wood with a chisel (again working alternately from each face of the block). When the groove is finished, round the edges of the rests with chisel, rasp and fine glasspaper ; a wax finish is easier to apply than a french polish.

If a box for the holders is required, proceed as follows :—

Wood required

Lid 10 ins. by $2\frac{3}{4}$ ins. by $\frac{3}{8}$ in.

2 long sides 10 ins. by $1\frac{3}{4}$ ins. by $\frac{1}{4}$ in.

2 short ends $2\frac{1}{4}$ ins. by $1\frac{3}{4}$ ins. by $\frac{1}{4}$ in.

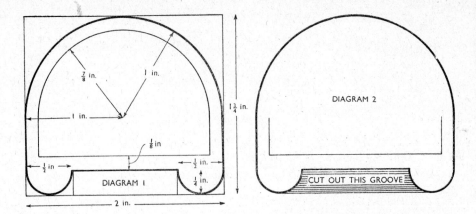

DIAGRAM 1

$\frac{7}{8}$ in.   1 in.

1 in.

$\frac{1}{8}$ in

$\frac{1}{2}$ in

$\frac{1}{2}$ in.

$\frac{1}{4}$ in.

2 in.

$1\frac{3}{4}$ in.

DIAGRAM 2

CUT OUT THIS GROOVE

---

1 base 9½ ins. by 2¼ ins. by ¼ in.

Pair of 1-in. hinges.

1 catch (or a pair).

The sides of the box are glued and pinned round the base, commencing with the short ends and following with the long sides. It will be advisable to drive the ¾-in. veneer pins part way into the sides before gluing, as this will facilitate the fixing. Punch in the pins, fill holes with plastic wood, then clean up the box with a finely set plane and attach the lid to the box with a pair of 1-in. hinges. **Finish.**—Polish or wax the surface.

PAPERCRAFT

Cut Paper Mats, Calendar, Boxes and Picture

PAPER MATS

MATERIALS

Cardboard, 6½ ins. square.

Gummed coloured paper.

A piece of Perspex 6½ ins. square.

Black passe-partout picture binding.

Method.—Cover the cardboard with the coloured paper chosen for the background. Enlarge the silhouette of the hen, duck, or cock; trace on to the coloured paper and cut out. The border is made by folding, colour to colour, a square of gummed paper as shown in the diagram on page 229. Trace an eighth of the pattern on the folded paper and, holding the folds firmly together, cut out parts marked for cutting with the scissors, then placing the folded paper on a piece of cardboard cut the other parts with a knife. Cut out the centre piece and unfold the paper when the border and centre opening will be found to be complete.

Damp the back of the paper and stick the border on to the coloured paper. It is better to do this in sections starting with a quarter of the border and sticking it down, then proceed by damping each piece between the folds until the mounting of the border is completed. By this

MODELLED FOR THE NURSERY. *A delightful example is given above of what can be done with gummed paper and a little ingenuity. At bottom left is a nest of boxes covered and decorated with coloured paper ; at bottom right is a cut paper mat ; at left side a calendar, and top, a brilliantly coloured cut paper picture.*

means the border can be put down without creasing.

Now damp the back of the silhouette and stick it to the background placing it nicely in the opening as shown in the diagram.

Border the Perspex with strips of passe-partout giving a quarter of an inch frame to the mat. This edge should first of all be sandpapered.

Turn the Perspex face downwards, place the mat in position, damp the outstanding edges of the binding, one edge at a time, turn over and stick to the back.

CUT PAPER CALENDAR
MATERIALS

White cardboard, 6¼ ins. wide by 8½ ins. deep.

Coloured paper with gummed back.

A small calendar about 2¾ ins. wide by 1¾ ins. deep.

Method.—Enlarge the diagram shown on page 230 of the church, trees, sky, and so on, to the required size, and trace the whole design noting the colours by numbers as shown. Carefully trace the design on to the piece of white cardboard and then trace the colours on to their appropriate coloured paper. These must be cut out with scissors and it is this cutting which gives such a unique character to cut paper work.

The sky must be stuck down first, each piece of blue fitting into the traced outline on the cardboard. The orange roofs come next, then the grey shadows; the black trees are then stuck into position and help to complete the form of the church. Cut the light green foreground in one piece if possible; it can include the dark green shapes which are much more easily stuck on the light green than fitted in a space left for them. The dark green trees at the right are also cut in one piece and the light green tree stuck on top. Cut out the window shapes, which are in buff, and fix in position. Cut and fix the black windows on the buff shapes and cut and fix the little black fence. Don't forget the tiny black weathercock at the top of the spire. If a small pair of tweezers are available they will be found very useful for picking up small pieces of coloured paper.

Bind the outer edges of the cardboard, mount with dark green, fix the calendar in position and stick a loop of coloured tape on the back.

CUT PAPER PICTURE
MATERIALS

Cardboard 9 ins. wide by 13 ins. deep.

A white cardboard mount 9 ins. wide by 13 ins. deep, with opening measuring 5½ ins. wide by 8½ ins. deep.

Coloured paper with gummed back.

Glass, 9 ins. wide by 13 ins. deep.

Black passe-partout picture binding.

Method.—Enlarge the design of the toucan, and the foliage, to the required size and make a careful tracing of the whole picture noting the colours by numbers as shown on the diagram.

Two drawings on the diagram show an easy way of enlarging a drawing. Suppose a tracing of a drawing has been made and it is required twice the size of the tracing. Rule quarter of an inch squares over the tracing numbering them at the top and left-hand side; rule half an inch squares on a piece of drawing paper, number them as on the tracing and carefully dot the position of the outline as it crosses the squares following its course on the small tracing. It is probably better to dot only a small portion at a time and connect these dots by a pencil line and so the drawing will gradually grow until the picture is complete; the enlargement will then be twice the size of the tracing.

Stick a piece of pale buff paper over the whole of the cardboard and when dry trace the design on to it.

CUT PAPER MATS FOR THE NURSERY

COLOURED PAPER MOUNTED ON CARDBOARD AND COVERED WITH PIECE OF PERSPEX.
EDGES BOUND WITH
PASSE-PARTOUT
PICTURE BINDING

PASSE-PARTOUT BINDING

BORDER PATTERN

BACKGROUND

GREEN

SILHOUETTE

LIGHT ORANGE

WHITE BORDER

$6\frac{1}{2}$ in. SQUARE

DIAGRAM SHOWING BORDER
FOLDED, DESIGN MARKED ON,
READY FOR CUTTING WITH
SCISSORS AND KNIFE

THIS PIECE
CUT OUT

FOLDED EDGE

FIRST FOLD

THIRD FOLD ON
DOTTED LINE

SECOND FOLD

NOTE. (FOLDED BORDER)
    A. CUT WITH SCISSORS
    B. CUT WITH KNIFE

PURPLE   BORDER

BLUE

WHITE

GREEN
BORDER

YELLOW

BLACK

$4\frac{5}{8}$ in.

CUT PAPER PICTURE AND CALENDAR

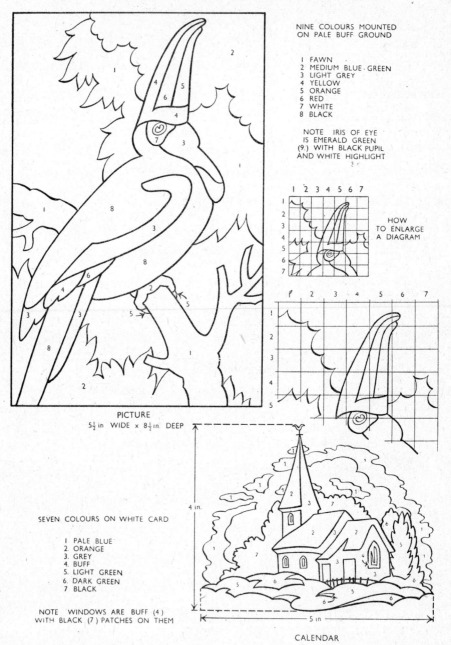

NINE COLOURS MOUNTED
ON PALE BUFF GROUND

1 FAWN
2 MEDIUM BLUE-GREEN
3 LIGHT GREY
4 YELLOW
5 ORANGE
6 RED
7 WHITE
8 BLACK

NOTE IRIS OF EYE
IS EMERALD GREEN
(9.) WITH BLACK PUPIL
AND WHITE HIGHLIGHT

HOW
TO ENLARGE
A DIAGRAM

PICTURE
5½ in WIDE x 8½ in. DEEP

SEVEN COLOURS ON WHITE CARD

1 PALE BLUE
2 ORANGE
3 GREY
4 BUFF
5 LIGHT GREEN
6 DARK GREEN
7 BLACK

NOTE WINDOWS ARE BUFF (4)
WITH BLACK (7) PATCHES ON THEM

4 in.

5 in.

CALENDAR

The next step is to trace and cut out the mass of fawn trees and the tree branch on which the toucan is perched. The branch should be in one piece and go under the bird. Stick these pieces in position on the pale buff background.

The medium blue-green foliage in the top right and bottom left-hand corners come next. Then the whole body of the bird, with the exception of its beak, is cut out of one piece of black paper and stuck in its place. The entire beak is in yellow with the red and orange pieces added afterwards. The black tail is then fixed in position and the light grey pieces forming the throat, wing, and tail feathers are the next in order followed by the pieces of red and yellow.

The bird's foot and claws are cut out and gummed on the tree branch as shown. The picture is finished by fixing the white patch on the side of the head, and then the eye with its green iris, black pupil and tiny white high light. The numbers on the diagram, on page 230, make it quite clear where the different coloured papers are placed.

The next thing is to mount and frame the picture. Carefully measure the position of opening in mount and cut it with bevelled sides, if possible. The border lines around the opening can be omitted if desired.

Put several patches of liquid glue on the back of the mount and stick it on to the picture, fitting it exactly on the border lines which should be ruled on the picture when it is finished. The border line is shown on the outline diagram.

Prepare four strips of passe-partout picture binding, two to fit the sides and one each for the top and bottom of the picture. Stick the strips on to the edge of the glass so as to give a quarter of an inch binding. When dry turn the glass face downwards, place mounted picture in position, damp the outstanding edges of the binding, one edge at a time, turn over and stick to the back.

Glue a loop of coloured tape on the back of the picture and cover the ends with one or two pieces of passe-partout binding to make the whole thing secure.

NEST OF BOXES COVERED AND DECORATED WITH COLOURED PAPER

MATERIALS

Coloured paper with gummed back.
Cardboard for making boxes.
White or tinted paper for lining if strawboard is used.
About 2 yds. of gummed paper strip.
Large box, 1 piece of cardboard, $10\frac{1}{2}$ ins. square.
Lid, 1 piece of cardboard $4\frac{7}{8}$ ins. square.
" V " to " Z " box, 1 piece of cardboard, $9\frac{3}{4}$ ins. square.
" Q " to " U " box, 1 piece of cardboard, $8\frac{1}{4}$ ins. square.
" L " to " P " box, 1 piece of cardboard, $7\frac{1}{8}$ ins. square.
" F " to " K " box, 1 piece of cardboard, 6 ins. square.
" A " to " E " box, 1 piece of cardboard $4\frac{7}{8}$ ins. square.

Method.—Cut the pieces of cardboard to the required sizes for the boxes and one lid, but do not allow any margins. If made of strawboard the inside should be covered with white or tinted paper. When dry, mark out the shape as shown on the diagram and cut out the four corner squares which are not wanted.

To make the sides of the box bend up evenly; the pencilled lines of the square, forming the bottom of the box, must be lightly scored on the back with a knife and ruler. When doing this take great care that the knife does not go too deep otherwise the piece may break off when bent. Carefully bend up the sides and fix them together with a short piece

A NEST OF BOXES COVERED AND DECORATED
WITH CUT COLOURED PAPER

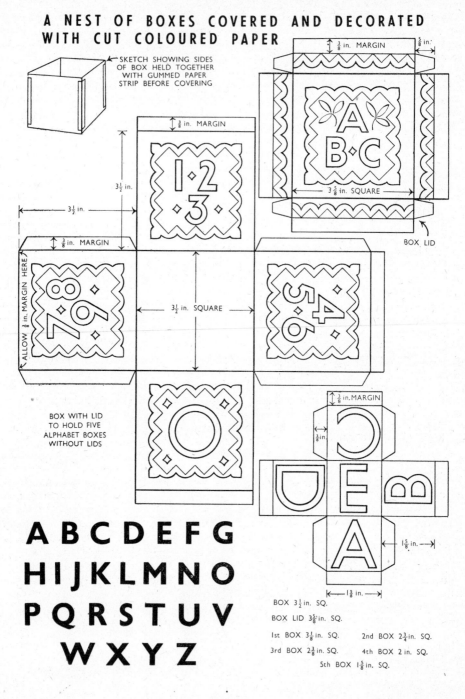

SKETCH SHOWING SIDES OF BOX HELD TOGETHER WITH GUMMED PAPER STRIP BEFORE COVERING

BOX LID

BOX WITH LID TO HOLD FIVE ALPHABET BOXES WITHOUT LIDS

ABCDEFG
HIJKLMNO
PQRSTUV
WXYZ

BOX 3½ in. SQ.

BOX LID 3⅝ in. SQ.

1st BOX 3⅛ in. SQ.   2nd BOX 2¾ in. SQ.

3rd BOX 2⅜ in. SQ.   4th BOX 2 in. SQ.

5th BOX 1⅝ in. SQ.

of gummed paper strip. The position of these pieces is shown on a small drawing on the sheet of diagrams.

The next step is to prepare the pieces of coloured paper which cover the boxes. If the diagram is referred to it will be seen that a margin is allowed on the top of each side piece and on the right and left-hand side of two side pieces. The $\frac{3}{8}$-in. margins on the side pieces cover the gummed strip and help to make a neat joint at the upright edges of the box.

When the paper is cut, with a soft paint brush damp the gummed surface of the square which covers the base of the box and carefully stick the box into position, pressing well down when doing so. Lift up the box with the coloured paper sticking to it and gently rub the paper on to the cardboard. Now damp one of the side pieces with the $\frac{3}{8}$-in. margin at the sides, and stick it to the side of the box turning the side margins over the gummed strip. Do not damp the top margins ; the sticking of these four pieces forms the last operation. Damp and stick the opposite side in the same way. Then stick the two remaining sides in position and finally damp, turn over, and stick the top margins on to the inside of the box. All the boxes and the lid are covered in this way.

The next step is to draw out the letters, enlarging and copying them from the alphabet on the diagram, and trace them on to the coloured paper chosen for each box. The letters are a little smaller than the squares of the smallest box and are the same size on all the boxes, the difference in the size of the boxes being counteracted by either one, two, or three marginal bands. This is clearly indicated in the reproduction of the boxes. A knife and scissors should be used when cutting the letters ; damp the back of the gummed paper with the soft brush and stick the letters in position,

bordering the larger boxes as previously described.

The " V " to " Z " box has three borders, the " Q " to " U " box and the " L " to " P " box have two borders, the " F " to " K " box has one border. When sticking on these borders always do the inner one first, then the middle one, and lastly the outer one. When cutting the inner and middle borders they should be made wider than shown to allow the next border to overlap, thus giving a much better edge than trying to fit two coloured edges together.

Having finished all the open lettered boxes attention can now be turned to the box with the lid. Make and cover the box and the lid in the same way as the others were made.

Draw and trace on to the coloured papers the zig-zag and curved borders, the " A.B.C." and the numerals. In this case it is better to do the bordering first starting with the zig-zag and following with the curved one. The " A.B.C." and the little leaf patterns are stuck on the lid and the numerals on the sides.

The box and lid shown in the illustration were covered with black paper, the zig-zag border was blue and the curved border green. The " A.B.C." and the numerals were in yellow with crimson triangular dots. The leaf patterns on the lid were in green with crimson stems. The " A " to " E " box was covered in crimson paper with letters in white ; the " F " to " K " box was covered in green with brown border and yellow letters ; the " L " to " P " box was covered in yellow with white and black borders and blue letters ; the " Q " to " U " box was covered in blue with green and brown borders and letters in yellow ; the " V " to " Z " box was covered in brown with green, white and crimson borders and pale grey letters.

TABLE MATS

Made with Odd Scraps of Leather

MATERIALS

Small pieces and scraps of leather of different grains and colours cut according to size of patterns shown in the diagram on facing page.
Cartridge drawing paper.
Cardboard for stiffening.
Skiver for lining the back.
Thread and thonging.

Method.—Cut the patterns from old postcards and select pieces of leather to fit. Draw the design on cartridge paper, place patterns on leather, mark round them with a pencil and cut out using the metal edged ruler and a sharp knife.

The outside pieces should have a small margin allowed on their outer edges which is cut away before thonging.

Paste the pieces of leather on the paper fitting them into the design. Mark a line $\frac{1}{10}$ in. away on each side of cut, make holes with the stitch spacer taking care that they come opposite each other and stitch the pieces to the paper. The stitching should stop about $\frac{1}{2}$ in. from the outer edge. Paste the back of the mat and stick it on to a piece of cardboard using stiff paste for the purpose.

Now cut a piece of skiver the same size as the mat and paste it on to cardboard. Put under a weight to dry. When ready cut the outer edges with knife and ruler. Mark holes with the thonging gauge, punch and thong the outer edges taking care to put two thonging stitches into each corner hole.

FOR GRANNY. *A charming choice of dinner mats made with coloured leather.*

TABLE MATS
MADE FROM SCRAPS
AND OFFCUTS

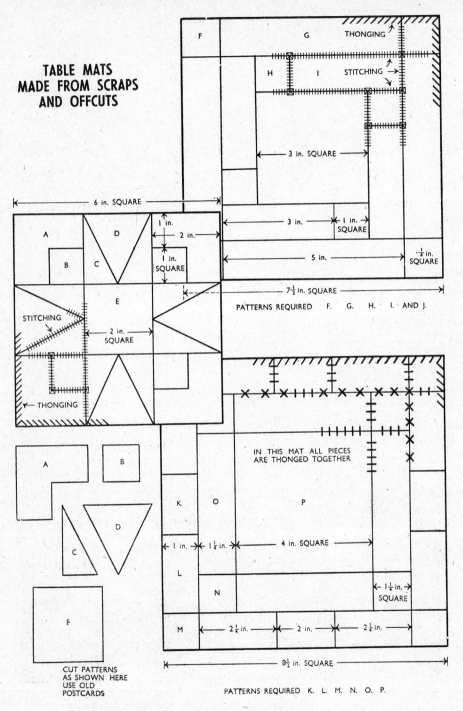

THONGING

STITCHING

3 in. SQUARE

3 in.

1 in.
SQUARE

5 in.

¼ in.
SQUARE

7½ in. SQUARE

PATTERNS REQUIRED   F.   G.   H.   I.   AND J.

6 in. SQUARE

1 in.

2 in.

1 in.
SQUARE

STITCHING

2 in.
SQUARE

THONGING

IN THIS MAT ALL PIECES
ARE THONGED TOGETHER

1 in.

1¼ in.

4 in. SQUARE

1¼ in.
SQUARE

2¼ in.

2 in.

2¼ in.

8½ in. SQUARE

PATTERNS REQUIRED K. L. M. N. O. P.

CUT PATTERNS
AS SHOWN HERE
USE OLD
POSTCARDS

SQUARE TABLE MATS

Crocheted in Cotton or String

MATERIALS

4 oz. coarse cotton or fine string makes one mat of each size.

Crochet hook.

MEASUREMENTS

Glass mat, 3½ ins. across.

Bread plate mat, 6 ins. across.

Large plate mat, 8 ins. across.

Centre mat, 10½ ins. across.

TENSION

5 rows of treble measure 1 in.

ABBREVIATIONS

Ch. chain, sc. single crochet, dc. double crochet, tr. treble, rep. repeat, ins. inches.

THE CENTRE MAT

Make 6 ch. and join into a ring with sc.

1st round.—3 ch., 2 tr. into ring, 3 ch., * 3 tr. into ring, 3 ch., rep. from * twice more, join with sc. to top of 3 ch. Finish all treble rounds in this way.

2nd round.—3 ch. (to represent 1st tr.), work 1 tr. into each tr. and 2 tr., 3 ch., 2 tr. into each of the 4 loops of 3 ch. which form the corners.

Rep. 2nd round 7 times more (35 tr. to one side).

10th round.—1 sc. into first 2 tr., * 5 ch., miss 3 tr., 1 dc. into next tr., rep. from * until 3 tr. remain before corner, 3 ch., 3 tr., 3 ch., 3 tr. all into corner, 3 ch., miss 3 tr., 1 dc. into next tr. ** 5 ch., miss 3 tr., 1 dc. into next tr., rep. from ** to corner, 3 ch., 3 tr., 3 ch., 3 tr. into corner, 3 ch. Work to end of round in same way, ending with 3 ch., 1 tr. into last st., thus bringing thread to top of loop.

11th round.—Work 5 ch., 1 dc. into each loop, working corners 3 ch., 3 tr., 3 ch., 3 tr. all into corner loop, ending round with 3 ch., 1 tr.

12th round.—As 11th round.

13th round.—Work 4 tr. into each loop along sides, with 1 tr. into each tr. at corner and 2 tr., 3 ch., 2 tr. into corner loop.

Rep. last 4 rounds three times more.

Next round.—* 5 ch., miss 3 tr.,

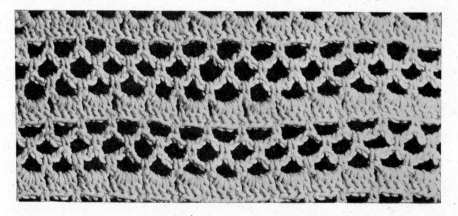

Close-up of stitch at side of mat showing the exact size.

THE YOUNG-MARRIEDS' GIFT. *A lovely gift for the home is this delightful set of square table mats crocheted in fine string. Instructions are given for making them in four different sizes.*

1 dc. into next tr., rep. from * all round, working 5 ch., 1 dc. into corner loop.

Next round.—Into each 5 ch. loop work 2 dc., 3 ch., 2 dc. Break off.

THE LARGE PLATE MAT

Work as given for centre mat to end of 7th round.

Now work 10th, 11th, 12th and 13th rounds 3 times.

Work last 2 rounds of centre mat.

THE BREAD PLATE MAT

Work as given for centre mat to end of 5th round.

Now work 10th, 11th, 12th and 13th rounds twice.

Work last 2 rounds of centre mat.

THE GLASS MAT

Work as given for centre mat to end of 3rd round.

Now work 10th round as centre mat, but leave only 2 tr. between each loop.

Work 11th and 12th rounds, then 13th round with 3 tr. into each loop.

Work last 2 rounds of centre mat.

Starch and press, pinning out to shape.

EARLY MORNING SET

Tray Cloth, Napkin, Cosy Cover and Guest Towel

MATERIALS

1 flour bag measuring 35 ins. by 35 ins. (after seams have been unpicked).

1 2-oz. ball of pale green crochet cotton.

Method.—Cut rectangles as shown on the chart (in the next column) and tack a narrow turning all round the tray cloth and napkin. For the cosy cover cut the two top corners in a slight curve and join with a row of stitching.

Hem the straight edge and also the long sides of the towel. Tack a narrow hem on the short ends of the towel. The first row of crochet is worked into the material over the hem and the stitches should be kept as evenly spaced as possible. It is worked in rounds for the

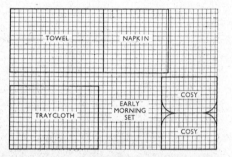

FOR THE HOME. *This attractive guest towel is made from part of a flour bag. It is finished with rows of crochet in pale green cotton at each end, and the bow and leaf motif is embroidered each side.*

FOR THE HOME. *A " visitor's set " consisting of tray cloth, napkin, and tea-cosy cover, all made out of one flour bag. The first row of the pale green crochet edging is worked into the material over the hem. The bow motif is worked with herringbone stitch, and three chain stitches make the leaves.*

napkin and cloth but in rows for the towel ends and cosy cover.

ABBREVIATIONS

Ch. chain, d.c. double crochet, tr. treble, d.tr. double treble.

1st row.—*1 d.c. into edge of material, 2 ch., miss a small space, rep. from * working 3 d.c. with 2 ch. between when turning corners.

2nd row.—*1 d.c. into 1st d.c., miss next d.c., 1 d.r. (thread over twice), 3 ch., 1 d.tr., 3 ch., 1 d.tr., 3 ch., 1 d.tr., all into next d.c., miss next d.c., rep.

from * working the group of st. without missing a d.c. each side when turning corners.

3rd row.—*1 d.c. into d.c., 1 d.c., 3 tr., 1 d.c., into each of the 3 ch. loops, rep. from *.

Any small flower motive could be embroidered instead of the bows shown in the illustration, but these are very quick to do. Trace the outline on to the material and fill it in with herringbone stitch. Three chain stitches make the leaves which decorate the bows.

TRAY CLOTH

In Openwork Crochet

MATERIALS

2 ozs. No. 20 crochet cotton.
No. 3 steel crochet hook.

MEASUREMENTS

16 ins. by 11½ ins.

TENSION

7 rows to 1 in.

ABBREVIATIONS

Ch. chain, tr. treble, d.c. double crochet, rep. repeat, ins. inches.

Begin in centre and make 264 ch.

1st row.—1 tr. into 4th ch. from hook * 2 ch., miss 2 ch., 1 tr. into next ch., rep. from * making 86 holes, 1 tr.

2nd row.—3 ch., 1 tr. into 2nd tr., 1 ch., 1 tr. into 1st hole, * 2 ch., 1 tr. into next hole, rep. from * ending 1 ch. 1 tr. into last tr., 1 tr. into turning ch.

3rd row.—3 ch., 1 tr. into 2nd tr., 2 ch., miss 1st hole, 1 tr. into next hole * 2 ch., 1 tr. into next hole, rep. from * ending with miss last hole, 2 ch. 1 tr. into last tr., 1 tr. into turning ch.

4th row.—3 ch., 1 tr. into 2nd tr., 2 ch., 1 tr. into next tr. * 2 ch., miss next hole, 3 tr., 3 ch., 3 tr. all into next hole, miss next hole, rep. from * ending with 2 ch. 1 tr. into 2nd tr. from end, 2 ch., 1 tr. into last tr., 1 tr. into turning ch.

5th row.—3 ch., 1 tr. into 2nd tr., 2 ch., 1 tr. into next tr., 1 ch. * 3 tr., 3 ch., 3 tr. all into 3 ch. loop, 2 ch., rep. from * ending with 1 ch., 1 tr. into 2nd tr. from end, 2 ch., 1 tr. into last tr., 1 tr. into turning ch.

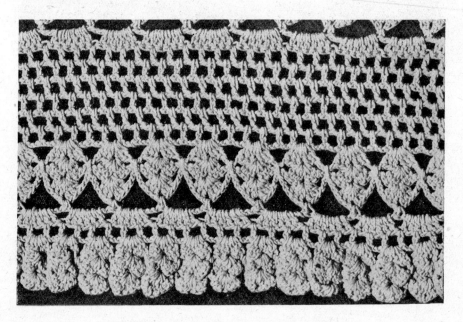

Close-up of the tray cloth stitch and border showing the exact size.

TO PLEASE ANY WOMAN. *A charming gift for the home is this attractive crochet tray cloth in cotton. It is in openwork panels with a gathered shell edging.*

6th row.—3 ch., 1 tr. into 2nd tr., 2 ch., 1 tr. into next tr., 2 ch. * 3 trs., 3 ch., 3 tr. all into 3 ch. loop, 3 ch., 1 d.c. into 3 ch. of 4th row working over ch. of 5th row, 3 ch., rep. from * ending with 2 ch., 1 tr. into 2nd tr. from end, 2 ch., 1 tr. into last tr., 1 tr. into turning ch.

7th row.—3 ch., 1 tr. into 2nd tr., 2 ch., 1 tr. into next tr., 3 ch., 1 d.c. into 3 ch. loop * 6 ch., 1 d.c. into next loop, rep. from * ending 3 ch., 1 tr. into 2nd tr. from end, 2 ch., 1 tr. into last tr., 1 tr. into turning ch.

8th row.—3 ch., 1 tr. into 2nd tr., 2 ch., 1 tr. into next tr., 2 tr. into 3 ch., * 6 tr. into 6 ch., rep. from * ending with 2 tr. into 3 ch., 1 tr. into next tr., 2 ch., 1 tr. into last tr., 1 tr. into turning ch.

9th row.—3 ch., 1 tr. into 2nd tr. * 2 ch., miss 2 tr., 1 tr. into next tr., rep. from * ending with 1 tr. into last tr., 1 tr. into turning ch. (86 holes).

** Work a further 5 rows of holes, then rep. from 4th to 9th rows. Rep. from ** once. Break off.

Work into the other side of the foundation chain to match.

For the edging work 4th, 5th and 6th rows all round, but leave only one hole between the groups of trs. in 4th row.

CROCHET MATS

For the Dressing Table

MATERIALS

12 oz. spool No. 20 crochet cotton.
No. 3 steel crochet hook.

MEASUREMENTS

1 motif measures 2½ ins.

ABBREVIATIONS

Ch. chain, dc. double crochet, tr. treble, db. tr. double treble (cotton over hook twice), rep. repeat, sc. single crochet.

Make 8 ch. and join into a ring with sc.

1st round.—(1 ch., 1 dc. into ring) 8 times, join with sc. to 1st ch.

2nd round.—9 ch. * 1 db. tr. into 1 ch., 4 ch., rep. from * 6 times, join with 1 sc. to 5th of 9 ch.

3rd round.—* 1 ch., 5 dc. into 4 ch. loop, rep. from * 7 times, join with 1 sc. to 1st. ch.

4th round.—3 ch., 1 tr., 3 ch. 2 tr. all into 1 ch., 3 ch. * 2 tr., 3 ch., 2 tr. all into next 1 ch., 3 ch., rep. from * 6 times, join with 1 sc. to top of 3 ch.

5th round.—1 sc. into tr., 1 sc. into 3 ch. loop, 3 ch., 1 tr., 3 ch., 2 tr. all into 3 ch. loop, 2 ch., 1 dc. into next 3 ch., 2 ch. * 2 tr., 3 ch., 2 tr. all into next 3 ch. loop, 2 ch., 1 dc. into next 3 ch., 2 ch., rep. from * 6 times, join with 1 sc. to top of 3 ch.

6th round.—Work as last round but with 3 ch., 1 dc. into dc., 3 ch. between

Detail of crochet flower motif showing the exact size of stitch.

EVERYWOMAN'S GIFT. *This delightful dressing table set is crocheted in small flower motifs joined to form one large mat, and two small mats. Fifty-three motifs were used for the set shown here, but the motifs can be joined to make any size mat according to particular requirements.*

the groups of 2 tr., 3 ch. 2 tr.

7th round.—Work as last round but with 3 tr., 3 ch., 3 tr. to each group and 4 ch. 1 dc. into dc., 4 ch. between each group.

Break off.

This completes one motif.

To join the 2nd motif to the 1st : work to end of 6th round of 2nd motif then, instead of working 3 ch. between the groups of tr. in 7th round, work 1 ch., 1 dc. into similar loop of 1st motif, 1 ch., join the next loop in the same way, then continue to end of 7th round.

To fill the square holes between motifs work thus :—

Make 8 ch. and join in a ring.

1st round.—12 dc. into ring.

2nd round*.—1 dc. into each of 3 dc., 7 ch., 1 dc. into loop where two motifs were joined, 7 ch., rep. from * 3 times, join with 1 sc. and break off.

To make the set in the illustration above, 53 motifs are required—9 for each of the small side mats and 35 for the larger centre mat, but the motifs can be joined to any size according to particular requirements.

TWO CUSHIONS

One is Oblong, the other is Round

CIRCULAR CUSHION

MATERIALS

1¼ yds. material, 36 ins. wide.
4 yds. 1½-in. bias binding for piping.
4 yds. cord for piping.
1¼ yds. featherproof material for inner cushion. Feathers for filling.

Method.—Cut 2 circles 19 ins. in diameter and join a 4-in. strip 60 ins. long for the boxing.

Make 2 strips of piping 60 ins. long by covering the cord with bias binding and stitch it with long running stitches close to the cord.

Tack this piping between the circles of material and the boxing strip leaving about 12 ins. open on one side for inserting the cushion. Machine together.

Embroider with scattered "large daisies" in bright contrasting wools.

Make an inner lining in the same way without the piping. Fill with feathers and insert in cover, stitch the opening.

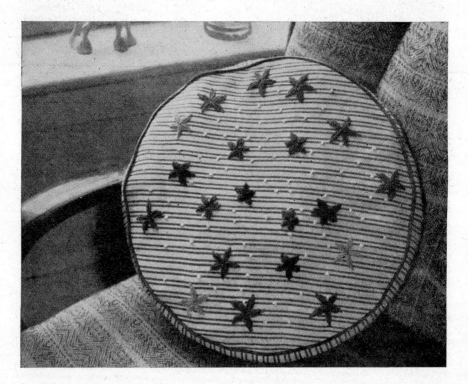

FOR THE HOME. *A charming circular cushion in striped material. The circles are outlined with piping in a contrast colour, and the front of the cushion is embroidered with large lazy daisy stitches in bright contrasting wools. The back is left plain.*

FOR THE YOUNG BRIDE. *A lovely gift for the home is this charming oblong head cushion. The original cushion was made from wide taffeta ribbon, trimmed at each side with braid and ball-fringe.*

OBLONG CUSHION

MATERIALS
3 yds. ribbon about 4½ ins. wide.
2 yds. braid 1 in. wide.
3 yds. ball-fringe trimming.

MEASUREMENTS
21 ins. by 13 ins.

Method.—Cut the ribbon and fringe into four equal lengths (27 ins.).

Cut the braid into three 27-in. lengths.

Join the braid and ribbon together alternately, beginning and ending with the ribbon.

Stitch a length of ball-fringe to the end pieces of ribbon, 1 in. from the braid.

Fold in half with the right side inside and stitch, leaving a 10-in. opening in the long side.

Turn right side out and stitch the other pieces of ball-fringe to the ends.

Insert cushion of suitable size and oversew the opening neatly.

Although the original cushion was made from ribbon, any strips of material, both plain and patterned, could be used. They should, however, be slightly wider to allow for the raw edges.

In this case use a foundation of book muslin and tack the strips of material to this. Leave about ¼ in. between each and do not turn in the edges.

Tack the braid over these joins and stitch, then finish as before.

DUCHESSE SET

Made with Bias Binding

MATERIALS

14 yds. bias binding in pastel shade.
Embroidery thread to match.

THE LARGE MAT

Method.—On a piece of strong paper, draw an oblong 12 ins. long by 9 ins. deep with a smaller oblong 6 ins. by 3½ ins. in its centre. Following Diagram 1, tack the folded bias binding on to the paper in the first stage of the design, then add the second lines as shown for the second stage. Keep the open edges of the binding to the inner sides of the curves in every case.

Diagram 2 can now be followed for tacking in all the shorter lengths which go to make up the design. These are inserted into the open ends of the main lines and stitched neatly.

When the design is complete in tacking, join the binding with faggot-stitch in embroidery thread. At the open edges of the binding, be certain to pick up both edges with the stitch and keep all first and last stitches on the top surface of the binding, as this side of the mat will be the wrong side. It must,

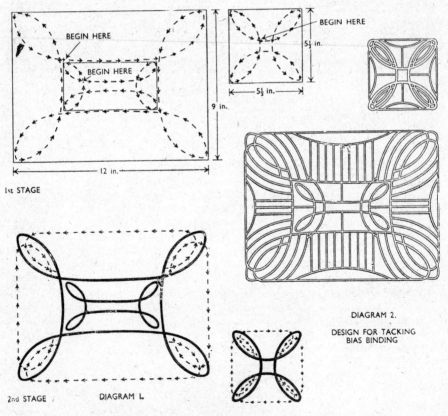

BEGIN HERE

BEGIN HERE

BEGIN HERE

5½ in.

5½ in.

9 in.

12 in.

1st STAGE

2nd STAGE

DIAGRAM 1.

DIAGRAM 2.

DESIGN FOR TACKING
BIAS BINDING

FOR THE SMART WOMAN. *Feminine yet practical is this charming and unusual duchesse set made with bias binding and embroidery thread. The binding is joined by faggot-stitching. The design is quite simple to follow from the diagram shown at the foot of facing page.*

however, be kept as neat as possible.

Where the strips of binding are parallel the faggot-stitching can be kept to an even width but where the space between is in an oval shape, as inside the loops, the stitches must be graduated according to the width of the space. Where there is an irregular-shaped space to be filled with one side forming an angle and the other a curve, a diagonal stitch should first be worked from the corner of the angle to the opposite curve. Subsequent stitches of varying sizes and at different angles can then be worked until the space is filled. Care should be taken that opposite corners in the design are worked to match.

Finish all the faggot-stitching before removing any tacking threads, then remove them very carefully and detach the mat from the paper. Press the mat carefully into shape with a damp cloth under a hot iron.

THE SMALL MATS

For these draw a square 5½ ins. each way, on strong paper and tack the binding on in two stages, as shown in Diagram 1. Complete the design with the shorter lengths, following Diagram 2, then join the binding with faggot-stitch and complete the mat in exactly the same way as the larger one. Make a second small mat to match.

SHOPPING BAG

Crocheted in Linen Thread

MATERIALS

3 oz. linen thread.
Bone crochet hook.

ABBREVIATIONS

Ch. chain, dc. double crochet, tr. treble, sc. single crochet, rep. repeat.

Make 10 ch., join into a ring with sc.

1st round.—3 ch., 19 tr. into ring. Join to top of 3 ch. with sc. (Join all tr. rounds in this way.)

2nd round.—4 ch., * 1 tr. into tr., 1 ch., rep. from * to end.

3rd round.—5 ch., * 1 tr. into 1 ch., 2 ch., rep. from * to end.

4th round.—5 ch., 1 tr. into 2 ch., 2 ch., * 1 tr. into next 2 ch., 2 ch., 1 tr. into same 2 ch., 2 ch. (1 tr. into next 2 ch., 2 ch.) 3 times, rep. from * to end.

Work 3 more rounds as last round increasing at regular intervals to keep work flat.

Next round.—* 5 ch., 1 dc. into 2 ch., rep. from * to end.

Next round.—* 5 ch., 1 dc. into 5ch., rep. from * to end.

Rep. last round 20 times (or until bag is depth required).

Next round.—* 3 ch., 1 dc. into 5 ch., rep. from * to end.

Next round.—3 dc. into each 3 ch. loop.

Next round.—1 dc. into each dc. Break off.

The Handles.—Divide the top into 4 equal parts and mark with pins.

Join thread to one marked place, make 60 ch. and join to next marked place.

Next row.—3 ch., 1 tr. into each of the 60 ch., sc. to edge.

Now work 1 row of dc. into the trs. and continue round top of bag to the beginning of this handle. Break off.

Work other handle in same way.

Work a row of dc. along the other side of the handles, continuing along the two remaining quarters of the top.

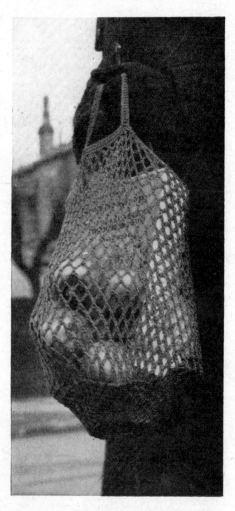

This handy-size family shopping bag is very simple and quick to crochet.

TABLE DECORATION

Attractive Flower Tray

MATERIALS

1 metal oven tray, about 12 ins. by 8 ins. by 3 ins. deep.

Few ins. of adhesive tape.

Small tins of enamel in cream or pastel shade and a darker, contrasting shade.

Method.—Wash the metal tray in strong, hot soda water and dry well.

From the adhesive tape cut a number of small star shapes and stick these on the outside of the tray, not in rows, but scattered about. Using the lighter coloured enamel, paint the outside of the tray and inside the four sides, covering the stars as well. If necessary, give the tray a second coat of enamel when the first one is absolutely dry.

When the enamel is finally dry, peel the star shapes off very carefully. The simplest way is to lift one corner with tweezers and pull gently. Now fill in the metal star shapes with the contrasting enamel, using a fine brush.

The tray can be filled with tiny, growing plants for indoors, or with rows of small jars for short stemmed flowers.

FOR THE FLAT DWELLER. *A metal tray, attractively decorated with small star shapes and filled with growing plants for indoors, or with rows of small jars for short cut flowers (as above), will make a lovely indoor garden for all the year round.*

OVEN CLOTH

To Protect the Hands

OVEN CLOTH

MATERIALS

Strip of strong furnishing cretonne or similar material, approximately 42 ins. long by 13 ins. wide (i.e., ⅜ yd. of 42 to 48 in. material).

2 pieces of interlining material each 15 ins. long by 6½ ins. wide.

2½ yds. of contrasting bias binding.

Method.—The oven cloth consists of a strip of material with two padded pockets, one at each end, into which the hands can be slipped when lifting hot dishes out of an oven. Any thick soft material, such as an old blanket or tweed material, can be used for interlining.

Fold the strip of cretonne in half, lengthways. Sandwich one piece of the interlining material in each end and machine-quilt the three layers together. Now fold about 7½ ins. of the quilted portions over towards the centre to make a pocket at each end and pin the two layers of quilting together. Trim off the outer corners into curves and taper the unquilted part slightly in towards the centre as shown by the dotted lines in the diagram. Tack the double layers of quilted material together on the outer edges of the pockets.

Fold a piece of bias binding in half, sew the edges together and stitch the ends to the top and bottom edges in the centre of the strip. This makes a loop with which to hang up the cloth when it is not in use.

Bind the inner edges of the quilted pockets, then bind right round the cloth, stitching the double layers of quilting together.

The pocket end of the oven cloth can be copied again to make a kettle holder into which the hand can be slipped. A diagram is given below and you will need about 4 pieces of strong furnishing material, each 7½ ins. by 6½ ins., 2 pieces of interlining each 7½ ins. by 6½ ins., 1 yd. bias binding.

Take two of the oblongs of fabric and sandwich one of the interlining pieces between them. Quilt all three layers together then make up the other pieces of fabric and interlining in the same way. Bind one short side of each quilted piece then place them one on top of the other with the bound edges together at the top.

Trim off the lower corners of both pieces into curves and tack together round the outer edges. Bind the two edges together, leaving the holder open at the top, of course. Use the remaining binding to make a loop and stitch it to one corner, at the top.

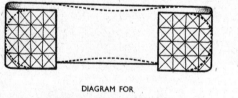

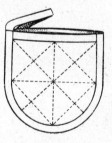

KETTLE HOLDER TO MATCH OVEN CLOTH

DIAGRAM FOR

OVEN CLOTH SHOWING QUILTED ENDS FOLDED OVER. DOTTED LINES SHOW WHERE CUTTING MUST BE DONE

FOR THE HOUSEWIFE.   *A useful little gift that is sure to please is this neat oven cloth to protect the hands when holding hot dishes.   The cloth consists of one strip of material with two quilted and padded pockets with bound edges.*

USEFUL COAL SET

Matching Apron and Mitt

MATERIALS

1¼ yds. of 36 to 40 in. wide material in black or dark colour.

2 yds. lime-green bias binding.

2 yds. cyclamen bias binding.

Strip of interlining material 36 to 40 ins. long by 5 ins. deep, and 2 oblongs, each 9 ins. by 7 ins.

The set consists of a padded mitt for picking up coal and an apron with its hem padded for kneeling. Any soft, thick material, such as old blanket, will be suitable for interlining.

THE APRON

Method.—Cut a piece for the apron, the full width of the material and 32 ins. deep. The sides will be selvedges so no hems will be necessary. Tack the long strip of interlining across the bottom of the apron on the wrong side and about 5½ ins. above the lower edge. Turn this edge up to make a hem 5 ins. deep over the interlining. Secure the two layers of material and the interlining together with machine quilting in large diamonds. Sew lime-green binding flat all round this padded hem.

For the bow trimming, cut pieces of binding in both colours each about 24 ins. long. If the edges of the bias binding are not already pressed, then turn them in and press them. Place the two strips of binding together, wrong sides facing, and tie into a bow. Arrange the loops and ends into a " lover's knot " arrangement to show the contrasting colours to the best advantage and pin and tack the bow in the centre of the padded hem. Slip-stitch along all the edges of the binding

to hold the bow securely in position.

The apron pocket must be large enough to hold the mitt when not in use. Cut an oblong of material about 7 ins. deep and 8 ins. wide, round off the two lower corners, turn in the outer edges and bind the top with lime-green binding. Now make a second bow of the two coloured bindings, as before, and sew it on the centre of the pocket. Stitch the pocket to the apron about 8 ins. from the top and 3½ ins. to the left of the centre as shown in the illustration.

Cut two strips of material, each 2 ins. deep and the full width of the material, and join two narrow ends together. Fold in half lengthways, right sides facing, and machine the raw edges together, leaving about 18 ins. in the centre unsewn. Turn the tie ends through on to the right sides, and press well, then gather the top edge of the apron up to about 18 ins. and set the gathers into the centre of the waistband. Press the apron well.

THE COAL MITT

Method.—To make a paper pattern for the coal mitt, place a right-hand glove of a suitable size palm upwards on a piece of paper ; draw round the outline and then cut out the shape. For an average size mitt the depth will be about 9 ins. and the width across palm and thumb about 7 ins.

Fold the material in two, wrong sides facing, pin the pattern on with the thumb to the right and cut out both layers for the front of the mitt. Reverse the pattern and cut two more layers for the

FOR MOTHER. *A practical yet decorative gift is this matching apron and coal mitt. The set is decorated with coloured bias binding in a "lover's knot" motif. The apron has a quilted hem to make it strong enough for kneeling, and the front of the mitt is quilted for protection.*

back. Now cut the shape twice in the interlining material, reversing the pattern as before. Sandwich each of the interlining shapes between two of the material shapes and machine-quilt the three layers together.

Make a third bow of the two coloured bias bindings and sew on to the back half of the mitt. Now tack back and front together and bind round the outer edges and along the wrist edges with lime-green binding.

DECORATIVE TILES

And Magazine Folder

PAINTED TILES

MATERIALS

Small tin heat-resisting jet black enamel, quick-drying.

Medium hogshair brush.

3 glazed tiles 6 ins. square.

Method.—Painted tiles are most effective and make a practical and original gift. The decorations shown here can be followed easily if you trace the outlines from the diagrams on this page marked 1, 2 and 3, on to a small piece of transparent paper and then transfer them to the surfaces of the tiles by means of a small piece of carbon paper between the paper and the tiles.

Work over the lines of the designs with a sharp pointed pencil, avoiding heavy pressure on the other parts of the carbon as much as possible. Remove the tracing paper and the carbon, and paint in silhouette in the quick-drying jet black enamel paint.

FOR THE HOME. *A decorative folder in which to keep your favourite periodical. It is made in acetate and the charming design can be traced from the diagrams given here and then painted. The edges are bound, and narrow silk cord is then threaded through the folder and the magazine to keep them in place. The delightful table mats are pastel-shaded tiles with the intriguing designs filled in with black heat-resisting paint. Full size diagrams of the quaint little animal motifs are given on these pages.*

Fill in neatly, using simple brush strokes, and keep your paint fairly thick so that it does not run, but experiment first of all until you get the right consistency.

These small motifs are most decora-tive when painted in the corner or centre of a plain tile (the originals were black motifs on pale green tiles), but care must be taken not to smear the work. Leave to dry (in as dust-free an atmosphere as possible), before use.

B

paper and assemble them in the positions shown in the illustration on the previous page with the lamb at the top, the horse on the left, the donkey at the bottom and the deer at the right side.

Now make a tracing of the border strip marked E and repeat the strip exactly as shown in the illustration until you have completely boxed in the motifs.

Place the sheet of paper with the design on it underneath the acetate and pin it to a board very securely, then paint the design straight over

C

ACETATE FOLDER

MATERIALS

Acetate 11 ins. wide by 12½ ins. deep (or to fit size of magazine).
1¾ yds. bias binding.
1 yd. narrow silk cord.
Sheet plain white paper.
Hogshair brush (medium, round end).
1 small tin cellulose enamel.

Method.—Make a tracing of each of the four designs marked A, B, C and D on a large sheet of tracing

D

the tracing on to the acetate.

When it has dried, unpin it from the board then cut a large sheet of plain white paper for backing, the same size as the acetate. Place this at the back of the acetate and bind the two edges together with bias binding, machine stitching the edges. Finish by punching two holes at the left side edge about five ins. apart. Corresponding holes are punched in the magazine.

E

Printed in Great Britain by Keliher, Hudson and Kearns, Ltd., London, and bound by Odhams (Watford) Ltd., Watford. S.1047.U.